HELEN WINTERNITZ

Helen Winternitz is a journalist who has lived and travelled extensively in Africa. She has reported from Africa for various newspapers, including *The Baltimore Sun* and occasionally *The Times* of London. She is a graduate of Harvard University.

Helen Winternitz

EAST ALONG THE EQUATOR

A Congo Journey

First published in Great Britain in 1987 by The Bodley Head.

Sceptre edition 1989

Sceptre is an imprint of Hodder and Stoughton Paperbacks, a division of Hodder and Stoughton Ltd.

British Library C.I.P.

Winternitz, Helen
    East along the equator:
    a Congo journey.
    1. Zaire. Description and travel
    I. Title
    916.75'1043

ISBN 0-340-49725-4

Printed and bound in Great Britain for Hodder and Stoughton Paperbacks, a division of Hodder and Stoughton Ltd., Mill Road, Dunton Green, Sevenoaks, Kent TN13 2YA (Editorial Office: 47 Bedford Square, London WC1B 3DP) by Richard Clay Ltd., Bungay, Suffolk. Photoset by Rowland Phototypesetting Ltd., Bury St Edmunds, Suffolk.

AUTHOR'S NOTE

This book would not and could not have been written without Timothy M. Phelps. It was originally his idea and began as a joint endeavor. He was a partner in gathering its contents and conceptualizing its form. He drafted some of the chapters and edited the chapters I drafted. His observations about what we experienced in Zaire, on every level from the personal to the political, are an integral part of the book. Above all, he believed in its worth.

ACKNOWLEDGMENTS

Many of the Zairians who helped us see their country have gone unnamed, because to name them could bring down upon them the wrath of the Mobutu regime. Some of them knowingly jeopardized their safety and they, first of all, have earned our thanks. In order to disguise their identities, I have given them pseudonyms and, where necessary, changed some details about them. The exception is Tshisekedi wa Malumba, who has risked himself time and again in public disagreements with the regime.

Thanks of the deepest sort also must go to Ann Rittenberg, the book's first editor. Along the way, the book gained a second editor, Ann Godoff, whose help has been invaluable. So too has been the help of my literary agents, Lizzie Grossman and Peter Matson.

Much useful information was patiently provided by Nzongola-Ntalaja, a professor at Howard University who continues to care about events back home in Zaire, and Stephen Weissman, staff director of the House Subcommittee on Africa.

I want finally to acknowledge the support of my father, Dr William Winternitz, and my stepmother, Madeleine Hill, as well as the help of friends who include Susan Cheever, Nancy Long, Michael Elder, Michael Massing, Fraser Smith, Eileen Canzian, Sally Millemann, Michael Millemann, and Constance Phelps.

There are many humorous things in the world: among them the white man's notion that he is less savage than other savages.

Mark Twain, in *Following the Equator*

I believe that the chief gift from Africa to writers, white and black, is the continent itself, its presence which for some people is like an old fever, latent always in their blood; or like an old wound throbbing in the bones as the air changes. That is not a place to visit unless one chooses to be an exile ever afterwards from an inexplicable majestic silence lying just over the border of memory or of thought. Africa gives you the knowledge that man is a small creature, among other creatures, in a larger landscape.

Doris Lessing, in the preface to *African Stories*

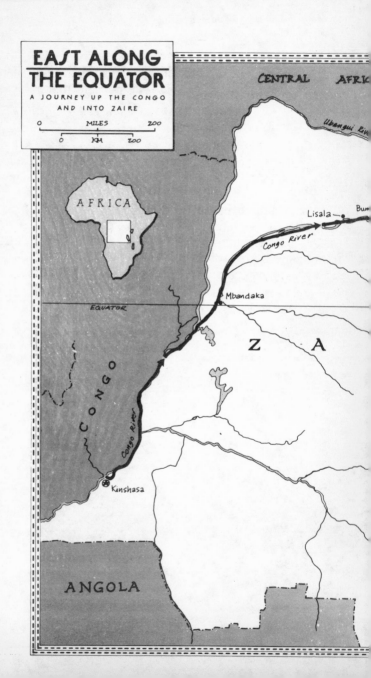

EAST ALONG THE EQUATOR

A JOURNEY UP THE CONGO
AND INTO ZAIRE

0   MILES   200

0   KM   200

AFRICA

CENTRAL   AFR

Ubangui Riv

Lisala   Bum

Congo River

EQUATOR

Mbandaka

Z   A

C O N G O

Congo River

Kinshasa

ANGOLA

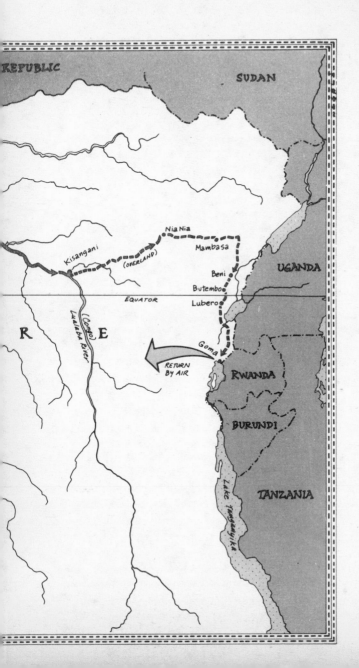

INTRODUCTION

The idea of traveling on the Congo River attracted me from the time I first lived in Africa fifteen years ago. I had a job as a young teacher at a school in Ethiopia, but when I wasn't teaching I was traveling as much as I could, for I was falling in love with the continent of Africa. Someone told me then that passenger boats still operated on long navigable stretches of the river, making it possible to journey deep into the heart of Africa. But, distracted by other African itineraries, it was quite a while before I got anywhere near the Congo.

Back home in the United States, I became a journalist and returned to Africa as often as I could to write about its countries and their politics. The more I saw of the continent, the more I loved its landscapes, the bounty of its space, and its people, strong and generous people who had time enough to share with a passing stranger. Although life was not easy or comfortable in Africa, it seemed to have immense meaning and power.

Following the Congo River as far as possible into central Africa was an idea that did not die away. It came alive years later when I was driving across northern Zambia on a road through lonely forests that spilled northward into Zaire. Hills undulated toward the border and continued past it into the blue distance, like unmappable waves in an undiscovered sea. Somewhere among those hills, in northern Zambia or southern Zaire, depending on contradictory geographic theories, lay the source of the Congo. I was fascinated by what I could see and even more by what I could not see. Somewhere beyond those distant blue hills lay the essence of Africa.

The potential difficulty of a trip up the Congo appealed to me as much as the idea that I could find Africa. It was a challenge of the sort I had been brought up to relish, having applied my childhood to such feats as swimming across a Connecticut pond inhabited by snapping turtles and climbing New Hampshire's White Mountains in storms. If the Congo was obdurate about protecting its secrets from the outside world, so much the better.

As much as anything else, though, I was drawn by the raw politics of central Africa, Zaire might be geographically remote but it is closely bound to the United States politically in a relationship that has brought much suffering to the country's people.

Zaire, the new name for what was once the Belgian Congo, has been an American client and ally for more than twenty years, ever since President Mobutu Sese Seko came to power. Mobutu's pro-West outlook was more attractive to American strategists than that of Patrice Lumumba, the country's first leader and only democratically elected prime minister, who was assassinated with the blessings of the Central Intelligence Agency.

During the two decades that Mobutu has ruled Zaire, he has amassed an immense personal fortune said to be worth five billion dollars and including a chateau complete with a moat and castlelike spires as well as two other houses, stables, and a park in Belgium; villas in France; chateaux in Spain, Italy, and the Central African Republic; and hotels in Spain and the Ivory Coast. Mobutu is one of the world's richest men and Zaire is one of its naturally richest countries, but its people are among the world's poorest and most powerless. Mobutu has held the country together under a dictatorship comparable in some ways to the regime of Ferdinand Marcos.

American policy toward Zaire has its own narrow logic as have had the other strategies pursued by foreigners during the unhappy history of the Congo's relationship with the Western world. There were powerful commercial arguments for the trade in slaves that ravaged the Congo and for the viciousness perpetrated by the Belgian King Leopold to collect fortunes of rubber and ivory from the same region. The Congo of Leopold's colonial era was the same territory of greed and insanity that

Joseph Conrad chronicled fictionally in *Heart of Darkness*. Now strategic minerals, such as cobalt and uranium, and geopolitical considerations, such as Zaire's useful location at the center of the continent, have replaced slaves and ivory as the prizes.

American policymakers have put a higher value on Mobutu's anti-Soviet stance than on the drawbacks of his domestic policies. President Reagan emphasised this in late 1983 just before I left for Zaire by inviting Mobutu for a state visit and embracing him at the White House. This was to be my only glimpse of Mobutu in the United States or in Zaire, since he seldom makes himself available for interviews.

Posing for photographers at the edge of the Rose Garden with his host, the Zairian president was dressed in his usual grand costume, featuring a leopard-skin hat and an elaborately carved staff that he has adopted as a symbol of his chiefly status.

From behind the cordon that keeps the press at a safe distance, an irreverent television reporter yelled, 'Hey, Mister Mobutu, that's a nice walking stick you got there.' Everyone laughed except Mobutu, who kept beaming at Reagan, and Reagan who kept beaming at Mobutu. Such an affront to the presidential dignity never would have been tolerated back in Zaire, but in the United States it was worth Mobutu's while to put up with it. The image of the two leaders together underscored America's ties to Mobutu, sending a powerful message to any Zairians thinking of opposing their president.

Beginning in highland savannas, the Congo gathers power as it arcs through Zaire, traversing the forested Congo Basin. A dozen major tributaries feed the Congo and are fed themselves by thousands of smaller rivers and streams, extending to the most remote corners of the rain forest. It reaches to the edge of the Great Rift Valley, a primeval rent in the continent's topography whose broad floor was the cradle of mankind. Some of the river's sources spring from high on the slopes of the Mountains of the Moon, the snow-capped peaks that crown

Africa's tallest massif. Other tributaries cut through the Ituri
Rain Forest, where the Pygmies still live as they did when
they first settled the forest more than 20,000 years ago,
hunting with poisoned arrows and handmade nets. The river
writhes across the equator, grows into a behemoth, and rolls
ponderously toward the Atlantic Ocean.

Even though I wanted wholeheartedly to take a trip up this
river, I wasn't going to set out alone. What I needed was a
good traveling partner. I knew that Timothy Phelps, the man I
lived with, would be ideal if I could overcome his understandable
caution about launching another joint adventure. But it was not
going to be easy if the trip to Guatemala, during which we both
came down with a strain of typhoid in a mountain village, or
the trip to Ethiopia, on which I lured him with tales of the
country's beauty only to take him to its drought-stricken,
sun-blasted Ogaden desert, were still fresh in his mind.

We met in the city room of *The Baltimore Sun*, where we
were working as reporters. Tim's first experience of Africa
had been in Egypt and the Sudan, where he had spent two
years as a freelance journalist contending with Cairo's
medieval-modern chaos and journeying up and down Africa's
other great river, the Nile.

We had traveled together quite a bit on the eastern side of
the continent. He had nursed me back to health after a mosquito
in Somalia infected me with dengue fever, a disease so debili-
tating that it is known in East Africa as 'breakbone fever.' We
had interviewed Cuban troops in the hostile Ogaden, had
reported on racism in southern Africa, and had learned to trust
one another in strange situations. When I first told him about
my trip in northern Zambia and about that view I had seen into
southern Zaire, speculating on what a journey on the Congo
would entail, he listened and set the idea aside as impractical,
uncomfortable, and perhaps impossible.

'Why can't we go someplace nice?' he asked. 'Just for once.'

But the Congo trip was one of those ideas that kept insisting.

Although clearly possessed of enough taste for adventure to
previously have quit a good newspaper job and set off for Cairo
where he knew no one, Tim did not respond as enthusiastically

to the prospect of adversity and discomfort as I did. But since he is a naturalist at heart, his interest perked up when he read about the rare gorillas living in the mountains of eastern Zaire, a landscape famed for its beauty. Reaching for cheerier thoughts, I promised him, falsely it turned out, that if we made it up the river, we could go searching for the shy mountain gorillas.

One incidental of traveling that worries Tim considerably, maybe because of his formal rearing as the son of a well-bred Rhode Island farmer, is the likelihood of encountering noisome toilets. He suspected that any riverboat on the Congo would have communal toilets and he wanted none of it. I promised him, truthfully this time, that I would consent to traveling first class with a private toilet if such existed. He at last agreed, and we set about trying to find out what we were in for.

Reliable information is scarce in today's Zaire. I made some preliminary inquiries around Washington, getting in touch with Zairians, experts on Africa, and officials at the State Department and asking advice. But none of them had traveled extensively overland in central Africa. This was an indication of the exigencies of traveling in Zaire and a shocking exhibit of how little information is available to Americans about a country that has been a loyal client for so many years.

Finally we received a response to a letter I had written to the American embassy in Kinshasa, the capital of Zaire. F. Weston Fenhagen, the embassy's public information officer who had lived in the country for many years, wrote us a long letter that was nevertheless shaky on many of the details.

The news about the first leg of the trip, the thousand miles between Kinshasa and Kisangani, our halfway point, was good. Fenhagen reported that colonial-era riverboats continued to run as far as Kisangani, a city in the interior formerly known as Stanleyville, with fair, although unpredictable, regularity. The diet of local vegetables and scrawny chicken he told us to expect on board sounded better than the 'rice full of weevils' that we had read about in a guidebook for low-budget travelers in central Africa, and each boat reportedly had a few cabins with private baths.

But beyond Kisangani, a city with a sinister reputation gained during bloody rebellions in the 1960s, there was no telling how we would be able to proceed.

'There are no scheduled boats beyond Kisangani, but, as you suggested, there is a railroad of sorts,' Fenhagen wrote. 'It will function between some points and undoubtedly not function between other points but it's very hard to get precise information in Kinshasa on the precise state of the art. My guess is that the railroad will run on a highly irregular basis,' he concluded guardedly.

He provided us with a Peace Corps memorandum saying that possibility of travel beyond Kisangani looked bleak. Aside from the problematic trains, boats either did not exist or, if they did, were not recommended because of their dismal condition and erratic schedules. 'I'd really advise against that river trip south of Kisangani,' the memo warned.

We had already decided that if continuing upriver was impossible, we would try to head east, through the land of the Pygmies, to the Uganda border and the habitat of Tim's mountain gorillas. But that too might be difficult. I learned from two former Peace Corps volunteers who had lived and traveled in Zaire's interior that the roads were almost impassable in the unpredictable rainy season. They told us stories about muddy roads that had potholes, pits really, so deep that cargo trucks disappeared into them. One of the volunteers recounted stepping from the edge of one of these holes to the roof of a truck stuck at the bottom.

Air travel was not reliable either, Fenhagen advised us. 'Please remember that schedules in Zaire mean absolutely nothing. Air Zaire cancels its flights without even thinking twice and the only thing you can safely predict is delays.'

Fenhagen warned us, too, about 'matabeesh,' the bribes that accomplish most business in Zaire. 'The whole economy is built on it,' he explained. 'It's simply the only way to get anything basic done. An extra one hundred zaires [about three dollars] left with the local ticket agent can make a big difference and you'll find this to be a most important consideration throughout your trip.'

Even with Fenhagen's cautions, we were greatly encouraged that at least part of the trip seemed feasible. We had no idea that, in the end, our greatest difficulties would come at the hands of Mobutu's security police.

The river, as it has been for millennia, was still the best highway into the tropical fastnesses of the Congo Basin. We were going to see firsthand, as few Westerners have, what has happened in the interior of Zaire as the result of America's sponsorship of Mobutu.

ONE

We both were jumpy on the long night flight from Brussels to Kinshasa. Despite the months spent theorising in the comfort of our Baltimore home, we did not have a clear idea about what was going to happen to us once we landed in central Africa. Our project to travel up the Congo River seemed more and more foolhardy the closer we got to our destination.

The Belgian jet carried us south over the Mediterranean, past the northern coast of Africa and through the empty night above the Sahara Desert, past the Sahelian savannas, and finally over the rim of the Congo Basin to Zaire. If it had been daylight, we could have looked down into that basin and seen a great tropical forest stretching from horizon to horizon. We also could have seen the Congo River cleaving through the greenery. It was far too late to turn back.

We were arriving at Njili airport on the outskirts of Kinshasa at midnight, and the passengers around us slept or grumbled about their fatigue in the claustrophobic security of the cabin. Most were with a pack of tourists heading on to South Africa. We were wide awake when the jet began its descent, peering through a scuffed porthole, straining to see something and then catching sight of the lights of the capital shining raggedly up through the darkness.

A woman, one of the tourists fleeing a chilly European autumn for the sunshine of Africa's racially segregated south, leaned into the aisleway to ask her guide what was going to happen at the stopover.

'Mind your own business and you'll not be molested,' the tour guide answered, and then explained that customs officials accompanied by rifle-toting guards would board the plane for an inspection. 'Be glad you're not getting off here,' he said as the plane touched down.

If we had had any choice in the matter, we would have arrived at high noon when the equatorial sun rises to the zenith and sears away the darkness, the ambiguities, and all but the most clandestine of shadows. Instead, we emerged from the airplane into blankets of heat that hung on the night. We breathed and then sniffed, sniffing again at the acrid air of the place. It smelled like something rotten burning. A tattered half moon threw an orangish light onto the landing strip, which was scattered with clusters of figures. Disoriented by the dark heat and the air's smoky burn, we were at a loss as to which way to go.

We had been hoping that Wes Fenhagen, the gracious information officer at the American embassy, had arranged to have someone meet us as we disembarked. We were expert at maneuvering through strange airports and normally would have been insulted by an offer of help. But security here in Kinshasa, even if it came from US officialdom whose role in Zaire was one of the things we had come to examine, was not to be shunned.

The other passengers had fanned out without any apparent pattern or purpose. No orderly stream of people showed us where to go so, clutching our gear, we headed toward some lights, prepared for the worst. As we neared the lights, we saw they were shining from the windows of a low building on whose step a large black man was standing. He was watching us and came bounding down with surprising agility for a man of his size. We stopped in our tracks.

'Alo! Alo!' he was shouting. 'Bonjour. Êtes-vous les journalistes des États-Unis?'

We were safe in the hands of an airport 'expediter,' a man with the singularly Zairian profession of getting travelers and their possessions through the airport. The fear that had been shrouding my vision dropped away. The expediter, talking and laughing, enclosed us in his confidence. He ushered us into a dim, confused passageway where people jostled each other. Having led us to a corner, the expediter told us to wait while he dealt with customs for us. We passed him our passports and, as a bribe, he sandwiched money between the pages. Within minutes he was escorting us past the customs stations, waved through by uniformed officials.

He said the airport was not as dangerous as it had been. Things had gotten so bad – travelers were being beaten up if they couldn't produce the requisite bribe money – that the government had hired Belgians to oversee the customs operation.

The officials let us through a gate into a room where luggage handlers were heaving crates and suitcases up a ramp, the backs of their orange coveralls soaked with sweat. Another bribe and we got our luggage, a collection of expeditionary and journalistic gear. The two of us were able to hoist and carry this gear, but only with a good deal more effort than grace. Crammed into two canvas suitcases and a lightweight duffel bag were a dozen plastic bottles of insect repellant (the most pungent, potent brand sold); a large spray can of insecticide (for bugs in general); a brass camping stove (compact and able to burn kerosene, a commonly available fuel in Africa where most people don't have electricity); a metal fuel bottle and funnel; two bulky US Army surplus mosquito nets; cotton clothes (to mitigate the greenhouse heat we expected on the river); long-sleeved shirts and knee-high socks (another barrier against the ravening swarms of riverine mosquitoes we expected); powdered Tang (to be hydrated and mixed with vodka for soothing the itch of mosquito bites and counteracting boredom or fear); twenty tin-foil packets of freeze-dried food (each packet labeled with a deceptively appealing name like 'Shrimp Cantonese with Long-Grain and Wild Rice'); notepads, pens, typing paper, and paper clips; a portable typewriter; letters of recommendation (addressed 'To Whom It May Concern'); books for inspiration, like *Heart of Darkness*, and books for information, like the unrelentingly dry US government handbook on Zaire; eighty-five rolls of film, two cameras, and five lenses; medicines (for killing bacteria, treating fevers, curing diarrhoea, preventing malaria, and purifying water); string; needles and thread; a portable shortwave radio; a flashlight and a candle lantern; a miniature alarm clock; a compass and binoculars; a Swiss army knife each; water bottles and a five-gallon, collapsible plastic water bag; extra batteries; padlocks, and an elaborate painter's color chart (an extravagance on which I insisted for the rendering of an accurate chromatic description of the river and the land).

Except perhaps for the knee socks and the lantern we were packing, we did not remotely resemble the grand expeditionary forces that had preceded us into Africa's interior in search of slaves, ivory, or glory. We carried no trading beads or rifles, and nothing like the portable boat one expedition had lugged across Africa. We were not out to claim anything in the name of civilisation, nation, or ideology. We were looking instead for an understanding of the impact the Arabs, Europeans, and Americans who preceded us had made on the Congo.

A baggage man, his coveralls disintegrating into holes at the elbows and knees, boosted our gear onto his shoulders with the supple ease usual in countries where most of the heavy work is done by hand. He balanced the whole load out through the front of the terminal, where passengers hoping to get seats on domestic flights slept bundled against the wall, to the expediter's car. Some boys and young men whose skinniness made them look juvenile were waiting outside the terminal. Hoping to grab up some morsel of our wealth, they closed around us like animals at feeding time. They clamored in the rough French spoken throughout Zaire, a reminder of the Belgians who imposed this delicate language on their brawny colony. Some begged outright for money and some insisted they deserved pay for guarding the parked car against the depredations of the others, while some others edged in looking for an unwatched pocket or satchel to snatch.

'Patron. Patron. Give us money, please, please.'

'You see your car is safe. We have guarded your car well. No one has damaged your tires. No one has taken your mirror. You can see.'

'We are hungry. We are hungry. You must give us money.'

They pleaded in high-pitched shouts and threatened with pitiful ultimatums. I tried to look as if I were ignoring them, heard nothing they said, and did not care. Years ago in Ethiopia, I had learned to pretend to stare past beggars, even the most heartbreaking, the lepers with their eaten-away faces, and the blind children who slept in paper sacks. To give to every one would have been impossible and to care about every one would have driven me insane. But behind my façade, I have never stopped being wrenched by Africa's many beggars, who so crudely illustrate the gulf between the rich and the poor, between health and sickness, between me and them, between my country and theirs. We slammed the car doors and the expediter handed out some small change.

'Please, patron, please help us. Please. Patronn, patronnn.' Their pleas lengthened. They pursued us with their voices as we drove off into the streets of the enormous slum that lies between the airport and downtown Kinshasa.

Kinshasa is a city worthy of its fantastic location on a southern bank of the Congo River, just above the place where the river changes from a placid giant to a furious cataract plunging down through the Crystal Mountains to the Atlantic Ocean. From a balcony of our small hotel near the city's port, we got our first look at the river rolling past the tin-roofed port warehouses. The opposite bank was miniature in the distance and the thick rumpling of the river's current suggested its submerged power. Seeing the Congo for the first time, I was impressed by the river's purposefulness, its huge and unstoppable sweep toward sea level and the ocean's anonymity. Other rivers I have seen, including the Nile and the Mississippi, do not have this same precocious sense of destiny.

From the hotel, we watched the bustle of people moving through the port gates, merchants and passengers bound upriver or arriving downriver from some backwater. We planned to take one of the aging riverboats that continue to ply the Congo's longest navigable section from Kinshasa to Kisangani deep in central Africa's great rain forest.

We had reserved space on a boat that promised to depart

the day after our arrival in Kinshasa – at least *'en principe,'* as
Zairians would say. Everything here runs in principle if not in
reality. The riverboat stuck to its schedule *en principe*, which
meant that it could depart any time of any day, or not at all. In
the coming weeks we were going to relearn this lesson and
some of its corollaries.

On the first of the three days we ended up waiting in
Kinshasa, we got a good piece of advice from one of the
watchmen who guarded the hotel's front door. On the way out
to look for some breakfast in the unfamiliar city, we asked the
watchman, the 'sentinel' in Zairian French, how safe it was to
walk around. He answered with a warning about *les gendarmes*,
the soldiers policing the city's streets.

'Les gendarmes sont les grands voleurs,' the old watchman
said, screwing his weather-beaten face into a grimace to under-
score the gravity of his words. 'The police are the biggest
thieves. Always watch out for them.'

Fortunately, we didn't see any soldiers that first morning
we walked out into the downtown streets of Kinshasa. Trees
laden with elephantine leaves edged the side streets, casting
deep pools of shade. Other trees hoisted crowns of purple and
flaming orange blossoms toward the pure tropical blue of the
matitudinal sky. The streets were busy. Quick Fiat taxis darted
through the traffic streaming along wide boulevards, past stores
and restaurants, churches, embassies, and the big buildings of
the government mining and transportation bureaucracies. It
looked like any modern European city, with high-rise office and
apartment towers rising from the sidewalks.

Unfortunately, we didn't have a good idea of where we were
going. The hotel sentinel had directed us to a place a few blocks
away, but we missed it, doubled back, and missed it again.
Frustrated and getting hotter as the sun climbed steeply into
the sky, we headed off in another direction, presuming that
we would eventually find something to eat. We had gone about
ten blocks from the hotel and the downtown highrises and,
because the sidewalk had disappeared, were walking in the
street when a shiny, high-sprung Chevrolet jeep pulled up. Its
tires left fresh tread marks in the dust at the edge of the street.

'Jump in,' said the driver, a woman with a Texas drawl. We hesitated.

'I guess you're the reporters from Baltimore. I'm Angier Peavy,' she said by way of explanation. 'I work for Wes Fenhagen. I was looking for you back at the hotel and the sentinel said you'd walked this way.'

Angier Peavy worked under Fenhagen at the United States Information Agency, whose worldwide centers dispense American culture, ideas, books, and information. The agency beams its version of the news around the world, a function the Reagan administration has used heavily to disseminate propaganda. Peavy was in charge of organising visits to Zaire by American speakers and cultural groups, like the dancing troupe she was going to meet that morning across town at the Intercontinental Hotel.

'This isn't a great street to be walking down,' she said after we had climbed into the front seat. 'I stopped once at this corner and two men jumped through each front window to try to grab my purse. They didn't get it, but in case you ask, that's why I keep the windows rolled up.'

Peavy laughed and drank back a slug of Tab from a can, a drink she was seldom without as she made her way through the heat of Kinshasa's days. Unlike many of the Americans posted in Zaire, she enjoyed the country, at least what she knew of it from life in the capital. She had been a Peace Corps volunteer in Asia, and Third World places appealed to her Texan ruggedness. Not that living abroad as an official American is so physically hard. Peavy was about to move into an attractive house near the river and was awaiting the importation of her personal car.

We got some breakfast at the Intercontinental's coffee shop while Peavy went to round up the American dancers for a little shopping tour she had promised them. At the doors of the air-conditioned Intercontinental, Kinshasa's only posh hotel, we had crossed back into the privileged and comfortable First World. We could have been in any city in any modern upper-class hotel, with views over landscaped grounds whose palm trees gave the only clue to the surrounding geography.

Five of the dancers came back down with Peavy and we all left for the *Marché d'Ivoire*, the Ivory Market, the only touristy place in Kinshasa. Driving toward downtown with Peavy and company, we began to see what lies behind the city's seeming modernity. Much of the commerce moved along the streets in rickety carts. The men who push these carts, homemade wheelbarrows for hauling loads, hire themselves out cheaply, for less than what it would cost to get a taxi. Muscle power is still cheaper in Kinshasa than machine power, an equation that has been absolutely reversed in the United States.

We noticed, too, that the strange acrid smell that had greeted us at the airport pervaded the city's atmosphere.

'I smelled it at first,' Peavy informed us. 'But you get used to it. I don't smell it anymore. It's the normal Kinshasa smell.'

We drove by one of Kinshasa's finest buildings, a new international trade center financed by the French. Impressive as it was, rising white and clean above the roofs of the surrounding buildings, it was losing its tenants. The building's central air conditioning would not work properly and its windows couldn't be opened, turning it into a stifling disaster.

On the jeep's front seat, concealed in a straw basket, Peavy kept a heavy-duty communications radio. Sputtering out static and messages, the radio kept her patched into an American-run substitute for the city's telephone system. Kinshasa's telephones work sometimes, but so sporadically that the Americans avoid depending on them. Peavy told us a story about a telephone in the house of a diplomat who waited three years before the phone successfully received an international call. It just would not work right until one night in the middle of a thunderstorm, as lightning struck around the city, a long-distance call made it through. To maintain a modicum of efficiency, the US embassy and the US agencies issue walkie-talkies and communications radios to all official Americans. This radio network is linked up through a Marine command post set up behind bullet-proof glass in the embassy building's foyer.

The Ivory Market sits on a dusty lot next to the traffic circle that marks the culmination of Kinshasa's main street, named

Boulevard de Trente Juin, June 30th Boulevard, in tribute to the date of Zaire's independence from Belgium in 1960. The boulevard was laid out on a noble scale with wide medians, but the tall trees that once lent it grace were cut down on the orders of President Mobutu Sese Seko to make room for military parades.

When we arrived at the market, its merchants came to life, calling us and gesturing toward the tables on which they displayed the gaudiest of the bounty that comes down the river from the interior: carved elephant tusks and ivory trinkets; beetles, hearts, and other baubles made from swirly green malachite; the skins of snakes and crocodiles; figures made from ebony, mahogany, and other rain-forest hardwoods; ritual masks with bulbous eyes that can fix you with eternal stares. Some merchants were selling small gray monkeys and bright-plumed parrots captured in the forest miles upriver. The monkeys, shocked at being wrested from their aerial freedom, huddled in the corners of their wire cages and gazed blankly at the Fiats clattering past on the boulevard. Imbued with more bravado than the monkeys or blessed with lesser sensitivity, the parrots flapped their clipped wings and sang in imitation of the passing cars, 'Whoosh-whoosh, weeoosh, woowoo.'

Peavy proved to be an old hand at this market, which she frequented to build her collection of carved ivory animals. Within minutes she had bought an exquisitely detailed crocodile, while most of her charges milled around uncertain how to go about bargaining for one of the trinkets. There were no set prices and the buyers had to debate the cost of each item with tourist-hardened sellers shrewd enough to know the wealth of most foreigners.

A lofty pedestal dominates the market scene, but it rises upward vacantly, supporting nothing, commemorating nobody. The huge likeness of the Belgian King Albert I, who ruled when Zaire was a colony of Belgium, has been toppled and its pieces hauled away. But the memory of the Belgian has hung on. Everyone calls the commemorative spot 'ex-Albert Place,' renouncing yet clinging in a perverse way to Zaire's unhappy colonial history. Albert was not the only figure in Zaire's history to have been memorialised so emptily. He was nephew to one of the most infamous colonialists of all time, King Leopold II of Belgium.

Leaving Peavy and the dancers at the market, Tim and I walked to a park over by the parliament building, where we found a solid, flat plinth that was missing its original statue of Leopold. Having seen an old photograph of this park, I knew that Leopold's statue had represented the Belgian king astride a prancing horse, a sculptured king looking handsome and brave like a great leader rather than the tyrant that he was. In his name, wholesale massacres and atrocities were carried out against the people of central Africa.

Kinshasa also has an ex-Henry Morton Stanley site on a bluff looking out over the city and the river. Gone, too, is the statue of the first white man to solve the geographic riddle of the Congo's course and open its watershed to outside exploitation. Stanley established the original series of foreign trading stations along the river, including one on a bank of the river just above the cataracts that plunge to the Congo's estuary. He named this station Léopoldville in honor of the Belgian king who hired him to open the Congo. Léopoldville became Kinshasa.

The most stupendous empty monument of all is the parliament itself. From King Leopold's plinth, we looked through a fence and across a lawn to the parliament building, the shell for a democracy that died in its infancy. A parliament still meets here, but its members all belong to the same political party, the only one allowed by Mobutu Sese Seko, who rules with the absolute authority of a king.

Since 1965 when President Mobutu seized power, with American help, he has refrained from building any monuments to himself, solving his ego rather by assuming messianic titles like 'the Guide' and living in grand style. The country's official dress, too, is the Mobutu suit, so called because the president himself designed it.

All over downtown Kinshasa, we saw men of prestigious position in the Zairian hierarchy wearing these Mobutu suits, ridiculous outfits given the heat that engulfed the city. A Mobutu suit looks like a partly unbuttoned version of the famous Mao suit, but the Zairian costume is commonly tailored from dark, oppressive wools. We saw bankers, bureaucrats, and businessmen sweating through the afternoons and proving their fealty to the president's regime.

On our first evening in Kinshasa, we were sitting in an outdoor café opposite our hotel when night fell quickly down around us. Since we were not sure when our boat was going to depart up the river, we were making tentative plans for the coming day. The port officers had not allowed us to get anywhere near the riverboat, and so we still did not know what was in store.

'If it's got rats, then we don't have to go ahead with it,' Tim said, reviewing an agreement we had made. If the riverboat was truly disgusting and unlivable, then we could back out and abandon at least that part of our plan. I had agreed not to put up a strenuous argument for forging ahead, which Tim knew I would want to do.

'That's the deal,' I assured him, even though I was not sure that I would keep the promise.

Out in the street, some men were scraping together a pile of twigs and dried grass, refuse and crumpled paper, heaping the rubbish against a curb. They set the pile afire and settled down in the circle of light, cooking something in a blackened tin can. The nearby streets, too, were dotted with fires. Our realisation was sudden – these street fires were the source of the bitter-smelling smoke that gave Kinshasa the evil perfume we first noticed at the airport. Trash is the fuel of the poorest of the city's millions of poor people.

At night we did not walk far from the hotel, never venturing beyond the light cast by the nearer garbage fires and beyond the scrutiny of the teams of watchmen who guarded every building that might be worth burglarising. We feared thieves, both regular thieves and uniformed ones. Almost everyone we ran across had advice about how to avoid getting robbed or some story about getting robbed.

To protect against pickpockets, I took safety pins and

fastened down the flap of the canvas satchel I carried. Tim had a couple of pins closing off the pants pocket in which he carried his wallet. But we did not have any countermeasures against official thievery.

A government clerk whom we had met down by the port told us about an encounter he had with a gendarme on a downtown street. He was shopping and carrying quite a bit of money.

'A gendarme saw that I had this money and grabbed me right there by the arm. He said he would arrest me unless I gave him some money. I said I had done nothing wrong and he could not arrest me for nothing. This went on and on, and we finally agreed that if I paid him one thousand zaires [about thirty-five dollars], he would leave me in peace.' The clerk shrugged. 'I paid him.'

If a gendarme grabbed us, our safety-pin system clearly would be of little use. Better not get grabbed at all, which is the strategy the American embassy recommends to its staff. It issues a manual to arriving Americans that instructs them not to cooperate with officials, to quash their impulse to obey the police and trust authority. The manual tells them never to roll down the windows of their cars when they are stopped by police officials and never to hand over their driver's licenses or travel documents. They are to show their papers through a rolled up window and from behind a locked door, the manual advises. The gendarmes are known for robbing with impunity not only on the city streets but also at fraudulent roadblocks, where passage is granted for money or for an impromptu gift, like a pack of cigarettes or a wristwatch.

This is merely a symptom, though, of the corruption that has come to pervade Zaire from President Mobutu's office on down to the streets. Often, the gendarmes do not get even their meager pay because their officers have stolen much or all of the payrolls, following the eminent example of the president and an inner circle of powerful politicians who habitually loot the national treasury.

Our second day in Kinshasa, we made preparations toward our potential departure and spent much of the day getting stocked up on supplies. To our surprise and convenience, we found a 'supermarket' filled with imported clothes, china, and appliances. The store was like an old-fashioned American department store with wooden floors and wares displayed in glassed-in cases.

We were interested in finding vodka and portable foods. The liquor section offered high-quality European stuff at wonderfully low prices. Two bottles of Gilbey's vodka cost us less than what we would have paid in England. We passed up a shelf of English jams and a cooler of Belgian cheeses. By American standards, the store was less than opulent, but in the African context, it was obscene.

Importing luxury goods like those in the supermarket means spending foreign currency, which is in terribly short supply in Zaire and a host of African countries whose own feeble currencies are not accepted on the international market. Since foreign currency is desperately needed to import gasoline, medicine, spare parts for railroads and machinery, and foodstuffs, many countries in Africa restrict luxury imports, reserving foreign exchange for nationally vital imports. But not Zaire, where Mobutu has catered to his circle of wealthy political henchmen while the country's foreign debt has grown so massive that he must periodically beseech the International Monetary Fund for new loans and for postponements on repaying its old loans.

Just before our visit, Zaire had reached another agreement with the international fund for a bail-out loan of $300 million. To get this financial infusion, the Zairian government promised to clamp down on corruption, not for the first time, and agreed to a drastic devaluation of its currency. A meteoric leap in the price of basic food and fuel, which surprised the Western economists who thought they understood the workings of the Zairian economy, had made life that much more difficult for the city's poor.

The supermarket did not sell anything as basic as the kerosene we still needed for our little camping stove, so we left to look elsewhere. Outside, a few blocks from the American embassy, two beggars were trying to catch the attention of the shoppers, many of them women in high-heeled shoes and Parisian dresses. One of the beggars was a man afflicted with elephantiasis, a disease that had caused gigantesque swelling of his legs and testicles. To garner the shoppers' pity, he squatted by the door and pulled aside a cloth hung around his loins to show his swollen parts. The other beggar was a blind woman accompanied by a child who snatched up the fluttering paper money dropped by an occasional shopper.

We went next to the outdoor market, where most people do their buying. Kerosene was essential to our hopes for staying healthy in the Zairian interior, where malaria, yellow fever, and cholera flourish. (The Congo is such a fertile breeding ground of tropical diseases that medical investigators are blaming the region for incubating AIDS.) Both of us had suffered already from several tropical illnesses and this time we were determined not to get sick. We planned to cook our own food, if necessary, and boil our drinking water.

The market, a conglomeration of stalls, sheds, and tables from which thousands of merchants were hawking their wares and foodstuffs in the classic African style, was the size of a couple of baseball stadiums. Our search began among the vegetables, heaps of potatoes, pyramids of cabbages and sacks of manioc, the starchy root that looks something like a fat parsnip and is the staple food all over Zaire. The manioc area was in uproar. Those looking to buy were arguing with the merchants, ranging up and down the lines of sacks and demanding lower prices. A gunnysack of the roots was going for twenty dollars, a price that had doubled since the devaluation to more than the average government teacher earned in a month. We traversed the vegetable section and got thoroughly lost on the dirt pathways that twisted through the places for cloth and clothes, second hand spare parts, smoked snakes, dried fish, spices, plastic shoes, baskets, used gunnysacks, just about anything a Kinshasa resident might need. We finally stumbled across the kerosene near the section devoted to the resale of tin cans and plastic bottles, and then retreated to the relative order of the downtown streets.

Nearly everyone we saw was carrying some kind of purse

to hold money, just to have enough cash to buy several dollars' worth of food. Some people were hauling around footlockers full of money they needed for larger transactions. People leaving the national bank had stuffed their money into cardboard boxes. One zaire, the country's basic unit of currency, is worth less than three American pennies. We changed a couple of hundred dollars and filled half a suitcase with stacks of zaires. Even the Marines assigned to the embassy carried satchels and purses.

That evening we went to a reception at the American ambassador's residence given for the visiting folk dancers by the ambassador's deputy. We walked to the residence in the late afternoon down shady streets where houses of the rich stood protected in high-walled compounds. Flies prospered in the sultriness of the ending day and, hunting them, purple-tailed lizards stalked in slow motion on the branches of flowering trees.

I sensed the tropical forest that once blanketed the city's location. With the arrival of dusk, mosquitoes, gnats, and other winged insects emerged from their hideaways underneath leaves and roof corners. Fruit bats chased the insects, which swarmed in cloudlets on the Congo's banks. In the tall trees along the river, we saw that people had stretched nets to catch the bats for their own eating. We continued out along the river on whose opposite bank we could make out Brazzaville, the capital city of the Republic of the Congo, Kinshasa's geographically close and politically distant neighbor.

We had no trouble finding the ambassador's house, for little red, white, and blue lights strung in the shrubbery around the residence declared the American presence on the Congo. The evening was warm and waiters served drinks and hors d'oeuvres to the guests on the lawn. The hostess, the deputy chief of mission's wife, fussed with candles meant to illuminate the veranda that kept getting blown out by gusts of wind coming in off the river. Since we had not had any dinner, we gratefully took the proferred meatballs on toothpicks and sausages wrapped in pastry.

Among the guests was Wes Fenhagen, who turned out to

be a wiry, soft-spoken man in his sixties. He told us how much he envied us our trip up the Congo. He had himself never been up the river that defines Zaire's interior, but he relished the idea a good deal more than some of the other diplomatic and foreign-aid officers to whom he introduced us.

'Oh, I've known about those riverboats for years, but I never considered taking one. I think they're pretty crowded,' one man said.

'Riverboats?' asked another. 'I didn't know boats went up the river. Sounds like something out of a movie.'

'It might be a pretty rough trip,' said another. 'They've got all kinds of things in that river. Crocodiles, hippos, diseases. The German diplomatic residence was near here, the German ambassador went for a dip in the river and a crocodile got him. All that was left was his hat, which they found floating on the river.'

A Greek businessman, a very successful man who lived upriver in Kisangani, told us to forget the whole idea.

'If you want to see the river, take an airplane to Kisangani and I will have you taken out on the river in a motorboat for an hour, two hours. That's all you need to see. The river is just a river. You needn't study it for a thousand miles.'

Those few days we were in Kinshasa, one Zairian in particular took interest in showing us the harsher side of the city. He worked in the office of an American company that does business in Kinshasa. He told us how difficult life was, even for the relatively well-to-do, and how unhappy the people had become with Mobutu's government.

'If the people were free, this government would be finished in a week,' our Zairian friend said once we had left downtown and arrived at a place where he felt he could talk safely. We had settled into the darkened corner of a bar deep in the outlying slums.

Mobutu's critics are careful not to speak loudly in public places or to speak softly to the wrong person. We understood why, because we had read and heard about Zaire's security police. Their power to arrest suspect dissidents without charge, interrogate them, torture them, and even kill them is limited only by presidential whim. When Zairians talked to us about their government, we were careful not to reveal their names, giving them code names even in notebooks and pseudonyms in our writing.

Our friend kept talking about Mobutu and the United States. He had worked nearly twenty years in one American business or another around the city and had grown to admire Americans for their efficiency and their friendliness, so different from the customary aloofness of the Belgians. But the American government's official policy toward Mobutu troubled him.

'The day will come when God will reach down and take Mobutu to his rest. When that happens the people will rejoice and they also will remember that Mobutu was the Americans' man. The Americans were for Mobutu and Mobutu was for the Americans, but they forgot about the people. The Americans are inheriting Mobutu's unpopularity.'

We were all three drinking from big, almost quart-sized bottles of Zairian beer. Tim and I drank and listened, but our friend forgot about the beer in front of him, so vehement was his monologue. He was bearlike, heavy and strong. His eyes, set wide above the generous planes of his cheeks, were merry but as he told us about himself tears brimmed in his eyes. His wife was gravely ill with cancer and he had six children to care for and finish educating, responsibilities compounded enormously by the fact that he lived in Zaire.

'I have been desperate trying to get treatment for my wife,' he said. 'I have to make sure she is going to get medical care and medicines. Taking her to the hospital makes no guarantee of treatment. So I had to borrow five thousand zaires and I had to go here and there, giving a bribe for the nurse, for the doctor, for the bed.' He mimicked himself passing out wads of money. 'In Zaire, nothing happens without a bribe. Even mercy has a price.'

He also had to find bribe money to put his children through Zaire's schools.

'For my oldest son to enter university in Kinshasa, it was not on the status of his marks. No, it was because I gave the necessary bribe. The same for secondary school.

'Everywhere, everywhere people ask for bribes. Starting at the top. Mobutu is the biggest crook of all. He has stolen so much from the country's wealth that everyone else has to scramble and cheat to get a share of the leftovers,' he said.

Zairians like to boast about their country, which has been truly theirs for just a quarter of a century. They are as proud as Texans about the size of Zaire, the third largest country in Africa, as big as the portion of the United States lying east of the Mississippi. They marvel at the immense natural wealth of their country – a mineral bounty that includes cobalt, copper, diamonds, gold, and iron as well as the Congo River itself, which possesses untapped hydroelectric potential and provides the country with a whole network of waterways.

But boasting was easier a decade ago, when prices on the international market for copper and other minerals were higher. The country's healthy export earnings buffered the growing corruption in Mobutu's increasingly authoritarian government. The burden of government corruption is no longer so bearable, copper prices have fallen, and little is left over for the people after those in power take what they want.

'I used to say that Zaire has problems but don't judge too harshly because the country is so young. It has to learn how to be a country. I used to say that my country was rich and would be taking its place among the advanced countries of the world. I don't make that argument any more. I think Zaire has learned how to be a bad country, a rich country of poor people,' our friend said.

'I will show you what I mean,' he said. He led us out of the bar into the bright streets and byways of the slum called 'La Cité.' It had been established by Belgian colonialists, who dictated that all Africans live in districts at a remove from the much pleasanter city center.

The most striking things about La Cité are its size and its sameness. Driving out to the bar, we had passed mile after mile of miserable shanties. People filled the streets – pedestrians dodging cars and bicycles, petty entrepreneurs hurrying on commercial errands, boys looking for something to do. The buses plying the larger streets were so jammed that passengers stood on the fenders and sat in the windows. Most of the residents of Kinshasa have their homes in this megalopolis of shanties. Three million people live here, perhaps more. No one has taken an accurate census of the number of Zairians who have flocked to Kinshasa, hoping for better lives than the ones they left in rural huts or towns, but finding instead *La Cité*.

An open sewer paralleled the street where we commenced our walk. Chickens pecked along its banks and a couple of goats wandered nearby, looking for weedy fodder growing at the sewer's edge. Three men were scouring the banks for bits of broken glass, which they were separating carefully into piles, one for brown shards, another for green, another for clear. Our friend explained that at the end of the day, the men would haul the glass to a junk collector and earn a few pennies.

'They'll make enough so that they won't have to worry about being hungry again until tomorrow,' he said.

He led us from street to byway, across wooden planks that bridged sewers and along pathways of dirty sand. I lost all sense of direction. Almost all the buildings were one-storey, some of cinderblock and many of mud brick. Women and children carried buckets of water from community taps to lean-to kitchens where they fixed their meals over wood and charcoal fires.

Our friend talked as we turned down another side street where our shoes sank into the sand. He said that the devaluation of the country's currency had been hard.

'The president has used up the people's goodwill. The people cannot even buy an aspirin when they are sick. They do not have shoes. They cannot afford school fees. I tell you, he has used up his credit. The Zairians have fallen to the ground,' he said. He halted his stride to underline his words. *'Les Zaïrois sont par terre.'*

Our friend was making his judgments on what he had seen happening in Kinshasa, because he had not been into the country's interior in years. Even for Zairians, the country is a difficult place to travel.

TWO

On the morning the riverboat was finally ready to depart, the port came alive. The first of the passengers arrived with the dawn and kept arriving, carrying with them every sort of baggage. They streamed through the gates, across the wharf, down a shaky metal stairway that landed on a stack of plywood pallets, and along a greasy steel dock that floated on the river. They lugged oil drums, metal trunks, bundles, baskets, children, suitcases, chickens, sacks, cartons, wheelbarrows, bolts of cloth, bags of salt, and hundreds of other possessions. They wrangled, wrestled, and argued with the stevedores, who could be paid to load the heaviest things. All the passengers were trying simultaneously to get themselves and their goods aboard and stowed safely away in some corner of the riverboat or its flotilla of passenger barges.

The boat itself was a four-deck relic from colonial days named the *Major Mudimbi*. It was powered by two enormous diesel engines whose task was to drag and push the five barges, which were lashed with steel cables to the *Mudimbi*'s blunt prow and battered sides, each as long as the riverboat itself and each soon crammed with people, animals, and merchandise.

About 1500 steerage-class passengers were going to ride the barges upriver. Two of the barges were flat, but the others were topped with tiers of metal-walled, cell-like rooms that were superior only to the aisleways and open decks where the poorest passengers settled in for the journey. A lucky few found comparative peace in odd niches in the cargo holds below decks. The hundred or so passengers who could afford first-class tickets took cabins on an upper deck of the *Mudimbi* herself.

We must have looked strange as we boarded, hauling our assorted gear, which now also included a bag stuffed with stacks of Zairian money, and followed by a porter we had hired to carry our five-gallons of purified water. But we were soon surrounded by fellow passengers who were too harried to stare at the spectacle we made. We had booked a *'cabine de luxe,'* one of two top-class, supposedly luxury cabins originally designed to provide the requisite comforts to high Belgian officials. In the weeks preceding our trip, we had allowed ourselves to imagine that our berths might be pleasant, and perhaps even grand. Having a fertile imagination, Tim optimistically pictured a wood-paneled stateroom, a bedroom with elegant bunks hinged to the walls, and a bathroom done up with copper fixtures and gleaming tile.

Only when we boarded the boat on the day of departure did we realise just how much the *Mudimbi* had aged since its commission in the Belgian colonial service shortly after World War II. Nothing about the squarish old riverboat was quite shipshape, from the pair of banged-up lifeboats at her stern to the chipped white paint at her prow. The gunwales were missing random sections of screening, giving the boat a gap-toothed look.

Up on the second deck we found a steward, a short man who wore a starched white uniform but padded down the deck barefoot. He unlocked the door to our cabin. Tim walked in first and looked around.

'Oh no,' he said.

He told me later that he had wanted to take the next plane back home when he saw the metal box of a room, low-ceilinged and absolutely lacking in luxury.

Years' worth of cobwebs and dusty gunk hung in the corners. The walls were a malevolent light green splotched with stains of unidentifiable origins. Two sagging cots and a couple of small tables competed for space with an imposing wooden armoire, one of whose scarred doors had come permanently unfastened and hung out over the beds. A door opened onto the bathroom, which had all of the necessary fixtures – cold-water sink, cold-water bathtub, and toilet – all of which were filthy. Beneath the inside rim on the toilet bowl cockroaches hid, attracted by the damp semidarkness. They were king-sized and had wings.

I stopped worrying about whether the topnotch accommodations were going to isolate us from the reality of the Congo. Tim braced himself for yet another uncomfortable trip, wondering when he was going to learn that traveling with me was never going to be easy. But his real problem was that he also had become fascinated with the idea of this journey. He could blame it on me, suggesting that he would have been better off with a more sedentary woman, but he knew he would have been bored with a more predictable partner.

We set about trying to clean up the cabin. Tim knocked down the cobwebs and levered open the metal shutters that had been rusting closed over the windows, while I sewed patches of mosquito netting over rents in the door screens. We scrubbed at the grime in the bathroom but with little result, so deeply was it ingrained. Being the strategist among the two of us, Tim went to war with the band of cockroaches in the toilet and the whole larger army of them that infested the cabin and outnumbered us by a ratio of hundreds to one. He attacked with our can of insecticide and, when he hit them with the fatal spray, the roaches went into frenzies, buzzing upwards before falling in drunken circles onto the floor.

Meanwhile, the steward returned with sheets. By pulling the sheets taut, he made the cots look flat and neat, at least until the sheets settled into the sags and came untucked at the edges since they had not been wide enough to begin with. I tried to start a conversation with the steward.

'We thank you very much,' I said in French. 'Please, we want to know your name.'

He backed toward the door, his boyish face clouded.

'Jimmy,' he said, pronouncing it 'Jeemee' as a Belgian would.

'Is that your real name? Or is that the name the Belgians gave you?' I asked.

'Jimmy is my name,' he said, and sidled toward the door.

'Okay. Jeemee it is,' I said, trying to reassure him with a friendly tone. 'How many years have you worked on the riverboats?'

'Thirty years,' he answered, offering no elaboration, bowing, and making his escape.

Including the luxury cabins, the *Mudimbi* had five classes. Our cabin, which was at the very stern of the boat, shared a deck with the first-class rooms. These were narrow, unventilatable rooms meant for two, and often occupied by as many as eight, passengers. At the end of the deck was the first-class dining room, whose carved mahogany bar and white tablecloths spoke to its former grandeur and whose warping floor spoke to its current neglect. Second-class tickets bought spaces in bunkrooms on the upper tiers of the barges and third-class in smaller, hotter rooms below, where most of the river merchants, or *commerçants*, established themselves. Fourth class, which seemed to be comprised mainly of threadbare students and itinerant soldiers, entitled the passenger to whatever spot he could claim on an aisleway bench or the unfurnished deck.

Preparing the *Mudimbi* for departure was a daylong event, during which order and purpose frequently capitulated to disorder and dispute. The hubbub made slow going of an exploratory walk I took around the boat. At the bottom of the stairway to the riverboat's lower deck, someone had stacked some cylindrical wicker baskets, inside which a couple of dozen yellow and black chickens fluttered. I had to make my way over this obstacle without crushing the chickens and also without hiking my cotton dress, which I wore at mid-calf length to satisfy African propriety. The Zairians who were nearby pretended not to watch, polite above all even when confronted with the sight of a white woman with long blond hair trying to find a path through the hodgepodge they were so familiar with. I hid my own doubts and curiosity behind a studied nonchalance, acting as if stepping over a pile of chickens in a long dress while maintaining a sense of grace in front of strangers was something I did every day.

Starting back toward the barges, I squeezed past a man carrying a spotted goat around his shoulders like a shawl, holding its hog-tied feet at his chest. Three women followed him, each with a gunnysack of something balanced heavily on her head and the last with a vinyl suitcase atop the sack. I edged my way along the dockside railing to the main gangplank, where a crew was hoisting aboard crate after crate of beer. Beyond them, two stevedores were raising a ruckus, gesticulating and shouting at a man in a Mobutu suit who was standing on the wharf and shouting back. The stevedores were broadcasting their outrage over the humiliatingly small sum he had paid them for carrying his goods. When their arguments failed to persuade him to augment their wage, first one, then the other, threw down the precious money and stalked away.

To get forward from the *Mudimbi* proper, I had to leap across a trough of water and onto the end of the first barge. A wide corridor partway along this barge was being transformed into a marketplace by a couple dozen *commerçants*, who were laying out the wares they would trade with the people upriver.

I threaded my way through a group of them, nodding my head and saying, '*Bonjour. Bonjour.*'

A young woman with a pretty face and large, almost diamond-shaped eyes nodded in reply but said nothing.

'*Mbote,*' I then said, trying to pronounce the greeting accurately.

The woman jerked her head up and snapped her eyes on me.

'*Sango nini?*' I asked.

'*Sango te,*' she answered before clapping her hand to her mouth and breaking into laughter. Some other *commerçants* who had overheard the exchange laughed, too, and called out explanations for the amusement of those who had not heard.

I had said hello and asked the news in Lingala, a Bantu tongue that is spoken the length of the river and has become Zaire's main commercial and military language. She had given the polite answer, telling me there was nothing going on.

The *commerçants* all spoke the rough French that is the lingua franca of this country of more than two hundred tribes and an equal diversity of languages. They were accustomed to foreigners who came speaking French, but to hear me say something in one of their own languages cut close to their hearts. People here are acutely aware of the tribe and the region from which someone comes and language plays a large part in defining tribal and geographical identities. Although my Lingala was limited and halting, the few sentences I could manage never failed to cause a sensation.

Working the crowd of boarding passengers like stadium hawkers, a number of boys were trying to sell skewers of roasted meat and cheap jewelry. Since I was a white foreigner and therefore rich beyond the dreams of most Zairians, a couple of these boys pursued me doggedly, finding it hard to believe that someone of my wealth would not buy at least one stick of meat. They gave up eventually, though, after I pushed forward through a crowded corridor and onto a lead barge.

More river merchants were busy on this flat barge, constructing tents by rigging canvases into makeshift shelters for the bales of used clothing and the other goods they were going to trade on the way upriver. The rusty deck and the odd assortment of flapping tarpaulins gave the barge a forlorn air. But it also gave me the feeling that it might metamorphose at any minute into a boisterous fair.

Gleaming in the late afternoon sun near the prow of this barge, I spotted a full suite of livingroom furniture upholstered with circus-red plastic that would have looked at home in the window of a discount furniture store somewhere in middle America. Several men were sitting on the sofa and chairs arranged in an intimate circle around a coffee table upon which were the dishes left from a meal. They invited me over to have a seat.

I answered their questions about where I was coming from and going to and they taught me some more Lingala. The owner of the furniture, a balding and paunchy man named Simon Kepe, said he was taking the suite to a store he ran in a town near the equator. I couldn't imagine who would be buying it. But, with its occupants, the suite did serve excellently as a living figurehead for the floating jumble on which we had embarked.

Before the *Mudimbi* pulled away from the dock, I jostled my way back toward the stern, feeling happy about being in Africa again. It was going to be impossible to feel lonely on this boat ride.

When I got back, the sun was setting. Tim was standing at the railing, having finished sorting out the cabin as much as was possible. Tall and with an Irish fairness, he looked out of place in the middle of a cluster of youths who had overcome their initial wariness and were pestering him in bad French to give them a lesson in English. Tim's face was clenched in concentration as he tried to decipher their many demands.

Suddenly, startling us all, the *Mudimbi*'s whistle blew. The diesels kicked on and modulated into a low roar, pushing the barges slowly away from the dock.

By the time the boat nosed into the Congo's heavy current, the sun was dunking into the water and splattering the sky with the color of ripe tangerines. Across the river the beckoning lights had come on in Brazzaville, to where Zairians periodically flee to find sanctuary in the socialist and relatively peaceful Republic of the Congo. We stood at the stern rail, watching the waterfront lights of Kinshasa and Brazzaville shrink in the distance until they seemed to join into a flickering arc above the aqueous darkness.

Darkness closed in on either side of us as the *Mudimbi* churned northeast across Malebo Pool. More lake than pool, this is where the river flexes sideways and bulges to a width of fifteen miles, frustrated in its onward rush by the Crystal Mountains. A dry and stubborn range, these mountains act like a dam thrust across the river's path, squeezing it below Kinshasa into a chute of water that plunges and twists down toward the Atlantic Ocean. The river drops a full 1000 feet through a horrendous series of cataracts, 200 miles of white water that end at the river's estuary 100 miles yet from the ocean. It was these cataracts that worked for centuries to keep most of the world ignorant of the regions through which the Congo runs.

On a map, the river looks like a snake and its tributaries like a profusion of tails, curving through the middle of Africa, its head at the Atlantic and its longest tail far miles inland. Malebo Pool resembles the lump a freshly swallowed monkey, or other luckless jungle creature, might make in the gullet of the ophidian river.

Once night had fallen on the river, we could discern little of what was around us, seeing only shadowy intimations of the pool we were traversing. Long silhouettes of marshy islands stood out darker than the darkness of the water, their inscrutableness broken here and there by the solitary flares of fishermen's campfires, which lit clumps of wide-bladed river grasses and made them seem to dance.

A couple of small patrol boats sped by, their lights appearing and disappearing in straight lines. They were out to catch smugglers crossing the river, the international border between Zaire and the Republic of the Congo, under the cover of night. The goods that get smuggled across the river include such a quantity of Zairian-mined minerals that the Congo republic has become an important exporter of diamonds, even though it produces none itself. The smuggling of goods costs Zaire tens, if not hundreds, of millions of dollars each year. Like other corruption, smuggling fuels the black market whose illegal businesses dominate the economy.

On the night river, dugout canoes slid by surreptitiously, most easily twenty or thirty feet long. A few measured fifty feet, in testimony to the sheer size of the trees nourished in the equatorial humidity of the rain forest, from whose trunks the canoes were chiseled by hand. Clumps of uprooted vegetation swept past also, torn from the mud of distant banks and swirled down by the river's currents. Our riverboat would keep chugging against those currents, going night and day, stopping only at the larger riverside towns and trading stations.

This first leg of the trip, the thousand miles to Kisangani, was supposed to take nine days, if all went well. By our calculations, this meant that the *Mudimbi* would heave its way upriver at an uninspiring speed of four or five miles an hour, about as fast as a quick walk or a slow jog. Greater speed was not possible, despite the strength of the diesels that drove the boat, pounding away round-the-clock with a vehemence that shook all of the boat's four decks. That the *Mudimbi* was able to make any upriver progress at all was impressive. The diesels were hauling a floating contraption more than two hundred yards long and forty wide, weighing who knows how much, while simultaneously fighting the countervailing power of the river.

The Congo's ever-gathering descent to the ocean is so powerful that the river by itself could produce thirteen percent of the world's hydroelectricity. Measuring 2,900 miles, the Congo ranks fifth in length among the world's rivers, but it is second greatest in volume, spewing very nearly 1.5 million cubic feet of water every second into the ocean.

The river swings counterclockwise through Zaire beginning with a grand piece of dissemblance. It rises in the Katangan Plateau and runs first northward with unswerving determination, until it takes an unorthodox bend to the west, before bending again, impossibly, toward the south. It crosses the equator twice – the only major river to cross it at all – gathering waters from tributaries that originate both north and south of the earth's midline. Part of the Congo's watershed is always under deluge so that a dry season south of the equator is balanced by a rainy season north of the equator and vice versa, giving the river an extraordinarily steady flow. The Congo drains almost a million square miles of the rain forest that grows in the Congo Basin, a topographical saucer of huge proportions, and abounds even today with trees, plants, and insects that have not been identified.

Within the country, the river is no longer known as the Congo. It has been renamed the Zaire, along with the country and the currency, in an effort to erase memories of the colonial Belgian Congo. The name Zaire most likely comes from a Portuguese mispronunciation of an old Bantu word, *nzadi*, which meant 'the river that swallows all rivers.' Internationally, however, the river continues to be called the Congo.

That first night the engines throbbed away rhythmically and assuringly as the *Mudimbi* threaded its way through the channels of Malebo Pool, its spotlights the only aid the boat's pilot had in navigating the nighttime river. Their beams swiveled across expanses of water and swept along the edges of the islands, revealing a patch of swampy grass or a mudbank. At the rate we were going, it would take until midnight to travel the pool's twenty-mile length. The noise from the barges, a mix of voices, music, clattering, bleating, laughing, shouting, and crowing, kept up far into the night as the riverboat chugged deeper and deeper into the forest that stretches more than halfway across Africa.

THREE

We were awakened at dawn by the paired roar of the diesel engines reversing at full power. The *Mudimbi* was stuck on a sandbar invisible beneath the opaque rush of the river. The engines roared and complained, paused and roared. Then abruptly the whole contraption, the riverboat with its five barges carrying its hundreds of people and menagerie of edible animals, swung loose off the bar. The barges surged free into the river's currents until their binding cables brought them clanging back against each other, jarring and toppling the braziers on which women had been boiling morning tea over redhot charcoal. Steaming water scalded those passengers who, sunk in early morning lethargy, were not quick enough to leap out of the way.

I jerked up from an uneasy sleep, having lain awake long into the night imagining what lay ahead on the river. The shaking of the diesels made the metal cot legs rattle against the cabin floor and the metal edges of the cots rattle against each other. Tim and I had pushed the cots together, trying in vain to add a touch of romance to the grim interior of the cabin. At least a score of the cockroaches had succumbed to the insecticide Tim had sprayed, although undoubtedly many more still lived. The bodies of the dead roaches crunched underfoot as we dressed and hurried out to the railing.

As it turned out, that dawn was only slightly noisier than those to come. The *Mudimbi* never quieted. Someone was always dancing, talking, shouting, arguing, bargaining, or singing, and usually many people were. Although the sun had barely risen, the music already was going full blast. Rock music, the hypnotically rhythmic tunes of the Zairian electric bands that are the undisputed favorites in Africa, was blaring from beer parlors that had opened overnight on the barges. From early morning into the middle of the night, the music played, amplified to full volume through hoarse sound systems and rasping speakers.

Now that we were moving again, the repetitive thrum-thrum-thrum of the diesels also blended into the music, sounding like big, mechanical base drums that never stopped beating, pounding out an unchanging rhythm. The engines churned, the speakers scratched, roosters crowed, and goats bleated, joining in a timpanic cacophony.

The morning had dawned misty, and was surprisingly cool given the fact that we were steaming toward the equator. But the fog soon burned off under a sun that was rising fast and that stung where it hit my skin. At dawn the sky had been colored a rich cobalt but the glaring light soon bleached it to a pale blue. The fog's clearing revealed a series of steep hills, the low outlying ranges of the Crystal Mountains, rising from both banks.

The view unfolding around the boat looked like a dream landscape. Recurring for mile after mile, nearly identical hills crowded the river. Settlements, clusterings of huts, huddled in the scattered shade of palm trees on the riverbanks. Scrubby patches of trees clung to the ridges, but the flanks of the hills were bald and seared. These baking hills mark what used to be the westernmost periphery of the Congo Basin forest, but the original trees have been hacked down and used to stoke cooking fires as far away as Kinshasa.

We had not had time to absorb the view when Jimmy came scuttling down the deck balancing a tray laden with plates of toast, butter and jam, and pots of coffee and tea. '*Chop*,' he said. '*Chop, chop*,' telling us in colonial-era idiom that food was served. Having set the tray down on the low table under the near-defunct air conditioner that occupied one wall of the room, Jimmy made for the door hastily in a sideways hustle. We were too startled to thank him.

'Just look at this,' I said, lifting the lid on a pot and delightfully confirming the smell of fresh coffee. 'Coffee and cream. Even sugar. Jam. What more could we want?'

'There don't seem to be any weevils anywhere,' Tim replied, inspecting the jam pot with equal pleasure. We felt a little smug about our good fortune, on our way into the heart of Africa, eating buttered toast and gazing out onto the Congo.

As soon as I finished eating, I pulled out the painter's chart, unrolled it, and hurried out onto the deck to take a reading of the Congo's color. I looked at the water, then at the many shades of blues on the chart and then at the many more shades of brown; I squinted at the river and stared at the chart, not wanting to accept what I saw: the river water was plain brown, ordinary brown, mud brown. It had no rubiginous hint or ochrous tinge; it was brown as the river's banks and there was nothing subtle, or indecisive, about it.

Although the *Mudimbi* had not yet traveled a full day upriver, we had crossed to the other side of a gap in time and into a region beyond the reach of all but the most haphazard influences of modernity. On the riverbanks, the tin sheeting used on an occasional hut instead of the traditional grass and palm-leaf thatch, caught the sun and glinted. The settlements were small, none larger than a couple dozen huts of sun-baked mud crowded together to deny their loneliness. No roads wound through the hills to join them to other places. The river was their sole connection to the outside, to the world of commodities and currency, the world that produced tin sheeting, galvanised pots, bottled beer and the riverboats loaded with tradestuffs. There was only the river, flowing as it always had from one age into the next, navigated since before the time of Christ by fishermen, traders, and warriors.

This stretch of river might have been very different, if foreigners had not devastated the early civilisation that flourished here. The story of the first meeting between Europe and the Kongo Kingdom, of the delight with which the whites were welcomed, is almost too sad to tell. But to ignore it is to assume that savagery is native to the African continent and that Westerners had nothing to do with the brutality that has marked Africa's history.

Portuguese explorers first came upon the Congo's estuary back in the fifteenth century, and they realised immediately the import of what they saw. So much river water was pouring into the Atlantic that it stained the ocean mud-color for miles around and led the explorers to think they had found a ready-made path into the center of Africa. When the Portuguese sailed their wooden-hulled caravels up the river's estuary they found themselves blocked by the lower cataracts. But they did hear reports of an African empire near there, the news of which caused great excitement at home. They believed this might be the realm of Prester John, the legendary Christian king rumored to rule somewhere on the African continent.

In 1491, a year before Columbus reached the Americas, a band of Portuguese hiked in from the mouth of the Congo through the forest to the kingdom's capital of Mbanza. It was a glorious time, this innocent meeting between African and European. The people of the Kongo Kingdom were not afraid of the white strangers and greeted them effusively, according to a chronicler of the time who wrote:

'So great was the multitude who ran to see the Portuguese Christians that it seemed the whole country was covered with people, who loaded them with kindness, singing and making sounds with cymbals and trumpets and other instruments.'

After three days' marching, the Portuguese reached the outskirts of the capital and were greeted by nobles of the Kongo court, who escorted them through their city of straw houses to the place where large trees bathed the king's palace in pleasant shade. Upon being ushered into the presence of the Mani Kongo, who sat on an ivory-inlaid throne dressed in a resplendent combination of furs and fine cloth, the leader of the Portuguese expedition knelt and kissed the king's hand. In his turn, the African king pressed a handful of dust against his heart and then against the heart of the Portuguese, making a ceremonial bond of brotherhood. The Portuguese had brought proof of the goodwill of their own king and presented the African with gifts that included bolts of silk and satin, gold and silver jewelry, and a lovely flock of red pigeons. So began an extraordinary alliance between European and African based upon respect and equality.

The Portuguese had discovered one of several great Iron

to the coast. The white slavers bought off local chiefs with liquor and firearms, fomented tribal wars, and encouraged crime. By despoiling the fabric of traditional African society, they were able to acquire enslaved prisoners and make deals with corrupted chiefs willing to carry out slaving raids.

The slave trade was contagious, tainting even the Portuguese artisans, teachers and priests who had been sent to the kingdom to help King Affonso but who became middlemen in the dealing in human beings. Nevertheless, King Affonso refused to let go his vision of taking the best of European civilisation and grafting it onto African society. He persisted in appealing to the Portuguese king for relief from the rampant slaving.

'We cannot reckon how great the damage is,' he wrote his royal colleague in Portugal. He explained that the slave 'merchants daily seize our subjects, sons of the land and sons of our noblemen, and cause them to be sold; and so great, Sir, is their corruption and licentiousness that our country is being utterly depopulated.' He wrote that his people needed from Portugal 'no other goods but wine and flour for the holy sacrament; that is why we beg of Your Highness to help and assist us in this matter . . . because it is our will that in these kingdoms there should not be any trade in slaves nor market for slaves.'

King Affonso's optimism was staggering. He wrote letter after fruitless letter to Portugal. One of the most pathetic of these missives sought information about ten youths, his royal relatives who had not been heard from since being sent to Portugal for schooling. The reason for their disappearance was that the youths had been seized and sold into slavery.

In the century following the Portuguese arrival in central Africa, a half million slaves were shipped from the Congo region and twice that many were taken from neighboring Angola. As the Kongo Kingdom failed, the slave trade prospered. Finally, the Portuguese invaded the kingdom in 1556. By the nineteenth century, the former splendor of the Mani Kongo had been all but forgotten. As many as ten million slaves were exported from central Africa before the trade was abolished.

When we traveled up the river, almost five centuries after

the first Portuguese arrived at Mbanza and seventy years after the last of the Kongo kings died a pauper, the original alliance between black and white had long been shattered. I could only wonder what might have happened along the banks of the Congo if the early cooperation between Portugal and the Kongo Kingdom had not been ruined but had become a model for relations between Europe and Africa, if friendship and enlightenment had superseded profit.

FOUR

Overnight, each of the *Mudimbi*'s barges became a floating village. The merchants had organised themselves in just about every available space along the corridors that cross-hatched the barges. The corridors were further clogged by passengers encamped with their possessions. Chickens ran underfoot and women tended to their cooking pots and babies. Boys lowered buckets fashioned from large tin cans over the railings and into the river to draw up water for washing, drinking, and cooking. The boat community had bars, outdoor barbershops, and even its own prostitutes.

The merchants were ready when the first fishermen arrived by canoe. Tim and I leaned over a gunwale to watch them, entranced by our first look at the people who live on the banks of the Congo. Two men and a woman were heaving in unison against their paddles, standing as they paddled, balancing with their feet apart on the wet, rolling bottom of their canoe. The front man leaped for the riverboat's lower railing, catching it and lashing on a rope from the canoe. On the bottom of the pirogue, as the dugouts are called, a fresh catch of Congo catfish glistened in the sun. Each several feet long, the fish fought to regain the river, arching and flapping as they suffocated in the air.

More canoes soon followed, and then a dozen more, laden with fish to trade with the *commerçants* for food, medicine, clothes, pencils, and hundreds of other commodities from the world that exists beyond the reach of the stoutest pirogue. Women on the *Mudimbi* were soon hacking up catfish for the first fish stews of the trip.

Worming along the passageways on the barges, Tim and I

stepped around fishermen dragging fish along the decks in slippery bundles and haggling with the *commerçants*, who had spread out their goods in raised baskets. As we went, we took a casual survey of what was for sale. Displayed in rows and piles were bars of soap, blue-steel fishhooks, batteries, loaves of bread, new clothes, old clothes, polyester shirts, woolen baby socks, cans of condensed milk, and tubes of toothpaste. There were also plastic shoes, nylon fishing line, bottles of fingernail polish, earrings, razors, razorblades, cigarettes, notebooks, syringes, bolts of cloth, underpants, powdered milk, thread, needles, cookies, skin lotion, bottles of warm soda and warm beer, creams for lightening skin, nails, sugar, loose tobacco, watches, candies, matches, and cloth, brightly patterned miles of it.

Other merchants had heaped their baskets with colorful assortments of drugs, capsules, tablets, and lozenges. The drugs were not labelled so we asked one of the riverboat pharmacists what his medicines were for.

Red and yellow capsules: 'For fever, normal fever,' he said very seriously.

Red capsules: 'For fevers that ache in the head.' He lowered his head into his hands, imitating pain.

Blue pills: 'For fevers that bring aches to the bones.' He rubbed his elbow joints, then tugged his hair. 'The blue ones also keep the hair from falling out.'

White pills: 'For diseases of the heart and mind, bad thoughts and evil desires,' he said.

Yellow capsules: 'For diseases when men and women are together. Very bad problems. Ten pills will cure the sufferer.'

Smaller white pills: 'For malaria.'

Perhaps the medicine merchants occasionally sold someone the correct drug, but I doubted that it happened very often.

In general, the *commerçants* were a gregarious bunch, always shouting jokes, telling stories, whispering gossip, and plaiting each other's hair into tufted spikes that stuck out in all directions and looked like palm trees. They did whatever they could to amuse themselves during the long days on the barges where they virtually lived year-round, disembarking for a few days in Kinshasa and then re-embarking with replenished stocks of trade goods.

On one of the barges I found the slender young woman with the striking eyes who had joked about my Lingala the first evening. Her name was Marie Thérèse and she possessed the broadly graceful features typical of many Zairians. She was sitting behind a flat wicker basket in which she had arranged a row of soda-pop bottles, a row of plastic sandals made in Hong Kong, and a stack of plastic bags filled with rationed measures of sugar.

As soon as I appeared in the passageway where she and some other women *commerçants* had staked out space, she beckoned and unfolded an extra chair. Her year-old son toddled over and stopped a few feet away. He looked at me hard and then let out a shriek that descended into hysterical sobs. He had never before seen a white person close up and he found the sight appalling.

'He thinks you want to eat him up like a little forest monkey,' Marie Thérèse laughed.

'I no eat you,' I stammered in bad Lingala, which only made the boy cry louder and the woman laugh harder.

Sitting with her tradestuffs, Marie Thérèse looked as delicate as any American department-store counter clerk fresh out of high school. That was until I saw her sell a Coca-Cola. She clamped the top of the bottle in a sideways bite and levered off the metal cap with a snap of her teeth. I flinched.

From the first day on, I spent a lot of time with this group of women merchants in their corridor, which was invariably stifling hot because a bulkhead blocked off any possibility of a breeze. It was here that my Lingala lessons began for real, the women taking turns teaching me words and phrases while we all sweated in the heat.

'Sugar,' I learned to say, then, 'sandals,' then, 'salt.'

Since I already knew how to say Coca-Cola and to count in Lingala, I soon was prepared to bargain with the fishermen who came sauntering watchfully down the aisle looking at the merchandise. When they saw me sitting there with Marie

Thérèse, their eyes popped open and they had to struggle to regain their composure. But when they asked the price of something in Marie Thérèse's basket and I answered, they could not keep from laughing at the foreigner who spoke the clumsiest Lingala they had ever heard. And I could not keep from laughing with the joy of being back in Africa.

The centerpiece of Marie Thérèse's basket was a glass bottle containing a liquid with a yellowish cast to it, what everyone called 'Zaire whiskey.' Brewed from corn and potent as anything drunk in the back hollows of Appalachia, it is central Africa's match for moonshine. Marie Thérèse had a glass placed upside-down over the bottle's neck and she filled it for the price of one zaire. The most rugged of her customers would quaff an entire glass in a couple of minutes, grimacing and then breaking into smiles as the stuff hit home. Marie Thérèse tried to get me to drink a free sample of it but I refused because its smell made my stomach clench.

Except for the heat, Marie Thérèse had situated herself in an ideal place on the largest barge. She and the other *commerçants* sat in two rows in the main corridor on the bottom deck. The rows faced each other so that the women could talk when they were not dozing in sling-backed chairs behind their baskets.

The *Mudimbi*'s senior merchant, an old and worldwise woman, had taken the best place in the corridor. Her basket was at the end of the row nearest a railing where the canoes tied up, which gave her the first shot at buying what came on board. Age had concentrated in her eyes, which drooped into wrinkles and were dimmed by milky-blue cataracts and she slept in her chair with her mouth agape, but she commanded respect. She was the chief arbiter in setting prices for the 200 or so river merchants who tried to keep a common front to the fishermen.

When Marie Thérèse was not around, I sat with the old woman. I helped her clean rice, picking out dirt and bits of rubbish from the grains she shook out across a shallow basket, and listened to her talk.

She complained bitterly about the value of the zaire, predicting the day when money would be worth less than plain paper. Speaking in French for my benefit, she remembered the days when ten zaires was a significant amount of money. She talked about the river, too.

'You can never understand this river until you have lived with it for years, and then you come to know it and to love it forever.'

She shook more rice across the basket. 'I have lived on this river thirty years, maybe more, for I do not count the years as they pass. I measure time by the number of days it takes the riverboat to arrive where it is going.'

She smiled a broad smile and started into a Lingala lesson. Chuckling, she taught me the word for my nose, for my hands and feet. Then, she patted my buttocks and told me to repeat the word. Everyone within hearing distance guffawed, and the brother of Marie Thérèse who was as noticeably handsome as his sister was beautiful, looked away in embarrassment. Marie Thérèse had no husband, so her brother came along as protector and assistant.

With each passing mile, the scenery was getting lusher. The foothills of the Crystal Mountains descended into flat swampland where elephant grass and shrubs wrestled for space.

The boat made such a racket as it went that the riverine wildlife we might have seen was frightened away. Even with his pair of bird-watching binoculars, Tim was frustrated in his efforts to observe the tropical fauna. But he spent hours anyway watching the Congo's sweeping landscapes that kindled his love of pure nature. He developed a routine of dragging one of the chairs from our cabin out onto the shaking deck where he would sit for hours, steadying his binoculars and watching the riverbanks, taking notes in his journal. He was beginning to think the trip was not going to be so bad after all.

As I was befriending the *commerçants*, Tim was following

our upriver progress on the maps we had brought, calculating where we were each time the *Mudimbi* chugged past any sizable village. He predicted the points where the major tributaries were joining the main stream and tried to guess what views lay around the next bend.

To get a better view of the river, we climbed up to the pilothouse where we talked to the *Mudimbi*'s captain, who had piloted boats on the Congo and its tributaries for more than thirty years. From his elevated wooden chair, he surveyed the river ahead, looking for the wooden signposts nailed to occasional trees that were his only navigational aid except for a book of charts on a shelf in front of him. He told us he could tell the location of the sandbars, which shifted constantly, by watching the dancing of the water on the river's surface. It was hard enough to steer through the maze of identical-looking islands by day, but at night the captain had to rely on the two searchlights playing along the riverbanks and illuminating the signposts.

Fresh fish from the Congo was the standard fare for most of the *Mudimbi*'s passengers. A fish stew was made simply enough, if ruthlessly, I learned while watching a woman go to work on a large silver-scaled fish. Wielding a dull knife, she scraped off the scales, letting them fall in an arc on the deck where they shone in the sunlight like metallic petals. She reached into the gill slits, pulled out the respiratory filaments, and flung them overboard. She kept the head, though, hacking it off and throwing it into her pot. Next, she sawed the fish horizontally into chunks, the way you would cut a loaf of French bread. She pulled the guts from the middle of each chunk, throwing the warm spaghetti of the viscera into the river and the rest into the pot. She added river water and hot pepper and put the stew onto her charcoal stove. Then, noticing that I was watching all this intently, she waved. I shouted a few words of Lingala.

About half an hour later, we heard a knocking on our cabin

door and opened it to find one of the boys from down on the barge holding out an enamel bowl of his mother's steaming and tasty fish stew.

Most of the time, though, we did not get to eat Congo fish. For the first lunch, the passengers who dined in the first-class dining room were served pork chops and fried potatoes with greasy gravy.

Even though Belgian officers were no longer around to enforce their customs aboard the riverboat, the *Mudimbi*'s crew carried on in the colonial manner. White tablecloths, worn but serviceable, were spread on the dining room tables. The pair of waiters wore unbleachably stained white coats and worked barefoot. They performed bravely, refusing to notice that the tables wobbled or that the ceiling had a hole in it, and, with platter in one hand and two spoons in the other, they served food in the most formal fashion. They had not quite mastered the technique, though, which meant we all had to wait as they shoved clumsily at each portion of food. But the waiters took their serving seriously, as if this imported etiquette had a higher purpose or possessed some meaning that transformed its essential ridiculousness. Nobody appeared particularly concerned about the pair of tame green monkeys that ran up and down the wooden bar, chattering, shrieking, and shitting.

The only other whites in the dining room were two German men whose looks we did not find reassuring. They came stomping through the door in what seemed to be motorcycle boots, heavy, scuffed black leather boots with thick soles. Their beards and hair were long. The shaggier one we had noticed when we first boarded the *Mudimbi*. He had been sitting on a railing sunk in a Teutonic scowl, watching the river and the clumps of water hyacinths swirling down it. Although we exchanged names in the dining room, we could think of little to say to them during the first few days.

Prepared as we were for bad food, we felt pampered that first time the waiters served pork chops. They were filling. Dinner was the same, except that the potatoes were mashed. We ate pork and potatoes day after day, the pork being replaced occasionally with fried beef liver so tough that we had to saw at it with our sharp-bladed pocket knives. All the meat for first-class had been loaded before the *Mudimbi* left Kinshasa and stored in the boat's refrigeration room, and I suspected that some of it had been stocked weeks or months earlier, leftover from one trip to the next.

The explorers, missionaries, and big-game hunters of colonial times used to bring not only their customs but also enough luggage and portable furniture to provide a semblance of home: tent, bed, chairs, table, lanterns, a pharmacoepia of medicines, collapsible bathtub, kettles, pots, pans, utensils, tinned food, tea, coffee, biscuits, pet dogs, liquor, and anything else needed to provide comfort or satisfy habit. To make it more complicated, the stuff had to be parceled into boxes so that porters could carry it. This demanded a considerable amount of labor, given that some travelers felt they needed a ton or even two tons of equipment to survive in the wilds of Africa. Unpacking an expedition's baggage could take half the day.

One British gentleman who journeyed up the Congo at the turn of the century had more than four dozen crates of gear, which he discovered belatedly had not been labeled. As he recounted the story in his journal, his equipment had been loaded onto a river steamboat, the prediesel, wood-burning kind. Night was falling when he realised he could not tell which box contained the camping bed and which the smelling salts. He suffered what he considered a most uncomfortable and unsupplied night.

Life in first class was not without its concerns. We were worried that our gear might be the target of some of the *Mudimbi*'s more desperate characters. We had two padlocks for the cabin door, but we feared a thief might pry open one of the windows and make off with things we could not stand to lose, like our notebooks and camera equipment, which was stashed in the bottom of the armoire, whose door persisted in swinging open invitingly.

I was sitting in the cabin and writing one afternoon when I glimpsed the head and shoulders of a man outside the side window. He disappeared immediately and I went back to my work. When I looked up again, he was back outside the window. When Tim got back from the barges where he had gone to buy sweet bananas, I whispered an urgent warning about the man being a lurking thief.

'Oh come on,' Tim said, refusing to believe me.

But conceding to my panic, he crept out the door, aiming to catch the strange fellow by surprise. He was back in a minute to report the man was not about to leap through the window. I went out and found the wretched man handcuffed to the heavy metal grating bolted around the outside of the air conditioner.

This grating turned out to be the *Mudimbi*'s principal jail. The ship's railing just opposite also was used for handcuffing miscreants apprehended by the boat police, who happened to be headquartered in the cabin next to ours.

(If the police had not taken advantage of the air conditioner's grating, the machine would have been of almost no use, since it cooled the air in our cabin only feebly and reluctantly. In the afternoons, when it became too hot to think or do much of anything, we would flip on the cold-air switch and huddle against the air conditioner, taking deep breaths and sucking in as much coolness as we could, while we could. After a few minutes, the thing invariably quit.)

The *Mudimbi* had eight police and, I believed, at least one person who worked for the security police. We had been warned that security agents kept close watch on the occasional foreign journalists who came to Zaire. The man whom I suspected was so guileful that I called him 'the spy.'

The prisoner stayed locked to our air conditioner for half the day before the palaver over his case began. A knot of people, relatives and friends of the handcuffed man, had come to defend him before the captain of the regular police, a muscular young man who held court at the doorway of the headquarters cabin. The prisoner had been caught trying to conceal a suitcase full of bullets for which he did not have the necessary permits. The captain, acting as prosecutor and judge, asked the man if he had stolen the suitcase.

'I bought it in Kinshasa,' he replied, twisting against the handcuffs that held him against the grating.

'Then where are your papers?' the captain asked.

'The police at the port said I didn't need papers,' the hand-cuffed man shouted.

'How much bribe did you pay the police at the port?' the captain asked.

'He is an honest man. You must give him his freedom,' one of his defenders said. 'Give him his freedom.' 'Give him his freedom,' the people chorused. 'Yes. His freedom.'

'You pay me the same amount you paid at the port and I will count this as your permit,' the captain said. 'Three hundred zaires.'

'Okay, two hundred zaires,' said a man in the crowd.

'Okay,' the captain said, no more loath to make money than most other Zairian officials. 'Two hundred zaires for his freedom and two hundred zaires for the suitcase.'

The man who had done most of the talking stepped forward and said, 'Okay, four hundred.' Money changed hands and the prisoner was freed.

The regular police were straightforward about what they did, even when they took payoffs. But the fellow I thought was working for the security police was different.

The spy had come around the back of the boat to our cabin after dinner one evening and introduced himself in English, rather than the usual French. I stood in the doorway and he leaned on the jamb, tall and thin, flicking his eyes over my shoulder as we talked. Tim was sitting on one of the cots inside looking at a map and taking notes. I had a box of matches in my hand because I had been trying to light our camping stove.

'Would you give me a cigarette?' he asked.

I told him I did not smoke.

'Then what are the matches for?' he asked. 'What are you trying to burn?'

I told him I was too busy to talk. After a couple more minutes of struggling with the stove, I glanced up at a window and saw him looking in. But he was gone when Tim and I went to the stern railing to watch another evening settle on the river.

FIVE

The *Mudimbi* heaved its load of passenger barges upriver and the swampland gave way to the forest. Plants, bushes, vines, and trees shot up along the riverbanks and intertwined to block the view like solid walls. Here and there, we could see the huts of fishermen, whose canoes were pulled up on the banks, perched precariously between the vegetation and the river, which cut the only path that could not be overgrown.

Our third morning upriver from Kinshasa dawned into a humid silvery haze that enveloped the boat and magnified the dull thump, thump, thumping of the diesels. The sun had hardly evaporated the haze when the engines went dead and the boat glided to a halt off a low river bank. We had no idea what had stopped us and there was nothing to indicate where we were, except that the riverscape had changed with heavily forested islands now breaking the Congo's expanse.

Getting information aboard the *Mudimbi* was not easy since public announcements were not part of shipboard protocol. Tim and I suspected that something had gone seriously wrong with the *Mudimbi*'s engines. Thinking that the Germans might be better informed, we went around the corner to their cabin. Gunther, the shaggier of the two shaggy Germans, had been hanging out down in the engine room ogling the big diesels since the first day. But they did not have any idea either about what was going on. Gunther shrugged and surmised from the sounds that the engines had been shut off intentionally.

We followed a flow of people moving forward. Making our way through the barges, we encountered the only other whites, Elly, a likeable Dutch woman, and Andrew, an unpleasant Scot, who had boarded in Kinshasa. They were not booked into first

class with the rest of us. Instead, they laid their bedrolls out
on a piece of decking. Although they were aiming for South
Africa, Andrew had less than two hundred dollars left and Elly
only a little more. Elly, who was a nurse, was traveling through
Africa for the simple joy of it. Light-spirited and curious, she
was an opposite to Andrew, who imitated a colonial posture by
sneering at the Africans around him. She had met and joined
him in West Africa after an original traveling companion turned
back for Europe.

Andrew was an unlikely version of the intrepid traveler. He
was awkward, beset with a lingering adolescent lankiness, and
his skin had a fairness unsuited to the raucous African sun that
burned his face and arms. Andrew was forging through the
middle of Africa not because he liked the place but because he
was trying to meet a challenge he had devised for himself, to
make it from Dundee, Scotland, to Dundee, South Africa.

'Dundee to Dundee,' Andrew had said. 'No doubt it will
establish some sort of a record. Overland. No frills.'

When we ran into them that morning, Elly told us that
someone had died a little while earlier, an event that had sent
sadness and fear washing through the barges. Contagion was
an omnipresent possibility on the crowded riverboats. When
an epidemic had broken out on one of them a few years ago,
the boat became a pariah and towns along the river refused to
let it dock. The passengers were hungry and desperate when
they finally were herded into a mass quarantine in Kinshasa.

Pushing our way forward again, we saw that a board had
been put down to the shore as a gangplank. Near the prow of
the front barge, women of all sorts had gathered and were
singing in Lingala, which is a mellifluous language that lends
itself to the cadences of lament. They were singing dirges for
a child.

The story we heard was that the child was a sickly boy who
had been too thin for too long. Prolonged malnutrition had
killed him. The rest of the passengers had no contagion to fear,
other than the general epidemic of penury that has settled
everywhere in the country.

The child's mother was standing off to the side and weeping.

She was a prostitute who worked in the claustrophobic corners of the barges for ten cents a trick. The T-shirt she was wearing declared in black letters that arched across her breasts: 'Momilo Germicide Soap.'

The singing women took the corpse and wrapped it in a blue cloth so that only the face showed up dark against the swaddling color. Some men found enough boards to nail together a simple coffin. Once this was accomplished, a stream of several hundred people balanced down the plank, bearing the body in the coffin, to the shore, on whose swampy edge water hyacinths bloomed in a tribute of purple. The mourners wound up a path through dry yellow weeds to a village. Some huts, their mud walls dried to a khaki color, stood in a clearing of hard-packed dirt that thrust back into the forest to make a peninsula of space. A few homemade stools, whose joints were reinforced with twine made from forest vine, and some enamel basins for washing were scattered about. A few goats wandered around the clearing whose only amenity was a stout mango tree with thick shiny leaves. Under the mango, someone was playing the guitar, gently and slowly, a dark form in the tree's shadow.

The procession continued to a little cemetery by the village, where the graves were marked by wooden crosses that rose level with the weeds. A child-sized grave was dug, the coffin lowered and covered. The mourners sang Christian hymns in French, the familiar melodies rising in testimony to the far-reaching impact of missionaries who spread their religion through the Congo Basin as their countrymen colonised and profited from it. The sounds of the hymns and the dirt thudding into the newest grave were quickly swallowed by the forest's immensity.

When the *Mudimbi* got underway again, Tim and I stood at our habitual observation spot at the stern rail and looked at the massed hyacinths diminishing to a band of color, to a resplendent line, to a speck, and then to nothing, lost to the distance. I was wondering why a country so well endowed – with rivers, forests, animals, rain, diamonds, gold, copper, cobalt – should allow any of its children to die from lack of food.

Zaire is no Ethiopia. Along with its mineral wealth, the

country has been blessed with year-round rainfall that makes it one of the wettest and greenest places on earth. It has plenty of space, huge areas of virgin land that have never been farmed or timbered. Game and fish are abundant. Since men began recording history, Zaire has never suffered a drought like those that have turned Ethiopia into a place of nightmarish famines. Yet Zaire is one of the world's ten poorest countries.

According to recent World Bank calculations, Zaire's gross national product per capita was less than $170 a year, the fifth lowest in the world. Zaire ranked right behind Ethiopia, Bangladesh, Mali and Nepal, all countries with severe geographic, topographic or, climatic problems to help explain their miseries.

Malnourishment is Zaire's single biggest health problem, one that afflicts children first of all. One medical study of children in Kinshasa under the age of five found that about forty percent of them are malnourished. In the country's interior away from the big cities, malnourishment is worse.

Nearly one-third of the children treated at Kinshasa's main hospital suffer from kwashiorkor, a stage of hunger on the way toward fatal starvation. When this stage is reached, the body has begun to eat its own protein and devour its own muscles. Hunger stunts a child's body and mind, making him easy victim to diseases a well-fed child could easily survive. Zairian children die of measles. They also die of worms, malaria, whooping cough, and severe malnutrition. In the United States, the survival of children is almost guaranteed. In Zaire, about one of every ten dies before reaching the age of five.

Leaning on the railing of the *Mudimbi*, I stared out over the river after the hyacinths had disappeared. This particular reach of the river had no islands, so that the opposing banks, which were three or four miles apart, became distant green strips that appeared to curve around and meet pincerlike in the down-river distance.

Tim had gone off to take a look at the maps and figure out

how much further it was to Mbandaka, right on the equator and our first official port-of-call. I stayed there, immersed in the scenery, letting it soothe the tension of the morning. I did not notice the police captain until he spoke.

'*Excusez-moi,*' he said, squaring his shoulders and pretending an authoritative tone despite his youth. 'Excuse me. We have a problem. A passenger has reported to me that you were illegally taking pictures.'

'Oh yes,' I said, startled but smiling and looking as ingenuous as I could. 'Just of the beautiful scenery and the many pirogues. I have made no trouble.'

I had been taking pictures of the funeral, knowing all the while that photographing just about anything in Zaire is frowned upon by the authorities, if not forbidden outright. I had been leaning on the *Mudimbi*'s railing and photographing the file of mourners, the huts of the village, the canoes on the bank, and several boys who had stripped off their ragged clothes and were washing in the knee-deep water by the riverbank. I knew that the government was paranoid about any stranger taking snapshots. Spots as seemingly mundane as traffic circles in Kinshasa were considered strategic, so that taking pictures of the wrong street was considered a breach of national security. I also had heard about erring photographers having had their cameras ripped away and smashed. One poor Associated Press photographer was arrested while taking pictures of scenic landscapes in eastern Zaire. Still, I could not figure out what I had done that was so offensive.

The captain told me.

'You were taking a photograph of a port. You are not allowed to take photographs of ports.'

I replied that I had not taken any picture of any port, that he must be mistaken. He asked if I had been photographing the funeral and the village. I admitted that much.

'And so, you are guilty,' he said.

The explanation was simple. Any riverside village was considered a port, because boats and canoes could stop there. Anyplace where boats of any kind stopped was a port.

Just then a familiar figure came sauntering down the deck,

looking out over the water. It was the spy. He glanced at us as he passed, revealing no more than a glimmer from the corner of an eye. Perhaps he was the one who had reported me to the police. I was sure he was spying, but all I could do was make some more excuses to the captain, who eventually seemed satisfied and turned away.

The mood aboard the *Mudimbi* stayed somber as the boat left the village of the funeral to its solitude. I could not tell whether the *Mudimbi* was chugging along the side of one of the islands, which again fragmented the river, or a bank of the river. The vegetation gave no clues. We had truly entered the forest, which rose all around with a luxuriance so grand as to rival the river's own presence. The forest concealed itself behind leafy walls that met the river and added to the mazy effect created by the islands and the channels that ran between them. Great fluffs of papyrus leaned out over the water's edge and behind that rose the tangled greenery. A million leaves sprouted into the air and stretched for the light, glinting back at the sun.

The sun was bearing down with a white heat that turned the islands into green shimmers when suddenly a commotion broke out among the passengers. I scanned the brown river and the green forest but could see nothing worth getting excited about. Tim had no idea, either. It took us several minutes to squeeze our way through the people who were jamming the railings of the upper decks and staring downward at a very large pirogue. Lying at the canoe's bottom in a pool of water stained bright blood red was a freshly killed hippopotamus. Its huge, decapitated head lay in the bow of the canoe looking backward, its mouth turned down into a flabby frown as if it were prepared to witness its own butchery.

A band of fishermen had hunted down the hippopotamus, loaded its bulk into the pirogue, and hauled it out to the passing riverboat. The beast represented a mammoth supply of highly prized meat. Almost everyone in the crowd was clamoring and trying to get in close enough to claim a hunk of it. Dozens of *commerçants* leaned over the railing waving money and trying to buy a wholesale-sized slab.

First the fishermen quartered the carcass, hacking away with machete blows that could have felled a tree. In order to grapple with the hippo's slippery flesh, the fishermen sliced handholds into the outer layer of skin and fat, one cut for the thumb and one for the fingers. It reminded me of the way bowlers grab a bowling ball. Each hunk of meat the fishermen threw up onto the deck was fought over by the crowd. Once they had disposed of most of the meat from the hippo's sides and belly, the fishermen wrenched off the legs at the hip and shoulder joints. Three or four of them working together hacked down to a joint and then grabbed the whole haunch, twisting it until the socket popped.

'*Hippopotam. Hippopotam,*' people in the crowd were shouting in French. '*Nguvu. Nguvu,*' others were shouting in Lingala. The merchants and the passengers were elated by the spectacle, by the gore, and by the idea of so much hippopotamus, which is judged to be at least as tasty as the coveted meat of the crocodile or the elephant.

After the butchery was finished, the fishermen stood barefoot in the bloody puddle and looked around, staring at nothing. Their mouths hung open. They had the exhausted and disconnected look of having survived something excessive. They had been brave, for a wounded hippopotamus can be murderous, and they had been lucky, for hippos are rarer on the river with each passing year.

The fishermen had made a lot of money selling off the hippo. Little did it matter that it is unlawful in Zaire to hunt the dwindling hippopotamus population without government permits, which are granted only for hippos that have gone on rampages, marauding farms and threatening villages. For the crime that had been committed so blatantly and with such public delight, the riverboat police did take action by arresting two of the band of hunters and confiscating their long harpoons. They were duly handcuffed to the railing by our cabin wall. But unlike other prisoners, they were at ease, squatting on the deck and talking. Within half an hour they were released. Their comrades in the meantime had presented the *Mudimbi*'s officials with a bribe, a hippopotamus haunch.

After their problem with the authorities was resolved, the hunters gave a mime performance of how they had killed their beast. They tipped the hippopotamus's head up on the stump of its neck and pried its mouth open to show a palate-pink cavern studded with yellow foreteeth the size of chisels. A couple of them picked up harpoons and, leaping and dancing around the yawning head, pretended to stab the animal, again and again, until the harpoons leaped from their hands, leaving them hauling on the attached ropes and enacting a Congo rendition of an old-fashioned whale hunt.

The hunting of hippopotamuses and the delectability of their meat became the talk of the boat. One man held forth on the best way to kill a hippo with a gun. He advised that the thing to do was to shoot it as many times as possible in the neck, because shooting it in the head would do no good, its skull being so thick that bullets would ricochet off it. He also claimed if a hippo was shot in the eye, the animal would not die right away but would attack the hunter in a half-blinded fury.

'How would you kill a hippopotamus if you didn't have a gun?' I asked.

A young man stepped forward from a group that was listening to our conversation, it being almost impossible to have a private talk on the crowded barges. He recounted a hunt in which he had participated as a youth.

'Arrows. That's what we used. We saw the hippopotamus in the grass by the river. My grandfather and the other men shot him with many arrows, twenty-five arrows or more. They wounded him so gravely that he leaped into the water. One hunter leaped after him with a knife and cut off his tail.'

'Why would you want to cut off his tail?' I asked.

'You will see why. Just listen. The hippopotamus bled to death from his wounds. The body floated to the top and we followed the path of the blood in the river.'

He stopped talking and folded his arms, his story complete.

'But why did you have to cut the tail off?' I asked again.

'If the tail had not been cut off, the hippopotamus would have sunk forever. The tail makes the hippopotamus sink.'

I did not believe him, but having come face-to-face with a real Congo myth, I stayed quiet.

For curiosity's sake, we wanted to sample some hippopotamus meat, but we could not find anyone willing to sell us even a taste of it. The most agile *commerçants* had stashed quantities of it in the refrigerator hold, planning to sell it later in the city at great profit.

In its way, the river had explained something about the child's death. The bounty of hippo meat was not going to be eaten by the *Mudimbi*'s poorer passengers. Rather, profits from it were collected by the fishermen who had illegally killed it, the officials who took a bribe to let them get away with it, and those merchants with enough money to buy the meat. Most of it would be eaten by members of the country's elite back in Kinshasa. The hippopotamus was as much a symbol of Zaire's natural wealth as the diamonds that are smuggled across the Congo. What we were seeing on the river was like some of the things we had seen in Kinshasa, where elegant shopping goes on next to profound poverty, where valuable foreign exchange is used to import English liquors for the few who live in anomalous luxury on the southern bank of Malebo Pool.

For most Zairians, nothing is in oversupply, not even trash. When we emptied our first bottle of vodka, we did not throw it away. We had used the liquor up quite quickly, mixing it with the Tang and sipping it in the evenings while watching the boat's wake meeting the velvety, descending darkness. When we finished the bottle, we put it under a chair by the door, the place where we put whatever trash we wanted Jimmy to take away for us since the cabin had no wastecan. When Jimmy came in the morning with our tray of toast and beverages, his eyes fastened on the bottle and he smiled.

'*Merci. Merci,*' Jimmy said. He bobbed into a couple of bows as he turned for the door holding the bottle in both hands. '*Merci.*'

Although he had become a little more talkative, Jimmy never

relaxed. He had been trained by Belgian colonials who, because of their conviction that Africans were more like children than men, were severe taskmasters. He reminded me of a dog that has been beaten and cringes at the gesture of a hand, fearing another blow or rebuke.

I saw him later that day cleaning the bottle under a washing pipe that funneled out river water from a tank set on a barge roof. High quality bottles, like the one that had held our Gilbey's vodka, are used to store drinking water. Similar empties are resold in the outdoor marketplaces. An empty vodka bottle is not to be scorned.

SIX

The works of men decay with a luxuriant relentlessness in the tropics. The equatorial sun bakes their edges brittle. The humidity rots them to their core. Exuberant moulds eat at their foundations and the vegetation riots, overrunning everything.

We awakened as the *Mudimbi* slowed and glided into just such a place of tropical rottenness, past a collection of derelict boats, old river steamers rusting into a promontory of mud, and past houses with crumbling walls and broken roofs. Their plaster façades, half hidden behind patches of tall grass and palm groves, peered out from the overgrowth like bleached white faces and their windows were filled by black shadows. These remains of the Belgian era stared down at the river, which refused to offer back any reflections as it coursed on its way through an overcast morning.

This was Mbandaka, the old trading settlement that sits on a low rise above the Congo at the point where the river rolls across the equator with sullen grandeur. Once called Equator Station, it served as a base of operations for the agents of King Leopold II, as they pillaged the countryside to appease the Belgian monarch's lust for rubber and ivory in what was then his personal colony. This settlement more than four hundred miles and five days out from the capital made a startling break in the forest. It has grown since the days of Leopold to a sprawling community of more than one hundred thousand.

The *Mudimbi* labored into Mbandaka's port past islands of floating hyacinths. A solid layer of clouds blocked the bite of the sun, radiating a tropical warmth downward as if a cottony electric blanket were suspended across the breadth of the sky. The port was announced by a crane that stood awkwardly, a foreign tower of structural steel on a flat lot beside the river. Some forgotten-looking barges were tied near the crane.

As soon as the boards used as gangplanks were slapped over onto the shore, we joined the passengers pushing to get off and do some trading at the market beyond the rusty gates of the port.

Across the equally rusty side of a port warehouse several messages were stenciled in French. The lettering was fading but we were able to decipher the short, sanctimonius homilies, which were ascribed to President Mobutu. One declared: 'The masses must understand that if each does as he pleases and follows his own ambition, that will result inevitably in anarchy.'

Just beyond the port another sign announced that we had arrived at the 'cradle of the revolution,' for Mbandaka is capital of the province of Equateur where Mobutu was born. This would-be revolution mainly has featured Mobutu's ascension to supreme power.

Mobutu has accomplished nothing if he has not followed his own ambition. He has accumulated a fortune estimated to be worth $5 billion dollars, although no one can be certain of that figure because he has cached much in secret European bank accounts and invested much in mansions and other properties on both the European and African continents.

At the same time, the country has slid into poverty and accumulated a terribly burdensome foreign debt amounting also to about $5 billion, the largest in black Africa. If Mobutu simply were to return his fortune to Zaire, he could relieve the country's insolvency and end its persistently grave problems with the International Monetary Fund and other lenders. That he has not is no surprise, since he has come to rule Zaire as if it were his own domain to do with what he pleases.

The stories of Mobutu's thievery are many and varied. One report has it that he once gave the proceeds of the country's entire coffee crop to his first wife, Marie-Antoinette, before she died in 1977. More recently, his second wife's personal secretary was caught trying to smuggle some $6 million worth of diamonds and other jewels through the Brussels airport in a valise.

Litho, the late uncle of Mobutu and a close adviser, probably was the most munificently rewarded of Mobutu's relatives. When Litho died in 1982, his assets were estimated at $1 billion. Dozens of other members of Mobutu's extended family also have enriched themselves under the presidential tutelage at inestimable costs to the state, as have members of Mobutu's entourage of politicians.

Mobutu was born in 1930 to a poor family in Lisala, the next sizable town upriver from Mbandaka. He grew up in Mbandaka and Kinshasa, where his father worked as a servant and cook for missionaries and colonial officials, but these humble origins are not what he recalls publicly. Rather, he has claimed as his home the ancestral village of his father's family, a place called Gbadolite in the far north of Equateur along the Ubangi River, a Congo tributary that forms Zaire's northern border with the Central African Republic. The village lies in the land of the Ngbandi, a relatively small tribe but one that prizes a warrior tradition suitable to Mobutu, who came to power through the ranks of the Zairian army.

Mobutu looks toward his own home province for political support and has around him a loyal corps of politicians, government ministers, army generals, and security officials from Equateur. When he decreed in 1971 that all Zairians Africanise their names, ridding themselves of European names as part of a campaign to rid the country of its colonial memories and make it more authentically African, Mobutu took the name of a relative from Gbadolite, a renowned Ngbandi warrior and diviner. Originally christened Joseph Désiré Mobutu, he changed his name to Mobutu Sese Seko Kuku Ngbendu wa za Banga, which means in rough translation, 'the all-conquering warrior who triumphs over all obstacles.'

From time to time, Mobutu likes to return to Gbadolite, which is no longer the unremarkable village it was. The only way to get to the capital from Gbadolite, which is separated from Kinshasa by six hundred miles of rain forest, used to be by taking some kind of boat down the Ubangi River to the Congo mainstream. That is no longer the case, for Mobutu has seen to the construction of a landing strip there sizable enough to accommodate a jet. He also has built a well-appointed presidential palace so that he can enjoy his rural retreats in comfort. Mobutu has had the village transformed into a model community, complete with an expensive mausoleum constructed to hold the remains of his first wife.

Gbadolite is part of the image Mobutu has tailored for himself. He has taken the skin of the leopard, the regally independent cat, from which to fashion his hat. He carries a sculpted staff as another symbol of his presidential status, the one that the White House press corps made fun of during his visit to Washington. He travels about the country chauffeured in Mercedes Benzes, flown in helicopters, or piloted on the Congo in his yacht accompanied always by a special presidential guard wearing immaculate uniforms and red berets. His photograph hangs in every public building, his likeness is printed on the currency and is copied onto enamel pins that loyalists wear affixed over their hearts.

Mobutu is chief of one of the most dictatorial political systems in Africa. He is president of Zaire and also president of the Mouvement Populaire de la Révolution, the Popular Movement of the Revolution, the only political party that is allowed to exist. The doctrine of this sole party is 'Mobutism,' an ideology meant to sound as grand as Marxism or Maoism but based on nothing sounder than the varying decrees of a dictator. Any doubts about whether a citizen of Zaire is free to make political choices have been cleared up by Mobutu's constitution, which states: 'Every Zairian is a member of the Popular Movement of the Revolution.' To be born in Zaire is to become a member of Mobutu's political party, automatically and for life.

Mobutu is not a profound political thinker, but he has been brilliant at one thing, keeping his grip on the country. He has bought off the upper echelons of the government bureaucracy and the military by allowing corruption to flourish. If the persuasion of corrupt profits isn't sufficient, Mobutu has other means of preventing challenges to his power. He does not let his ministers get too secure, shuffling his cabinet more than once a year on the average. He keeps a sharp eye on his army of 70,000 soldiers while moving the commanders around so that no single general can create a power base.

Although Mobutu is hardly a popular president, there is little chance of his losing an election in today's Zaire because he is the only candidate and the balloting is public. Under the scrutiny of soldiers and officials loyal to Mobutu, each voter must choose a green card favoring the president or a red card signifying a vote against him. Then, in plain sight of everyone, the voter must deposit the card in the ballot box. In the most recent election for another seven-year term, Mobutu won with 99.16 percent of the vote.

Mobutu nevertheless puts on great displays of electioneering. The last time he campaigned in Mbandaka, he arrived on his yacht with his helicopter parked on the boat's stern. Party and government officials had made sure a crowd was down at the river to greet him. Dancers were performing on the yacht's deck and each time Mobutu raised his staff, the crowd cheered. Dressed in his Mobutu suit and leopard-skin hat, the president went ashore, held a carefully orchestrated press conference at one of his houses and then hosted members of the foreign press aboard the yacht, feeding them imported European wines, smoked salmon, meats, and fruit. When it was over, the reporters flew back to the capital and Mobutu flew away in his helicopter.

At the market near the port, I bought some roasted caterpillars from a woman who wrapped them up for me to carry away in a fresh banana leaf. We had not gotten more than a few yards beyond the port gate when we were intercepted by a man in an olive-green uniform. Above his shirt pocket was a patch that said 'Immigration.' He wanted to see our travel documents, our passports and international vaccination certificates. We proffered the appropriate papers immediately, but he demanded that we follow him and set off at a stiff military pace down the middle of the town's main avenue.

It was a broad street laid out with a generosity that must

have been inspired by a vision of a prosperous future for this settlement midway between Kinshasa and Kisangani. The colonialists who planned this main street would find, if they could return today, that the palms planted the length of the avenue have grown to a stately height that lent an anomalous graciousness to the place.

Waist-high grass sprang from the avenue's median. The white stucco buildings lining the streets had wide verandas. It was in the protection of these shady verandas that white officials, traders, and missionaries must have spent long afternoons in decades past sipping hot tea and gossiping about the events of the day. But as we were marched past the verandas, we saw no pith helmets on the railings and no Europeans in clean white suits taking their refreshment. Plaster was peeling from the facades of the buildings, cracks defaced the walls and the moldy porch pillars. The roofs of red painted corrugated tin were falling in.

The immigration officer veered toward a building whose front porch sheltered a company of squatters. They had put mattresses on the porch floor and built fires on the steps, where they squatted to cook their meals. For fuel, they were mutilating a venerable shade tree adjacent to the veranda, hacking away at its roots and limbs. We looped past this encampment and around the side of the building to a door that had been left ajar and untended with the exception of a couple of goats basking sleepily in the sun. Our escort ushered us up a dim stairway to an office lit by an open window.

The officer sat down behind a desk and examined our documents with the time-consuming meticulousness of a bureaucrat practiced in the patient skill of exacting bribes. We knew our papers were in order, so we stood silently waiting as he scrutinised each of the dozens of visas in our passports, questioning me about the runic Amharic writing on an Ethiopian stamp, flipping every page with studious care. Eventually, he conceded the contest of patience, handed us back our passports, and led us to a smaller room where a man tottering with age examined our vaccination cards. He peered at the certificates and then at each of us through a pair of glasses that had one good and one shattered lens. Eventually, perhaps having verified the documents by feel, he handed them back to us.

Not long after we had escaped the toils of the town's bureaucracy, we saw the Germans being herded past the dozing goats and through the side door. To their misfortune, they were not carrying international certificates to document that they had been vaccinated against the worst of the contagious tropical diseases, which is required throughout Africa as a means of combating epidemics of cholera, typhoid, and yellow fever. To meet the law, they both should have been vaccinated and quarantined there in Mbandaka. It cost them each about one dollar to buy phony certificates of health from the old man.

When we turned off the main avenue onto an intersecting street we came upon an abandoned sedan, which lacked one whole wheel, the bare wheelhead being supported by cinderblocks. Half of its windshield, like the lens of the health inspector's eyeglasses, was shattered. In the back seat a boy was sitting, not moving, staring straight ahead at the blank street.

Although it was barely mid-morning, a general torpitude had clamped itself down around the town, so much so that the arrival of the riverboat caused no more than a few heavy ripples of excitement. Little disturbed the morning save for the crowing of a few wayward roosters bragging to the world about their scrawny masculinity and, then, the slow clumping of the boots of a band of soldiers on their way through town. Some of the soldiers rested submachine guns lackadaisically in the crooks of their arms. The sun appeared fitfully out of the clouds, delivering a stinging heat and producing sudden steamy fogs from patches of foliage where the humidity hung heaviest. Even the mosquitoes were flying about in slowed motion, moving so lethargically that we could swat them in the air.

Although it is one of the larger cities in Zaire, Mbandaka has sunk into geographic isolation, except for the river that slides ceaselessly by. Hundreds of miles of nearly trackless forest surround it and the roads that link it to Kinshasa are reputedly

so difficult that only a daredevil would attempt the through trip
these days.

Mbandaka was founded a century ago by Henry Morton
Stanley, the American journalist turned explorer who scooped
the world by finding the wandering David Livingstone encamped in the East African interior. It was from the great and
half-crazed missionary doctor that Stanley first heard about the
Lualaba River, which no one then knew was the southernmost
stretch of the Congo River. Dr Livingstone had convinced
himself that the Lualaba, flowing almost straight northward
past the Mountains of the Moon near the very center of the
continent, had to be the beginning of the Nile, and that its
source was holy. Livingstone died while wandering in northern
Zambia, still searching for the divine springs he thought gave
existence to the Nile. Stanley resolved to get to the bottom of
Livingstone's obsession and planned a daring expedition that
would take him across the breadth of the continent and through
its heart.

The nineteenth-century Western world had less of an idea
about what lay in the middle of Africa than the early Portuguese
who had befriended and then betrayed the Mani Kongo. During
the four centuries between Diego Cão's and Stanley's expeditions, the era of the slave trade, the West had come to
perceive Africa as a dark and heathen continent absent of
civilisation. The Congo remained a puzzle, so much so that
some of Europe's most renowned geographers and explorers
held to the theory that the Congo estuary was really the mouth
of the Niger River. To prove this theory, the British admiralty
sent an expedition to map the Niger whose members ended
up trying to scale the Congo's treacherous Crystal Mountains
only to turn back in failure and exhaustion, having proved
nothing about either the Congo or the Niger.

Tackling the problem from the opposite side of the continent,
Stanley set out from Zanzibar in 1874. He started with a
caravan consisting of three hundred and fifty-six porters and

soldiers and eight tons of supplies. They carried wire, beads, and cloth to trade with the local peoples for provisions. They took bedding, ropes, tents, medicines, ammunition, guns, scientific instruments, photographic equipment, shaving mirrors, ivory-backed hair brushes, eau de cologne, and meerschaum pipes. The most remarkable item was a boat Stanley had designed. Forty feet long and of shallow draft, it could be taken apart into five sections, each light enough to be carried by two men. Stanley christened it the *Lady Alice* after his fiancée, whom he had left behind in the United States.

Two long years later, Stanley arrived at Nyangwe on the Lualaba, an outpost for Arab slave traders on the upper Congo about four hundred miles above the rapids at present-day Kisangani. The Arabs had been stymied in their efforts to travel farther down the river by the forest that encroached from the north, by hostile Africans who lived on the river's banks, by deadly boa constrictors, and by ninety miles of rapids just above Kisangani. In tales brought back to Nyangwe by Arabs who had attempted to penetrate the tropical wilderness, gorillas were said to habitually rush down from the thickets of nearby mountains and attack passing adventurers by grabbing their hands and biting off their fingers one by one. This story was patently false, since gorillas are strictly vegetarian and naturally timid, but it speaks to the wild imagery that sprouts from the soil of the unknown.

Stanley, refusing to be daunted, pushed on. He found the deep, sunless forest almost impassable. When finally the members of Stanley's debilitated caravan launched themselves in the *Lady Alice* and in canoes upon the river, however, they found the going easier.

Writing in his diary, Stanley recognised the significance of this navigable stretch of river, even though he was yet unsure of what river it was: 'We have labored through the terrible forest, and manfully struggled through the gloom. My people's hearts have become faint. I seek a road. Why here lies a broad watery avenue cleaving the Unknown to some sea, like a path of light.'

But almost as soon as they were moving on the river,

they were attacked by painted Africans paddling immense war canoes. They pulled out guns and shot their way down the river, creating fear and precluding peace as they went.

Hardly had Stanley and his group gotten accustomed to constant harassment from the local people than they encountered the rapids. The travelers managed to portage their flotilla around the white water, dragging the boats along paths slashed through the jungle to finally relaunch at the foot of the rapids. Before Stanley continued downriver, he renamed the violent cataracts Stanley Falls in honor of himself. It was there also that he deduced that this river was not the Nile. He determined the river's elevation by measuring the temperature at which water boiled and found the altitude low. For the Lualaba to be the Nile, the river would have to flow uphill. And since the river took a big bend toward the northwest, away from the Nile, he guessed that he was following the Congo.

Stanley kept going down the next long stretch of navigable water, the same one we were traveling aboard the *Mudimbi*. But he had come west down the river, while we were going east along the equator on a mission very different from his. After more than two months and thirty-two battles with various river peoples, the explorer stood at Congo's estuary with the remnants of his caravan. It was August of 1877, and Stanley had taken nearly three years to trace the course of the Congo and open central Africa to the outside world – a world where the commerce in slaves was being replaced by other methods of profit-making.

Stanley's great trek was to end with personal pain. When he arrived back in Zanzibar, he got an eagerly awaited letter from his beloved Alice Blake that read: 'I have done what millions of women have done before me, not been true to my promise.' Stanley's Lady Alice had married someone else.

The Congo was more constant than the woman, and Stanley turned his attentions to trying to interest the British in developing the vast territory of central Africa that suddenly had been made accessible. But the British were unmoved by his vision of a colonised and profitable Congo, so Stanley looked toward King Leopold.

The Belgian king had been casting about for a colony for a number of years, since his little country was far behind in the European empire-building of the time. Leopold saw the imperial grandeur of Britain, another small country, and was envious. He had been hatching schemes to buy islands or hunks of land in various places around the world from South America to the South Pacific. He tried even to rent the Philippines from Spain, before finally realising that the unclaimed land at the center of the continent was his best opportunity. When Stanley approached him, he was ready. They suited one another, the explorer driven to prove himself with exploits, the king greedy for power and wealth.

Leopold dispatched Stanley on a mission of stunning difficulty: to build a road around the cataracts at the mouth of the Congo, establish a string of trading stations up the river, and procure the allegiance of local chieftains for a central African state to be run by the Belgian. This process of colonialisation, the bamboozlement of Africans who did not know that the treaties they were signing promised unhappiness, was not particularly unusual. What was unusual was that this territory was not to be the colony of another nation but the personal possession of King Leopold.

Stanley performed his mission well. He established Mbandaka in 1883, on his way upriver to found an innermost station at the foot of Stanley Falls. Steamboats connected Stanley's string of riverbank stations, forging a long chain representing Western civilisation across the Congo.

In 1884, a year after the founding of Equator Station, the European powers met in Berlin for what was undoubtedly the most arrogant single act in the colonisation of the African continent and the most far-reaching in its consequences. By the time the Berlin conference ended in 1885, the European leaders had simply parceled out the continent among themselves, using claims based on the travels of their various explorers, traders, and missionaries. Not a single African had been present. The Europeans had only the roughest idea of what they were dividing up, since their map of Africa was blank for whole regions, including most of central Africa. England,

Germany, France, and Portugal all were anxious about being geopolitically outmaneuvered and they ignored the needs of the continent whose fate they were debating. The Europeans drew lines on their maps of Africa that violated tribal boundaries, threw antagonistic tribes together, created territories that amalgamated Christians with Moslems or that were mostly barren land capable of supporting little more than nomads.

Among this group, Belgium was only of the slightest consequence, being a tiny, relatively young country with no colonies and a population that was not interested in building an empire. It did not seem that Belgium was in contention for a piece of Africa. But once the eight Congo trading stations were in place and Stanley off on other tasks back in Europe, Leopold went to work devising a scheme to gain international acceptance of his claim to the Congo. He played on the avarice of his fellow Europeans by promising to place the whole region at Africa's heart under a neutral association supervised by him. Free trade was to be guaranteed for all nations under the auspices of this association, which was to be devoted to the philanthropic development of the Congo Basin and the eradication of the last of the central African slaving. A territory eighty times the size of Belgium was handed over to him, even though he had never set foot upon it, and never would. By the time the rest of Europe realised that the promise of free trade was a sham, the so-called Congo Free State was well on its way to becoming Leopold's colony, its riches and resources his alone.

The slave trade had stunted the growth of central Africa, but Leopold's rule was anything but regenerative. It was ruthlessly commercial and introduced the concept of private property to the Congo with a vengeance. King Leopold discovered that he could finance his colonial state by the forced collection of rubber and, to a lesser extent, ivory. As the world market for rubber expanded with the industrial revolution and demand for rubber tires, Leopold's greed burgeoned.

The king installed Belgian agents at the river stations, paid them commissions based on how much rubber and ivory they collected, and imposed little restraint on the methods they could employ. Ethical and moral qualms often did not interfere, either, for many of Leopold's hirelings were from the dregs of European civilisation, mercenaries and profiteers who had shipped out to the Congo to escape strictures and failures at home. They were 'recruited amongst the pimps, non-coms, bullies and failures of all sorts on the pavement of Brussels and Antwerp' in the opinion of Joseph Conrad, who worked among them during his stint piloting a Congo riverboat in the Free State in 1890. Conrad concluded that they carried out 'the vilest scramble for loot that ever disfigured the history of human conscience and geographical exploration.'

Those Africans who tried to resist the Leopoldian regime paid a heavy price. The southern portion of the colony was ruled by a man named M'Siri who refused to relinquish his mineral-rich land to the Belgians. King Leopold dealt with the matter by ordering a military campaign launched against the obstinate African. M'Siri was shot and killed.

It was more than a decade after the Berlin conference that the rest of the world began to learn about what was really happening in the Congo Free State. Some of the first reports described Equator Station, where the daily round of life was regulated with military exactitude. One visitor observed that the days began punctually with a dawn reveille and roll call, after which the African workers marched to their tasks on the plantations and roads. The streets were kept militarily clean, with women assigned the job of sweeping the byways with palm leaves. Belgians drilled African soldiers on the central square. Laborers cleared land and struggled with the mighty trees of the virgin forest. One day the visiting traveler watched a hundred men haul a single giant trunk through the settlement. The orderliness seemed commendable, a thing to be praised and contrasted to the disorder of nearby villages, until the underlying evil was revealed.

An early view of what was really going on in Leopold's colony came from the Reverend J. B. Murphy, an American Baptist missionary based at the equator settlement, who described in an 1895 report how African soldiers in the employ of Leopold's state had shot some people on Lake Tumba, about fifty miles to the south of Mbandaka, and cut off their hands. Among the mutilated was a little girl, not quite dead, who subsequently recovered to live her life out as a cripple.

'These hands – the hands of men, women and children – were placed in rows before the Commissary [the Belgian agent], who counted them to see that the soldiers had not wasted cartridges.'

To enforce the collection quotas for rubber and ivory, the king's agents recruited African militias to do the work. To document that they were doing their job, the soldiers often came back with severed hands, supposedly those of villagers who had not met their quotas. The common rule was that a soldier needed to prove he had shot someone with his bullet, rather than having wasted it on an animal or other frivolity. A hand was proof that a human being had been punished.

The Congo was anything but a region of free trade. Immense tracts of land were declared the property of the Congo state, meaning Leopold owned them, and dedicated to the pursuit of profits. To attract capital, Leopold granted monopoly concessions to various companies giving them the exclusive rights to exploit rubber, ivory, palm oil, or diamonds. Having kept a majority interest in all these companies, Leopold grew rich as he supervised the ravaging of the Congo.

The raid described by the American missionary was one among frequent expeditions in which villages were punished for not producing their quotas.

The year after the Reverend Murphy's account, a Swedish missionary named Reverend Sjoblom recorded some of the scenes he had witnessed just upriver from Mbandaka. The Swede told of watching a soldier shoot an African and then order:

. . . a little boy . . . to go and cut off the right hand of the man who had been shot . . . The boy after some labour (the man was not quite dead) cut the hand off and laid it by a fallen tree. A little later the hand was put on a fire to smoke before being sent to the Commissary . . .

If the rubber does not reach the full amount required, the sentinels attack the natives; they kill some and bring the hands to the Commissary . . . The sentinels, or else the boys in attendance on them, put these hands on a little kiln, and after they have been smoked (to preserve them), they by-and-by put them on the top of the rubber baskets. I have many times seen this done . . . From this village I went to another, where I met a man, who pointed to a basket, and said to me, 'Look, I have only two hands!' He meant there were not enough to make up for the [small amount of] rubber he had brought . . . When I crossed the stream, I saw some dead bodies hanging down from branches in the water. As I turned my face away from the horrible sight, one of the native corporals who was following us down said, 'Oh, that is nothing; a few days ago I returned from a fight, and I brought the white man 160 hands.' . . . Two or three days after a fight, a dead mother was found with two of her children. The mother was shot, and the right hand taken off. On one side was the elder child, also shot, and the right hand also was taken off. On the other side was the younger child with the right hand cut off, but the child still living was resting against the dead mother's breast. This dark picture was seen by four missionaries.

The Swedish missionary's report continued.

On December 14 a sentinel passed our mission station and a woman accompanied him, carrying a basket of hands. Mr and Mrs Banks, beside myself, went down the road, and they told the sentinel to put the hands in the road that they might count them. We counted eighteen right hands smoked, and from the size of the hands we could judge that they belonged to men, women, and even children . . . I have seen extracts from letters in which the writers have freely told about hundreds of hands being brought by the sentinels. Another agent told me that he had himself seen a State officer at one of the outposts pay a certain number of brass rods (a standard trade good) to the soldiers for a number of hands they had brought. One of the soldiers told me the same . . . 'The Commissary has promised us, if we bring plenty of hands, he will shorten our service . . . I have brought in plenty of hands already, and I expect my time of service will soon be finished.'

The limits of human decency were shattered. It became practice for soldiers to hack the hands off living victims, not just dead ones, since it was hands not corpses that needed to be produced. Severed and smoked hands became a gruesome kind of currency, tokens for a soldier's work. As money was used in the American Civil War, hands came to be used in the Congo to buy a way out of military service.

The profiteering and the massacring reached a fever pitch. Viciousness blended into insanity as the turn of the century neared in central Africa.

The agent of one company, which had been given license to operate as it wished in an area upriver from Mbandaka, confessed to having assassinated one hundred and fifty villagers, cut off sixty of their hands, crucified women and children, and then cut off the sexual members and the heads of men, which were nailed on the fences of the village.

Another missionary, the Reverend W. H. Sheppard, writing about the same time as the others, described the massacre of eighty or ninety villagers, half of whose bodies were dragged off and eaten by the Belgians' raiders. At the massacre site, he stopped by three bodies whose flesh had been carved away from the waist down and talked to the chief raider, recording his conversation thus:

'Why are they carved up so, only leaving the bones?' I asked.

'My people ate them,' he answered promptly.

On the left was a big man, shot in the back and without a head.

'Where is the man's head?' I asked.

'Oh, they made a bowl of the forehead to rub up tobacco . . . in.'

Back home in Europe, Leopold led a grand existence, buying millions of dollars' worth of mansions and Mediterranean real estate, entertaining mistresses, chasing young girls, and donating huge sums of money to his favorite philanthropic projects. He continued to defend his Congo policies by arguing that his goal was to bring civilisation, the enlightened ways of Belgian learning, culture, and religion to the darkest fastnesses of central Africa. That the deeds performed in his name in the Congo were barbaric was not something he addressed.

Word leaked out from the Congo, from Mbandaka and other settlements along the river and its tributaries, but only slowly, impeded as it was by barrages of Leopoldian propaganda and by his policies of secrecy. He encouraged Belgian Catholic missionaries, rather than those of other nationalities, to establish themselves in his Congo because he believed they would be loyal to him, and they generally were. Leopold tried to cloak with fine words the terrible deeds his Belgian agents were committing in the exploitation of the Congo.

'Our only programme, I am anxious to repeat, is the work of moral and material regeneration, and we must do this among a population whose degeneration in its inherited conditions is difficult to measure. The many horrors and atrocities which disgrace humanity give way little by little before our intervention,' the king wrote in a surpassingly hypocritical letter to his agents.

Finally, twenty-three years after Leopold's unbridled experiment in capitalism began, international outrage forced the Belgian government to take over the Congo Free State from the king. Critics in Europe and the United States, including Mark Twain, who wrote a biting satire of King Leopold, demanded an end to the atrocities being committed. In 1908, the government of Belgium took over Leopold's colony and it became the Belgian Congo.

By then, huge areas of the Congo had been depopulated. Tens of thousands of the Africans who survived the massacres and the mutilations had fled across the river to the colony of Congo-Brazzaville administered by the French government. The population of the area to Mbandaka's south around Lake Tumba had been reduced by two thirds, by the reckoning of a British official who toured the Congo while Leopold still ruled

it. Across the length and breadth of Leopold's colony, as many
as six million people died, perhaps more in what amounted to
a central African holocaust. When Leopold died in 1909, he left
an estate worth $80 million, most of that enormous wealth
extracted from his personal kingdom in the Congo.

The question of why central Africa has endured such a brutal
history has many answers, no single one of them sufficient. Its
fertility and its wealth always have attracted intruders from
more temperate zones, where life is calculated and orderly,
far removed from the luxuriance, the surfeit of plants and
minerals, watercourses and forest, heat and rain, natural to
the Congo. Its isolation, the vastness of its protecting forest,
also has made it ripe for ravaging, since it is a place the rest
of the world can easily forget.

The Congo has sparked the interest of the outside world
only when something was to be gained, some raw material,
some vegetable product, some human slave, some useful
mineral or some geographic advantage. When foreigners have
come to the Congo, they have always arrived touting some
value of Western civilisation, talking about Christianity or
democracy, while dealing in violence and dictatorship. The
Congo has been cursed not by its own dark demons but by the
demons from afar.

The Congo's history shows in the sudden, stoical stares that
can transform the face of a Zairian from laughter to brooding,
and also in the omnipresent decay, the rejection of colonial-era
edifices. The government building where our papers had been
scrutinised by the immigration official, with its façade veiled
by the smoke of the squatters' fires, epitomised the lush
decrepitude into which the old Equator Station had fallen. When
we strolled back to the town's main avenue, I took several
photographs of the building and had barely finished when a
Zairian man came rushing up to us. He was angrily insistent.

'You will be arrested,' he announced.

He rightfully accused us of photographing poor people, which we already knew was considered an antigovernment act, and of photographing an official building. The man was not dressed in uniform so we were unable to decide if he actually had any authority. We denied having taken pictures of anybody poor, indeed of anybody at all. I said that I had been trying to capture on film the beauty of the palm trees along the avenue.

'You will be arrested,' the man maintained. 'You will be arrested unless you pay me. You must pay me two thousand zaires.'

If he had asked for twenty, we would have handed him the money, but the bribe he wanted was too extravagant. Thinking quickly, Tim started talking in English, switching from the French we all had been speaking.

'I do not understand what you are saying. I do not understand French,' Tim said.

The man had only the barest grasp of English, just enough to understand that Tim was saying he did not understand. He was as nervous as we were and apparently forgot that we all had been speaking French a minute earlier.

'*Il faut que vous me payer deux milles zaires,*' the man repeated in French.

Tim shrugged and turned to me, asking if I knew what the man was saying. Having caught on, I shook my head.

The man's face clenched in pained concentration and he tried to speak, stammeringly, in English.

'I want . . . I want . . . I want . . .'

He could not remember how to say two thousand in English. We walked away, leaving him staring at the middle of the street, and headed along the river and up a gentle slope toward a large yellow-stucco house and a stone church. We found that the house was enclosed by a stout ironwork fence and bars protected the lower windows. The building was the regional headquarters for the security police, the bars meant to prevent the escape of prisoners who had angered the Mobutu government.

Around behind the stone church at the top of the hill, we found a mission building that was falling victim to the forest. Three trees sprang through the tiling of its roof. Cutting back toward the port, we went past a building that advertised itself with high humor as the North Pole Restaurant. A sign on the door claimed the place was air-conditioned, but the door was locked. Beer-bottle tops littered the ground around the door, where on hot evenings the patrons of the North Pole must have sat out on the steps to catch a cooling breeze, or to put their arms around the prostitutes who frequented the bar.

As we were walking, the sun burst out from behind the morning cloud cover, a truly equatorial sun that seared into our skin until it prickled. We sought shelter in an unpretentious bar near the port that varied its hours according to the presence of riverboats. We recognised fellow passengers drinking there and settled down to a couple of beers.

I opened up the banana leaf I had been carrying around and bit into one of the charred caterpillars. It tasted and crunched like Fritos. I announced this to Tim, attempting to persuade him to try one, but he remained staunch in his refusal.

We fell into a conversation with the proprietor of the bar, a slender Belgian of about forty whose eyes weighed pensively at the corners. He had married a Zairian woman and Mbandaka was his home, where he was raising his daughter, a laughing infant to whom we were introduced along with his plump wife. The Belgian talked at length about the economic difficulties of his adopted country, the devaluation, the corruption.

'I think that things cannot go on like this. It is too hard for the people to survive. The prices are going up and up, so that business is very hard to accomplish,' he said.

Worse, the cost of corruption was keeping pace with the rising price of beer. Bribes – to government transport officials to deliver the beer, to local officials to allow him to stay in business, and so on – were doubling the cost of all his transactions.

'The people are suffering. Everything gets only worse than ever, worse than ever,' he repeated mournfully as he left us to go about his business.

Morning turned into noontime, while we sat at the bar table, listening for the ship's horn that would signal our departure.

Tim was anxious, afraid that we would somehow miss the boat and be left behind here in the middle of nowhere.

But not me. I was happy, happy to look out from the bar through a soft stuccoed arch painted in green and blue pastels and feast my eyes on the red flowers that engulfed the front of the building, happy to watch the orange butterflies dancing among the blooms seeking nectar, happy just to be there basking in the generosity of a warm climate. Time, like the mosquitoes, was slowed and flowed through a scene drenched in the peace of its own monotony, a scene of perpetual green where snow never falls and the days blend together as easily as the river's currents.

I didn't want to leave Mbandaka and its unfettered sky. Despite its history, Mbandaka was not a place of beaten people. It was a place of survivors, of Africans who knew the strength of their continent.

I felt that I might find a lost part of myself if I lingered long enough. But the *Mudimbi*'s horn sounded and we left the lugubrious Belgian, the bar, the vegetation, and the town. Back on board, I watched as Mbandaka disappeared, blending into the banks of the river and the somnolent, equatorial greenery.

SEVEN

Being less gregarious than I, Tim liked to sit at the prow of the *Mudimbi*'s leading barge and gaze at the river unfolding. This barge was comparatively peaceful. On its flat expanse, neighborhoods of makeshift tents had sprung up in the spaces between pieces of heavy cargo, which included a Volkswagen, barrels of gasoline and diesel fuel, bales of used clothes, and Simon Kepe's red furniture. It was almost quiet up there, far enough away from the straining engines so that it rode smoothly across the water as if pushed by some giant and benevolent hand.

Tim found a spot where he could lean against a low bulkhead and study the river that was wider with each mile we traveled in from the mountains that had choked its passage near Kinshasa. In the mornings the river still was brown, a uniform brown; it had no red tinge, no green hint, no blue possibility, nothing to proclaim it Africa's greatest river. But the rising sun changed its countenance. Under the bombarding light it took on a silvery sheen, and by noontime it gleamed like dirty sheet metal.

The farther we traveled upriver, the more difficult it was to tell where we were and where we had been. The river had become a skein of channels that split and merged and split again around island after island. Some four thousand of these islands interrupt the river, disguising its size, slicing its currents into mere insinuations of the greater watercourse. Each reach of the river looked the same, bend after bend, hour after hour, mile after mile. The only apprehensible change in the scenery was with the forest, which was getting thicker, always thicker. From the mass of foliage, an occasional palm or an old giant of the forest would thrust itself free, shooting straight up into the air and then blossoming into a lofty crown.

Sometimes, villages slid by, insignificant clearings in the greenery, a patch of rubiginous dirt and houses built of sticks and thatch. Sometimes, a few raggedly dressed people would look up from their chores to stare, startled, at the churning riverboat. Naked children ran along the banks, pursuing the *Mudimbi* as if to catch it, and then waving until the boat labored beyond their sight around some bend in the river or curve of an island.

Young men hung out on the foredeck, trading and smoking marijuana, and bathing in the patch of privacy provided by the bulkhead. Dunking buckets into the river water, they sloshed themselves mostly clean with the muddy water, bending and stretching and letting the water run down their lean bodies to the deck where it evaporated in minutes. Once they had washed, they, too, leaned back and watched the river.

The prow was the place to watch the pirogues coming in. Against the silver immensity of the river, the canoes that lay in wait for the riverboat formed a pattern of dark curves, chiseled to points at the ends like uncertain smiles. They were no different from those crafted by the early Bantu settlers who swept through the Congo Basin in a great migration before the time of Christ. The dugouts, the largest of them wide enough to hold a hippopotamus and long enough to carry forty people, were made to look impossibly delicate by the sheer size of the river rocking them down its currents. Warned of the riverboat's approach by a system of drum signals passed along the banks, the river people paddled out to the edge of the main boat channel, a pathway up the river that zigzagged around sandbars, muddy shallows, and islands. They waited then for the boat to draw abreast, standing with their long paddles still.

At an exactly figured moment, they flashed their paddles, bending from their waists and balancing with a grace practised down through generations, shooting their canoes toward the boat. As a dugout came sliding toward the side of the boat, veering and slithering in the turbulent water at the boat's side, the front paddler grabbed for a railing or another canoe, anything more stable than the rushing water. The riverboat plowed ahead, paying no heed to the struggling paddlers, not even when an occasional canoe bounced off its side or overturned in the turbulence.

The river people, some of whom travel for days from villages on the Congo's tributaries, came with the bottoms of their pirogues laden with fish, eels, oranges, and other fruits. Dying fish flapped and writhed on the lower decks, making it difficult to walk without stepping on the tail of some giant fish whose penny-sized eyes stared, glazing, toward death. A hundred varieties of fish were hauled from the muddy depths of the river to the muddy decks of the riverboat, from the placid carp whose meat is succulently plentiful to the slimy eels that are common riverine fare. The Congo breeds startlingly ugly fish, including a catfish that grows up to six feet long with a be-whiskered snout like that of a pig, and wonderfully delicate fishes, including an almost round variety with lustrous yellow scales that resembles an oversized gold piece.

The canoes served up a widening bounty of forest produce. We could buy fresh fruit like bananas, oranges, or papayas; mammoth snails, chewy and served in hot pepper sauce; the charcoaled caterpillars that tasted like Fritos; roasted crocodile, a delicacy; flying squirrel; antelope killed that same day in the forest; fat tree grubs, the larvae of beetles that are sauteed in curry sauce and are a prized source of protein; and monkey.

Dead monkeys, whose meat is highly regarded fare, began piling up all over the boat after we left Mbandaka. Canoe after canoe arrived at the *Mudimbi*'s side heaped with monkey carcasses, little green monkeys, brown furred monkeys, and rufous monkeys with elegant tails. The hunters wrapped the tails forward around the necks of the freshly killed creatures and then carried the trussed monkeys in bunches by the improvised handles of their tails. It reminded me of the way an American woman carries a bulky handbag by its strap, holding it out stiffly so that it won't bang against her thighs.

Besides the fresh monkeys, blackened carcasses of smoked monkeys were heaped in nearly every corner. They were smoked in the indelicate Zairian sense, which means roasted until charred into a state of long-term preservation. Unfortunately, the smoked carcasses still resembled monkeys. The high heat of the roasting had curled the monkeys little hands into fists and locked their mouths open, the thinner flesh of their lips burned away so that their teeth grimaced nakedly, transfixed forever in silent screams.

We ate some monkey ourselves, not the smoked kind but some fresh meat stewed in a gravy. Gustatory pleasure was not our aim in this meal and, in fact, we were perturbed at the idea of eating an animal that was so close to being humanly intelligent. But I thought it my duty as a journalist, as a student of the river, to try it when the Germans asked us if we wanted to share a monkey with them. They had persuaded one of the cooks to stew up a monkey that Gunther had bought, a beautiful one with a long tail and delicate face. Andrew and Elly came up from the barges to have some of it with us in the dining room.

The stew arrived in a big bowl. I had expected the meat to be cut away from the bone and its true nature disguised, but the limbs and various parts of the monkey's trunk were clearly represented among the chunks of meat floating in the gravy – a leg here, ribs there, a socketed hip bone. The waiter served it on piles of rice and, to my disgust, dished out on my plate one of the very identifiable hind legs, intact from hip to anklebone. Mustering my bravery, I took a couple of bites, enough to note that the meat tasted fine, gamy like a rabbit, if a little stringy. Not far from the table, the little green monkeys were running back and forth on the dining room bar.

I donated the remainder of my leg meat to Andrew, who ate prodigiously, taking three helpings and spooning up the last strands of meat. Then he sucked on the bones. Andrew was always hungry, always trying to eke out his money, living mostly off boiled manioc, which sold cheaply on the barges. For a couple of pennies you could buy a lump of the starchy vegetable, which comes out tasting like gluey tapioca pudding. One lump was enough to make you feel full for a few hours.

Even when he had eaten, Andrew looked hungry. He never looked quite healthy. His clothes were worn and dirty and his hair hung down lankly across his forehead. The tops of his feet were blistered by a case of scabies he had picked up sleeping on some filthy blankets on Mount Cameroon and were so raw that he could not bear to lace his sneakers closed. Andrew seemed unable to find the place in the world he was seeking, a place where his being no longer chafed and suffered.

One morning, a pair of fishermen hauled aboard several strings of the gold-piece fish and a jug of homemade palm wine. They swung their strings of fish in the air, making them look like glittering necklaces, and quickly sold them to one of the *commerçants*.

When the fishermen set the jug of wine out on the deck, a circle of passengers gathered around them. This wine is made from the juice of the generous raffia palms, whose fruits provide oil and whose fronds provide thatch, and it is a favorite drink in central Africa. The fishermen ladled out the wine with two plastic cups, charging six cents a cup. Among the drinkers were some soldiers in camouflage uniforms who quaffed down cup after cup and then moved off from the others, muttering and joking among themselves. They made me nervous, for they seemed to have no officer and no purpose other than to amuse themselves. I edged around to the other side of the wine pot, nearer to the fishermen, who took this as a signal that I wanted some of the drink, too. I did want to try it for the sake of curiosity, but I was afraid of it because of the possibility that it had been diluted with river water infested with any number of virulent diseases, such as schistosomiasis, which attacks your bladder and intestines, and amoebic infections that give you terrible dysentery. The fishermen held out a cup of their wine.

'Go ahead. Drink it. It is free. They want you to try it,' one of the drinkers advised. I did not want to try to explain my qualms so I took the cup and drank, praying that I wasn't drinking down any vicious bugs. The wine tasted like old lemonade.

I decided to follow these two fishermen and talk to them. They spoke only Lingala and a smattering of French, but they tried politely to answer my questions, bizarre as my interest in them must have seemed. They let me follow along, this pair of friendly men who undoubtedly could harpoon a hippopotamus and whose ancestors may well have been among the warriors who, with good reason, tried to kill Stanley.

Immediately after finishing with the wine, the fishermen bought some bread and wolfed it down, swallowing it without chewing. They had been paddling out from their village for more than a day, moving down their tributary through the night, steering a course through marshes and around islands whose geography they knew by heart, by daylight or by starlight. They could read the river by deciphering its bends and ripples as easily as I could read street signs back home.

They also bought two cigarettes, one each, which they puffed down to the smallest smokable stub almost without pause. Few people in Zaire are rich enough to buy a whole pack of cigarettes at once and smoke any time they want. The merchants who sold cigarettes on the *Mudimbi* doled them out, collecting a few pennies for each one. A sure dividing mark between the rich and poor nations is the way cigarettes are sold and possessions treated. In countries where material life is hard, everything a person owns is distinct. An enamel bowl, a cooking pot, a piece of cloth, a pair of shoes, a bar of soap, all these items are valued for their considerable worth.

The fishermen were brothers-in-law and neither was particularly prosperous. They wore no shoes and their hands were as heavily calloused as their feet. They wore cheap patterned shirts, the kind made in Hong Kong or Taiwan and sold everywhere in Africa, and their polyester pants were shiny with wear.

Most of the river people dressed up, if they could, for the excursion to the riverboat, wearing shoes if they had them. The women kept to the traditional patterned cloths that they wrapped and knotted around themselves, but the men liked to look modern. The height of Congo fashion was the jogging suit. Despite the heat and the humidity, an outfit of matching warm-up pants and jacket was the equivalent of the Sunday-best suit. Bright pastel suits – aquamarine, canary yellow, rose pink – were popular, and the sharpest male dressers added a further touch of exuberance by painting their thumbnails with red polish.

The fishermen held the money they had earned from the fish and wine in their fists and began touring the *Mudimbi*'s markets. Maneuvering through the crowded passageways, they compared prices, fingered bolts of cloth, examined the soles of plastic sandals, inquired about the freshness of manioc, and looked over baskets of medicines. This was their prelude to buying a few things. They bought a bar of yellow soap for washing clothes, two razorblades, seven unlabeled medicine capsules for 'fevers,' and another plastic cup. They also bought two notepads for their children, who studied at a school near their village run by a local teacher.

With the remainder of their earnings, the fishermen splurged. They climbed up to an upper tier and found a bar, where they bought beers, one each. The music was loud, scratchy, and insistently melodic. The fishermen sipped from their bottles, listened, and looked down at their feet. But as the music took hold and they finished their beer, they began dancing, really dancing. Zairians dance as if they have problems no longer, as if the poverty and the struggling have ended, as if their history were filled with triumph. The people at the beer parlor were dancing effervescently, men with men, women with women, men with women.

I joined in, dancing with the fishermen and letting myself go, as surprised to be dancing with them as they were with me, and as delighted. The people around us were moving for the sake of the music, their feet gliding from step to step, back and forth, their arms and their backs undulating toward their moving feet. The riverbanks were gliding past, the canoes gliding in, the feet gliding, as the barge was gliding, across the smoothly opaque water, going upriver in time, in tune with the pulse of the music, in time to a beat born in the Congo and reverberating across the Congo, dancing their way upriver, the rock music blaring and rasping and bare feet slapping out the rhythm on the metal deck.

The longer the fishermen stayed aboard the *Mudimbi*, the farther they had to paddle home, so after a while they had to leave the music. Before they untied their pirogue, I talked to them as best I could within the narrow territory of words we all understood.

They asked me if there was a river like the Congo from where I came in the United States. I told them what I could about the Mississippi and about the catfish from that river, that the fish are smaller and the river has few canoes and fewer islands, but still it is the biggest river the United States boasts. I explained also that if the Mississippi has fewer canoes, it has more boats and many more cities, many more people. They wanted to know how people caught fish on the Mississippi and I told them with hooks and nets, similar to what they used, but in bigger and more comfortable boats so that the work is not as difficult.

'We work very hard. We must fish under the sun when it is very hot,' one of them said.

'It is getting harder to live,' the other joined in with a complaint about the rottenness of the economy that we had heard from others and would hear again on our trip across Zaire. 'The prices are going higher. The money is getting smaller.'

It was late afternoon when the fishermen pushed away from the *Mudimbi*, standing at each end of their canoe, paddling toward their village somewhere in a clearing isolated in the green splendor of the forest.

EIGHT

Something was getting on my nerves as we moved farther upriver. Tim, too, was irritable. The constant heat, which persisted through the nights undaunted by the dark breezes that gusted sporadically from the forest, had a numbing effect on my mind, making it hard to think. The humidity, which became more oppressive the farther we went, gave body to the heat. The thumping of the diesels had become hypnotic and the nights insomniac. I would wake bathed in sweat, startled by the renewed rattling of the cots' legs against the metal floor, by a shouted argument from the steerage barge, or merely by some inarticulate fear, surfacing from inside my mind. The ill-fitting sheets would have come loose and tangled around my body.

Maybe it was the fact that, on the eighth day and about 750 miles upriver, each reach of the river looked like the one that came before and the one that would come after. In its struggle for space, the forest pushed over the edges of the islands so that its branches and fronds leaned into the rushing currents against which the *Mudimbi* was making her steady and uninspired way. Although the river had widened to eight miles, its breadth was obscured by island after island after island. The forest, too, went on and on and on, as if it had lost its beginning and its end.

At night we had been reading *Heart of Darkness* aloud to one another, and the novel did not leaven our mood. We had rationed the book to make it last until we got to Kisangani. It was set on this same stretch of river, where Conrad had piloted his steamboat during the era of Leopold's ravages. Kurtz, Conrad's fictional Belgian agent, went mad during his

assignment at the far trading station, the outpost that grew
to become Kisangani. Kurtz was driven insane by horror, the
horror of the inhumanities that supposedly civilised white men
were capable of committing when power, greed, and fear were
magnified by the steamy heat in a brutalised land.

Conrad's forest was appropriately inhuman:

It was like traveling back to the earliest beginning of the
world, when vegetation rioted on the earth and big trees
were kings. An empty stream, a great silence, an impen-
etrable forest. The air was warm, thick, heavy, sluggish.
There was no joy in the brilliance of sunshine. The long
stretches of waterway ran on, deserted, into the gloom of
the overshadowed distances. On silvery sandbanks, hippos
and alligators sunned themselves side by side. The broaden-
ing waters flowed through a mob of wooded islands; you lost
your way on the river as you would in a desert.

This stillness of life did not in the least resemble a peace.
It was the stillness of an implacable force brooding over an
inscrutable intention. It looked at you with a vengeful aspect.

The forest was inscrutable as ever, if not vengeful.

With every day, the spy was making me more edgy. Certainly
he was curious, if not suspicious about why we were traveling
upriver packing a typewriter and a bag full of cameras and
notebooks. Always, he seemed to be near our cabin, leaning
on the railing by a window, standing silently on the deck outside
the door, watching Jimmy clear the day's trash and the usual
littering of dead cockroaches from our room.

Tim liked to write observations in his journal while sitting
on the deck outside the stuffy cabin, and the spy would come
around and ask him what he was doing. He was particularly
intrigued with the maps Tim was using to calculate the
Mudimbi's progress, and wanted to know why Tim was noting
the names of towns along with descriptions of the river. I

thought the spy suspected Tim was mapping some byzantine invasion route and I finally persuaded him to stop taking notes outside the cabin even though he believed I was being paranoid.

Despite the heat and the monotony, life went on aboard the *Mudimbi* at a lively pace. During the days I continued to pass time with Marie Thérèse and the other *commerçants* in her circle. Produce was heaped in every corner, beside every chair, in every miniature cabin. Forest parrots, bought for resale in the cities, hung in wickerwork cages tied to the ceiling, birds with princely orange-red tailfeathers and newly clipped wings, prisoners in the name of riverine commerce. A man over in a corner, who sold batteries and razorblades, the batteries upended and stacked in short pyramids and the blades in individual paper wrappers laid out in straight rows, had acquired two live turtles, the larger one with a diameter the size of a bushel basket. They were tethered to a post by ropes that were looped through holes drilled in the edges of their carapaces.

After some practice, I learned a Lingala sentence that was endlessly successful as a comic line. I presented it haltingly and with such questionable pronunciation that the listener had to work at figuring out what I was saying.

'*Mbote, mbote. Tala nsima na yo, na okomona na malili ya yo,*' I would say. 'Hello, good afternoon. Look behind you, and you will see your shadow.'

The first time I tried it, my listener was concentrating so hard on the meaning that he turned around and looked for his shadow, not remembering that he was standing in a closed-in, shadowless aisleway. The expectant audience of *commerçants* who had painstakingly taught me the sentence were ready with guffaws. The line worked just about every time I tried it, and the *commerçants* loved luring in fresh victims to hear my Lingala.

As unstylish as I felt dressed in a travel-worn cotton dress and old leather flat-soled sandals, my belongings were envied.

Marie Thérèse never gave up asking me for my sandals. I would explain in French, the language we used when we really wanted to say something, why the sandals were no good for her.

'These sandals would not fit your feet and, more than that, they are wearing out. You can see the leather soon will fall apart,' I said.

'Yes, you may speak truthfully, but leather shoes don't hurt the feet like plastic shoes. And they are much prettier,' she replied.

She held up her foot in a green plastic Hong Kong sandal and winced for good measure.

Marie Thérèse was a seasoned trader and, like the other *commerçants*, thought nothing of overcharging the unwary. Foreigners were particularly easy game, Tim and I both learned several times during the trip. Marie Thérèse, who would give us oranges free after we got to know her, sold us half a dozen on the first day at a price five times the going rate. By tricking us, she had made thirty cents.

In the evenings, I was often found in *La Cave*, a popular bar in the hull of the barge below the *commerçants*' corridor. A flight of metal steps led down to the bar, which consisted of a couple of unadorned chambers with rusty walls, warm beer, and music so loud conversation was almost impossible. The stairwell was the only source of air, making the place stifling during the day and even hotter during the night, when all sorts of passengers pressed together on plank benches drawn up to long wooden tables that lined both sides of the main chamber. I liked to sit there, drinking beer and sweating as the riverboat chugged all the while toward Africa's very center.

La Cave was the one place on the boat where beer was available day or night, although through some act of Zairian illogic, its warm beer cost more than the cold beer sold in first-class. The bar's proprietor was a man with a sallow face disfigured by a puckered scar below the ridge of one cheekbone. His complaints, accompanied by a lopsided grimace that exaggerated the ugliness of the scar, were unceasing.

'I am going to die before we reach Kisangani. You must help

me, madame. You must give me medicine,' he told me several days out from Kinshasa and every day thereafter. His pleas were as persistent as the heat.

'You are sweating because it is too hot down here, not because you have a fever. I don't believe you are sick,' I responded.

He refused to give up.

'But, madame, I may be sweating but I also am dying,' he said.

It was ritual on his part, this attempt to wheedle something valuable from me. He wasn't alone. Many of the students, and the youths who claimed to be students to bolster their stature, also persisted in soliciting anything they could think of that I might have – matches, cigarettes, paper, pens, film, clean water, books. I possessed just about everything a person could want and they had very, very few of the many things they needed.

Our ninth day on the river dawned cloudless. The temperature had risen into the nineties by mid-morning, which would not have been too hot except that the humidity was somewhere close to ninety percent. It felt as if the rain forest were exhaling moisture. On a bad day, the Congo temperature and humidity combine into a hothouse atmosphere that saps your will and deflates your spirit. I was sweating that morning long before the sun reached its zenith in a panting blue sky.

The clouds came in the early afternoon. During the rainy season on the river, storms blow up suddenly and furiously. The clouds gathered, accumulating, piling into nebulous regiments, massing in the southern regions of the sky. They turned from gray to blue-gray to black-gray, flattened out and blew from one side of the sky to the other. They sank and their angry underbellies almost touched the tops of the big trees on the islands. Dull yellow rags of fog trailed on the rising wind. Just before the storm broke, the light changed, doubling, tripling its intensity, strangely, as if the storm were squeezing the light from the air. There were no shadows, only the light and the clouds.

The *Mudimbi* was near a long island choked by fringy palm trees whose leaves looked in the prestorm light as if they were glazed with chrome. Within minutes, rain came lashing down hard, slanting in under the roof and across the deck. Mist swirled in, wrapping the riverboat in a cocoon, obscuring our vision and making the river into a pond walled by fog. A gale raised waves on the river and capped them with mud-colored froth.

The storm sent the passengers scurrying for shelter, including the woman of hippopotamus proportions who was traveling in one of the first-class cabins. She customarily passed the day lying on the deck by her cabin, resting on a fleshy elbow, drinking beer from the bottle and eating bunches of sweet little red-skinned bananas. We passed her spot each day because her cabin was adjacent to the dining room, but she never talked to us. Other passengers said she was the wife of an important government official and businessman in the upriver trading town of Bumba. When the storm hit, the woman hauled herself to her feet and leaped into the sheltered dining room, the yards of flowered cloth with which she swathed her body billowing like cheerful sails in the precipitate wind. She settled herself onto a wall bench opposite the place where the ceiling had started leaking and rewrapped the bolt of cloth around her torso.

Lightning flashed and the storm boomed. To protect the *Mudimbi* and her barges, the captain steered the whole assemblage into the side of the island. The boat crashed into the vegetation, tearing limbs from trees and tossing a couple of empty pirogues against the bank. Another dugout was swamped, capsized, and carried out of sight on the wave-whipped current. The two people who had been paddling it struggled to the island's bank and crawled into the bushes to wait out the storm. The *Mudimbi* dragged to a halt against the riverbottom, canted by the thick mud.

Lunch, which had been underway in the dining room, continued without interruption. The waiters ignored the howling of the wind, the dripping ceiling, and the slanted floor. We diners stuffed the ends of the tablecloths under our plates to level them so that the gravy wouldn't slop onto the table-tops pitched at the same slant as the floor and the stalled riverboat.

We were as motley a group of diners as could be found in first class anywhere. Aside from the two Germans, there was a Zairian minister whom we disliked from the beginning, a pompous man who prohibited his wife from eating with him or drinking beer in his presence. He was a Protestant and enjoyed sermonising between mouthfuls of pork chop and potato about the immoral acts perpetrated by the prostitutes whom he had observed at work on the barges and even in first class.

We all had noticed Simon Kepe, the man with the red living room suite, and some of the other river merchants visiting the cabin of a woman up on the first class deck. She had taken the cabin for herself and three children, whom she herded out onto the deck when she had a man visiting.

'This is the problem with the people today – they go to prostitutes. They have no morality,' the minister said.

When he was not at meals, the minister was usually leaning back in the only deck chair on the boat, an open Bible propped on his belly and a bottle of beer at his side.

The spy also came to meals. He tended to sit with a half-caste Portuguese who had boarded by canoe at one of the barely significant upriver towns where the *Mudimbi* had paused for a few hurried minutes. We never figured out what this man was all about. He told us he was a trader on the Congo, as his father had been before he died of a fever on the upper reaches of a tributary that meets the Congo from the northeast. But the Portuguese would not tell us what he traded or where he lived. He was missing some of his teeth and the rest were brown stumps, but he had money and a habit of pulling bills off a fat roll he kept in a pocket of his pants, which were sheeny with grease. Like someone who has wandered far off the track of normal life, he seemed fundamentally lost, neither European nor African, neither of the forest nor of the modern world.

The spy and the Portuguese were sitting that day at the

table across from us. Like fast friends and accomplices, they hunched together. The spy curled his long back and leaned toward the Portuguese, whispering into his ear and paying little attention to the storm.

The storm, after a quarter hour of uproar, drove on northward over the forest, shaking the trees like pompons. A few clouds hung back over the river but they were drained of gray, a yellow-pink in color containing either the dregs of anger or a blush of fair weather to come, and perhaps both. The *Mudimbi*'s diesels, pushed up to full power, heaved the old boat out of the mud and shoved the barges out into the main channel. As we got underway, the sun came out and steamed the moisture from the forest's dripping leaves.

We usually ended our meals with Coca-Cola or beer. We could have the drinks cold if the steward who controlled the padlocked refrigerator behind the bar was around and properly humored with a small payoff. We would share the drinks in thick-rimmed ceramic cups in which we had drunk tea during the meal. It was over teacup beer that we became friends with the Germans. It took us a while, though, to get over our mutual suspicions. We had thought them odd and unfriendly. They judged us as representatives of the United States and therefore responsible for the deployment of American nuclear missiles in Germany.

They told us that they were touring Zaire overland, each on a big Honda 500 motorcycle. That explained their boots and grubbiness. Motorcycles, in fact, were probably the best way to get around on Zaire's deteriorating roads. We told them that we also were unhappy about our country's nuclear policies. Of the two Germans, Wolfgang was the more intellectual and talkative.

'Yes. We are on vacation making this tour,' he began in serviceable English, hissing on the plurals and growling at the vowels in the German way.

'Why did you come all the way to Zaire for vacation?' I asked. 'It's not the kind of place for tourists.'

'But you see we are not tourists,' Wolfgang said. 'We are neighbors. We come from Rwanda.'

Squeezed into a mountainous wedge between Zaire and Tanzania, Rwanda is a tiny country whose farmland is over-crowded and whose forests have been largely destroyed. Zaire's raw and expansive topography is altogether different and the Germans were reveling in it, admiring above all the forest, which is second in size only to the Amazon. The Germans, it turned out, were professional foresters working in Rwanda in a program to reforest some of the abused land there. We watched the forest and so did the Germans, Wolf-gang with his wirerimmed glasses and Gunther with his shaggy hair. The forest rolled past the sides of the riverboat, as if we were looking out at a slow-motion film that repeated itself, trees and vines and the brown river, vines and trees and the river.

The vegetable wall we saw squeezing in upon the river hid an efficient and sophisticated ecosystem. Like other rain forests, the Congo forest has evolved in an uninterrupted roll over millions of years, diversifying to support a myriad species of flora and fauna, each one filling a special environmental niche. The soil of the forest floor is extremely thin despite the huge trees it supports, but the rain forest is so efficient that it literally feeds on itself rather than the earth, re-absorbing nutrients from the dead leaves and branches that decay speedily in the humid heat. Almost as soon as a plant or tree dies, it is eaten by the other plants, broken apart by roots and creepers until its remains are sucked up again into the living vegetation.

'Like a big green cannibal,' Gunther interjected tersely during one of our conversations.

This vegetable cannibalism explains why the world's rain forests are ultimately so fragile. When the big trees are cut down, the soil beneath is no longer replenished and the thin layer quickly erodes. Although the remoteness of the Congo Basin has protected much of its forest from wide-scale timber-ing of the sort that has gone on in the Amazon, the big trees have not been invulnerable. The Germans, who were on the final leg of their tour, had ridden their motorcycles in a wide circle that took them through the forest and out onto its peripheries where they found it was being pared away by farmers clearing new land and cutting wood for fuel.

'The shame is that this country does not see its forest as a natural gift. No, instead, it is considered a blockage to development or a chance to make fast money,' Wolfgang observed unhappily.

He told us about a big German veneer company operating in the forests around Mbandaka, selecting venerable hardwoods to fell and then peel for their outer layers of wood. Once it has been exported, the veneer is used to make elegant furniture and paneling.

The future of Zaire's forest has an importance that goes beyond the country's borders, since the rain forests may be crucial to keeping the climate of the whole globe stable. Scientists are not certain what will happen if the equatorial forests of Africa, South America, and Asia continue to be destroyed, but their predictions tend to be grim. The burning of these forests, which is the standard way of clearing them, may be accelerating the so-called greenhouse effect by adding carbon dioxide to the atmosphere and trapping heat. The burning of fossil fuels does the same thing. The temperature of the globe could rise as much as five degrees, approaching a warmth not known since the age of the dinosaurs, melting the polar ice caps and playing havoc with weather patterns.

Every few days the monotony of our progress across the saucer of the Congo Basin was broken by a stopover at a town grown up around one of the original Belgian trading stations. Lisala, situated on the flanks and crest of a rare hill where the river curves back toward the equator for a second time, was one of the bigger of such towns. This was the birthplace of Mobutu, who memorialised his fiftieth birthday by buying hundreds of piglets and having them transported to the town as gifts for the people.

Even with the infusion of presidential pigs, Lisala was another place that had seen better days. A tarmac road cut up the hill from the river, but most of the town's activity was pedestrian. People climbed up and down the hill on a long flight of crumbling stone steps. At the water's edge, a couple of buildings, once places of commerce, were sinking into shambles. An old woman had found shelter on one of the building's porticoes, establishing her hegemony with some bundles of rags she had gathered around her. The rest of the building was empty, its original purpose lost in the flux of years, lost with the departure of the Belgians who had tried so hard to imprint their own order on the Congo. All along the river the scene was the same. The Congo was shrugging off its foreign trappings, turning back toward a past of villages, of simple baked-mud architecture, of small-scale farming, of forest hunting and river fishing.

Tim and I debated the meaning of this retreat from modernity. We argued about whether the ubiquitous decay was the result of some conscious choice, a rejection of colonial structures in preference to indigenous ones, or whether the power of the forest and its simpler ways of life was inexorable. Was it the result of government corruption, of a graft-ridden economy too enfeebled to support a modern society in the heart of Africa? Or did the people of Zaire prefer to live in dirt clearings and carry their water in cans and buckets up from the river? The conclusion we agreed upon was that, of course, Zairians were as hungry for modernisation as any other people, hungry for comfort and knowledge, advanced medical care, and all the benefits taken for granted in developed societies. But history and modern-day politics have combined to send their country sliding backward into the forest.

That afternoon, after pulling out of Lisala, the *Mudimbi* crossed paths with another of the big riverboats, which was coming back downriver laden with an equally outrageous assortment of barges and passengers. The captains of both boats cut their engines and steered together until the two behemoths bumped together, drifted apart, and then bumped again, hugely clumsy, like dinosaurs trying to dance.

The other boat was bristling with passengers, maybe as many as two thousand, and they all crowded to the railings to look and shout and laugh at us. After days of seeing only fishermen and tiny villages clinging to the riverbanks, the sight of another boat called for celebration. For an hour, everyone pranced and shouted, danced and waved from one boat to the other. The celebratory hullabaloo ended only when the boats moved off in their separate directions.

The chances of our getting to Kisangani on time were getting more and more remote. Several days earlier the *Mudimbi* had started losing power. The scenery began passing more slowly and the canoes paddling alongside seemed to pick up speed.

Suspecting something might have gone wrong with the engines, we went to find Gunther, who loved the *Mudimbi*'s diesels and was often down watching the boat's mechanics working on them. The engines, their greasy, steaming pipes and valves rising beyond the level of the first deck, were a general attraction for the passengers. While the mechanics labored in the infernal heat thrown off by the diesels, many passengers would spend hours gazing at them through a wire mesh fence and passing along inaccurate observations about the boat's mechanical health. Gunther would get down inside the cage with the mechanics, asking questions or offering advice. He loved any kind of engine.

Gunther explained to us that one of the diesels was out of commission, in need of a part that was not in stock aboard the boat but that the mechanics were going to try to jerry-build. They did eventually get the thing going again, but not half an hour afterward the other engine quit, in protest perhaps at having had to carry the whole monstrous load of boat and barges alone.

This became a pattern; when one engine was up, the other was down. Our pace, which had been no quicker than a fast man could walk in the first place, slowed for a few days to that of a canoe paddled stoutly upriver. Indeed, the canoes proved a match for the riverboat when the *Mudimbi*'s captain, concluded that the fifty or maybe sixty canoes tied up to the crippled riverboat's railings were dragging too much. That the canoes were a mere featherweight compared to the barges and the people, animals and freight did not matter. The captain ordered the dugouts to cast off and sent out the squad of boat police to enforce his decree.

Summoning what ferocity they could for the assignment, trying to look stern rather than silly, the police charged and jumped across the decks, waving their pistols, slashing the vine canoe ropes with axes, and shouting terrible threats. They fired their pistols into the air madly – a little too madly because one of the police shot himself in the arm. Worse, it was all to no avail, since the fishermen who had been cut adrift simply paddled around to the other side of the boat, laughing and singing as they retied their ropes. Within the hour, the police gave up and the trading on the lower decks returned to its nonstop normalcy.

The *Mudimbi* hobbled along on one or another engine for three days, until one midnight the working engine gave out, too. The *Mudimbi* stopped rattling. At the stern, I found Gunther standing by himself and watching with fascination as the currents took over and started drawing the boat back down the river. He was calmly enjoying the débâcle.

'How bad is it?' I asked.

'Can't tell. They could get it fixed within the hour or within the week. It's something with the piston again.'

'Do you think they have some kind of anchor?' I asked.

'No anchor is any good. This boat is too heavy to hold. The only anchor is an island big enough to block us.'

The *Mudimbi* and her barges began to gather downstream momentum, crashing crazily into islands but not anchoring, swirling free, heaving sideways, gouging great holes in the muddy banks.

'Watch out! Get down!' Gunther yelled, sensing a danger in the darkness that I could not see.

I crouched against a steel pole that supported the deck above us as a tree limb came smashing over a gunwale and splintered against the walls of the first-class cabins. Tim was up now, too, crouching down with me and asking Gunther the same questions I had. Unshaken, Gunther still was enjoying himself, leaning over the railing and peering downstream to see what we were going to smash into next.

After half an hour of this, the mechanics coaxed one of the engines to life. By the next day, miraculously, they had both engines going again and the *Mudimbi*, four days behind schedule, was once more proudly outstripping the fastest canoes.

Four lost days is a mere hiccough for Zaire's disease-ridden transportation system. Zaire is blessed among African countries, possessing 9000 miles of navigable waterways, the great Congo river system whose tributaries reach into the country's remotest regions. It is as if nature compensated for the difficulties of the rain forest by creating a network of natural highways to serve the forest and end its isolation. As it is, commerce on the river system proceeds at a hesitating pace.

On the Congo's mainstream, the *Mudimbi* crossed paths with only one or two other boats a day, even though this was the only means of supply for much of the country's interior. All along the river we saw abandoned riverboats, dead from neglect or a lack of spare parts, sinking into the muck of some forgotten riverbank.

Some of the problems of transport were documented recently by a team of men from the American embassy who traveled a southern portion of the Congo watershed. They went by rail and boat from Zaire's copper mining southern province up the Kasai River and down the mainstream to the Atlantic coast.

Starting in the railway headquarters at Lumbumbashi, the capital of the copper region, the Americans found nine precious locomotives sidelined. About a hundred diesel motors and numerous railway cars were also stalled. The Americans found, too, that huge volumes of fuel meant to keep trains and boats and generators running were being sold on the black market.

They reported, with rare candor, since the official position of the US government was that the Mobutu regime has been making great strides at curtailing corruption, that the illicit profits were filtering back on a separate highway of corruption to the center of power in Kinshasa.

One major city along the Americans' route, Kananga, with a population of one million people, was without electricity. This was supposedly because its diesel-powered generators were not working, but the American report implied that the fuel designated for the generators had been stolen and sold. The Americans calculated that the profits from the petroleum sales in this one city alone amounted to nearly $1 million a month.

At a town further down the line, 11,000 tons of freight were backed up in a switchyard, including fifty-two train cars of copper that should have been on their way toward earning foreign exchange, if not for the railroad at least for Kinshasa's élite. But probably the most pathetic thing reported by the Americans was the wholesale theft of motor oil from locomotive engines. Thieves drained the oil between stops, sometimes leaving the engines with no lubrication so that they ground to destruction.

The Americans found that all along the Kasai, as we had seen on the Congo itself, riverboats were abandoned. At one town, the Americans counted seventeen stacked up in a semipermanent wait for spare parts.

Zairian transportation officials who have had to deal with these problems day in and day out, year in and year out, get cynical. One Zairian told us about his job procuring railroad supplies.

'I buy supplies for people to steal,' he said.

The man, who had become deeply disillusioned with Mobutu, said, 'Before 1964, we were on the brink of a great hole. And then we made a big step forward.'

NINE

It was the twelfth night on the river, but it could have been the eleventh or the thirteenth, so much did the events of the days melt together. The engines pounded, the decks of the *Mudimbi* vibrated, the wake spread a fan of turbulence out across the mud-thick water. The heat of the day persisted through the night, caught in the unventilated passages and cubicles of the passenger barges.

Night and day, the canoes were lying in wait for the riverboat. Without cease, the river people hauled aboard the fish and the game they had netted and killed in the opaque water and the tangled green forest. And always, the farther into the forest, the more monkeys were hauled aboard, alive and dead, fresh and smoked. The *commerçants* were into the final stretch of their mercantile marathon and the steady arrival of the canoes permitted no pause. Their nights blurred into the days, there being no difference whether the sun was beating down on the silvery river or the riverboat lights were flickering and flaring yellow on the dark water. To sleep was to lose trade and to lose money.

The bars were doing a hot business, since beer and music were the best antidotes to the heat and the monotonous frenzy. Everybody with a zaire to spare was drinking beer, numbing and inspiring Congo beer, the *commerçants*, the passengers, the prostitutes, the police, the first-class minister, the hippopotamus lady, the Germans, the police, and the fishermen. Those who were stronger and crazier drank Zaire whiskey. The wounded policeman, the one who had mistakenly shot himself in the arm, was taking quantities of it as treatment for his pain. He had to wait for surgery to remove the bullet until the *Mudimbi* arrived at a town with a clinic. The man lay on a bed in the police captain's cabin, his arm bandaged, groaning and drinking.

At Bumba, just below the place where a wide tributary, the Itimbiri, rolls into the Congo, the *Mudimbi* docked alongside a long flat riverbank. A sandy street ran along the edge of the bank and its far side was lined with stores. Bumba's underpinning is commerce and the river trade. But the first store we entered was half empty. Tinned foods and some dry goods, like flashlights and pots, sat lonely on nearly bare shelves. Signs proclaiming perfume and stationery departments hung down from the ceiling over dusty showcases. The next store and the next were the same.

We took a side street that we assumed led deeper into town. But after forty paces it ended, merging into tall grass that formed a narrow belt between the backside of the town and the forest. The stores were almost stageprops, the town hardly wide enough to hold its own against the vegetation.

At the intersection of two streets, we came upon a little square where black weaver birds had built nests in some palm trees. Dozens of nests bent the fronds and made the trees look like umbrellas. Then, the boat whistle shrieked, setting us running toward the dock. Our feet sank into the deep sand of the streets, and by the time we got back on board we were panting. The *Mudimbi*, of course, did not budge for another hour.

The spy had gotten off at Bumba and never got back on board. He was to remain enigmatic, the quintessential character in a country where facts disappear beneath the surface of the day.

Simon Kepe, the merchant with the red furniture, also disappeared at the Bumba stopover, but only after borrowing ten dollars from us, with assurances that he would get some money from a business partner and repay us. He didn't, and we never saw him again either.

Back on board the *Mudimbi*, the metal walls and roofs bounced the heat around and magnified it. Frustrated and sweating, we fiddled with our cabin air conditioner, hoping that by some caprice it would work. We did revive it enough so that it blew out a thin jet of air for maybe two minutes before subsiding into silence. Tim banged on it and cursed. He was getting tired of the *Mudimbi*.

When we finally pushed off again, Tim and I went out and stood at a side railing to catch the little warm breezes the boat made as it headed again toward the equator, bearing down from the north on the line we had crossed earlier coming up from the south. The boat rattled, goats bleated, roosters crowed. The river's water looked like it was running beneath a thick layer of silvered grease and clouds piled up around the circumference of the huge hot sky.

By late afternoon of that day, darkening stormclouds had built up angrily in the sky, but they refused to let go of their rain. With the approaching night, the clouds parted, retreating again to the corners of the sky, and the sun sank like a cooked egg yolk westward over the river.

A new prisoner had been jailed on the railing outside our cabin, a man accused of stealing a basketful of soap from a cripple with polio-withered legs who had been selling it on a lower deck. With the night, lightning exploded in balls distantly over the dark forest, playing back and forth the length of the horizon. The searchlights of the *Mudimbi* swept the dense foliage on the shorelines ceaselessly. We heard the prisoner whimpering outside our cabin window when we went to bed, and I stayed awake for hours, sweating and tossing and listening to the thief. By the morning light, he was still at the railing, awake but quiet, subdued by his misery. Late in the day the police released him, but only after confiscating his stock, a basket containing a couple of bolts of cloth, sugar cookies in cellophane wrappers, and the controversial soap.

In regions close to the equator, evening is short lived. The sun, having no long angles to negotiate on its illusory descent to the horizon, sets with an unhesitating suddenness. It leaves no lingering twilight. The afternoon moves from flagrant illumination to flamboyant sunset, and the sunset is sponged swiftly from the sky by the blackness of an absolute night.

The dark caused me no trouble, though, as I made my way to *La Cave* the next night, for I knew the way to the bar in the barge's hull. I was going to buy some beer to share with Marie Thérèse and the senior *commerçant*.

Once down the stairs, I angled back along the railing that marked one of the fishermen's preferred landing spots, stepping carefully along a strip of decking slippery and muddy from the constant reception of fish and wet feet. I passed the three women who peddled tree grubs, which they kept alive in big baskets of loamy dirt so that they would be entirely fresh when bought and fried in curried oil the way most people liked to eat them. Next was a cluster of merchants selling clothes. One of these merchants usually wore a T-shirt that asked in bold letters: 'Where the hell is Pittsburg?'

The clothing sellers competed for space with a couple of men who specialised in buying fish and stashing them in the ship's freezer room just off the prow. They bought the biggest of the fish, dragged them around and between the clothes merchants, piled them up, and let them flap to death. Then they carved their initials in the fishes' fleshy sides, making bloody brands to distinguish one fish from another at trip's end. A lamp somewhere up near the pilothouse threw a soft light on the merchants and on a woman who was struggling to haul a mammoth catfish down the deck, using the fish's eyesockets for grips.

Next came the jump from the boat onto the first barge, which became more and more difficult as the journey proceeded. The problem was that you had to leap onto a metal step, then leap again up over a sill to a passageway awash with the sewage from the common toilets. Four metal cubicles at the end of each barge served as combination toilet-showers, having a hole in the floor and a pipe spouting water down from the ceiling. The steerage passengers overwhelmed this sanitation system early on and sewage was soon leaking onto the decks, getting deeper each day until it slopped over the sill and made the step treacherously slick.

I missed most of the sewery puddle, wetting only my heels, and went on past the benches bolted onto the corridor walls where young men played endless rounds of checkers using bottle caps for pieces. I then eased around the corner where the parrots hung in bamboo cages, and past the railing against which *commerçants* had been stacking packets of smoked fish tied with vines. So great had the stack become that I had to sidle sideways to get past. The railing kept people and animals from falling down *La Cave*'s rusty stairs, which were heaped with woven mats, carved stools, chairs, and coils of fibrous rope made by the river people in their forest clearings. I zigzagged down to the barroom.

The scar-faced barman was working hard, popping the tops off bottles, and music was rasping full volume from a loudspeaker set up on a beam. An unshaded lightbulb illuminated the main chamber and an overhead fan twirled the hot air in the room around and around, its blades cutting below the lightbulb and throwing out stroboscopic slashes of darkness.

The barman was sweating and mournful. But this time, before he could begin his ritual importuning, I gestured at the passengers and the *commerçants*, the whores and students filling his tables, and told him he was making lots of money, enough so that he should go out and buy his own medicine for malaria, for river fever, or whatever it was that afflicted him, if he really needed it. He shrugged and stared at me.

I had surprised him with my outburst. Maybe what was aggravating me was the claustrophobia, the surfeit of passengers who squeezed and struggled for space with a forebearance that Malthus never predicted. Maybe it was the engines that shook our cabin day and night, night and day. Maybe it was the shouting and singing from the bars that grew louder and more reckless with each day.

I carried some beer back up the steps and around another corner to the passageway where Marie Thérèse and the others kept shop. As was her custom, she snapped the bottlecaps off with her teeth. I gave her a bottle, passed one across the aisle to the chief merchant, who accepted it with the high cackle she reserved for her gladdest moments, and kept the last for myself. The old woman had been doing a good trade. She was cramming smoked monkeys into a cubicle, piling them so that the heads stuck out and made the stacks look like totems to a barbarous god.

It was even hotter than usual that night. As I drank and watched the searchlights beaming from the pilothouse, sweeping the sides of the islands, roving and seeking something in the vegetation, I wondered whether the forest's unfurling leaves released little pockets of heat as they grew. The river might be adding heat, too, holding it and then letting it go into a tropical night that had swallowed the shade.

'It's hot,' I said to Marie Thérèse. I was sitting on a stool by her chair with my legs drawn back out of the way. *'Lelo molunge mingi*. It's hot. It's very hot today, so hot that the hippopotamuses in the wide and beautiful river are sweating,' I said.

This was my most elaborate sentence in Lingala yet, and it brought praise from the women around me. A couple of fishermen stared.

'Come on, come on. She doesn't bite like the crocodile,' Marie Thérèse told them peremptorily, pinching my arm to illustrate that I was made of human stuff.

They came up and bought a glass of Zaire whiskey from Marie Thérèse. They then tried to buy me one, but I didn't want to get drunk. I stood up with my empty bottle and told them that beer was a sweeter drink, going back down to *La Cave* to get more. At the bottom of the stairs, a fat woman, a prostitute who was down at the bar every night dancing with men, then disappearing and coming back alone, grabbed my hand and said that I must come and dance. The fan strobed and the music ricocheted off the walls. The people dancing and the people sitting along the table were sweating in the flashing light. Instead of dancing, I got more beer and climbed back upstairs.

After awhile I climbed back down for more and, starting to feel the alcohol, I danced this time with the prostitute, who laughed with me and encouraged me as we joined other dancers prancing to the repetitive rhythms of the Zairian music.

It blared hypnotically, entrancing, mixing in brassy coun-
terrhythms, carrying a song, a mélange of Lingala and French
words throbbing and soaring with the rhythms. I danced
on and on and I didn't remember when I got back to the
cabin.

The following dawn was as sweaty as the evening had been.
Jimmy knocked and came in bearing a tray with toast and hot
tea. Tim had woken out of a fitful sleep, feeling queasy. He
thirstily drank down the tea even though it made him sweat
more. He was getting feverish. If he was going to come down
with something bad, all we could hope was that the *Mudimbi*'s
engines would hold out so we could get to Kisangani. We knew
enough about tropical diseases to understand the potential
gravity of any strange fever. Some of these diseases we
unfortunately had experienced firsthand.

Ever since Guatemala, we had always carried a thermometer. Tim had come down with a fever in an out-of-the-way
town, and I had bought a thermometer to measure the fever
at the ramshackle town pharmacy, but it was calibrated in
Celsius degrees. I began struggling to convert its reading to
Fahrenheit by means of some partially remembered formula
I had learned in junior high school. My calculations only confused me, until I realised that I wasn't thinking clearly. The
problem was that I was also feverish, coming down with what
was later diagnosed as paratyphoid, of which Tim had a less
severe case. One of the symptoms of the disease is photo-
phobia, which means that any light sends searing pain through
your eyes into your head. Tim helped me wrap my eyes in
layers of shirts and sweaters and led me to the town square,
got us on a bus back to the capital, held me on the jouncing
ride that left me sobbing with pain, and finally found me a
doctor.

Tim also saved me during the aftermath of the worst disease
I ever had, the dengue fever that I had caught while traveling
alone in Somalia. After the wracking fever itself had subsided,
I went on to Kenya, where I sank into a terrifying physiological
depression that made the whole world around me into a nightmare. Tim arrived from the United States to find me trying to

work and to write even though I was emaciated and nearly psychotic. He coaxed me back to normalcy.

That morning Wolfgang came around and asked if he could use our bathtub because the one he shared was clogged and filthy. He needed to wash himself, his clothes, and especially the cloth he used as a sleeping sheet, which was covered with chimpanzee shit.

The chimpanzee was a scared three-month-old orphan whom the Germans had bought from a river trader, hoping to tame the baby ape and carry him home to Rwanda with them. The people on the Congo draw the line at eating chimpanzees, which of all the apes are closest to humans on the evolutionary chain. But baby chimpanzees bring good money if they are sold as pets in the cities, so female chimpanzees are hunted and killed and their offspring captured. When they bought him, the Germans' chimp, was nervous and unhappy. Easily upset or frightened, he would run up and down the deck or leap from side to side of a cabin, howling for his mother and his lost forest infancy. To comfort him one or the other of the Germans would grab the chimp up into his arms and coo like a mother chimpanzee.

'Uouh, uouh, uouh,' the German would coo, pursing his lips in an apelike smile.

'Uouh, uouh, uouh,' the baby chimp would answer, and lean his head on the German's chest.

The Germans mothered him and fathered him, playing with him, feeding him, dosing him with antibiotics to treat a nasty rope burn around his haunches where he had been tethered, comforting him all the while in guttural whispers. The chimpanzee began to calm down and began to believe that the hairy, gentle Wolfgang, with whom he slept every night, was his mother.

We were happy to have Wolfgang use our bathroom and ushered him in, neglecting, however, to tell him why the typewriter was on the toilet, an explanation that went back to

Tim's years of living in Cairo. When rats infested his apartment there, he had to take drastic measures to get rid of them. He managed to corner several in the kitchen, and, using the only weapon available, beat them to death with a broomstick. He, of course, has hated rats ever since.

We had heard talk, believable but not confirmed, that there were rats aboard the *Mudimbi*, so Tim decided on a preemptive antirodent defense, one that concentrated upon the rats' most likely route of entry into our cabin, which, he had learned in Cairo, was through pipes. The only pipe in the cabin was in the toilet, which did have a wooden lid. All that was needed to keep the rats from, theoretically, crawling up the toilet pipe and pushing out from under the lid was something heavy and flat. We kept the typewriter on the lid and we had no problems with rats.

Wolfgang spent a long time in our bathroom, washing first himself and then his laundry. When he eventually emerged from the bathroom, he had a strained look on his face. He said nothing beyond giving his thanks.

It was not until later in the afternoon that happy-go-lucky Gunther asked me the question that Wolfgang must have discussed with him but had not had the courage to put to us.

'So, why do you type your articles on the toilet?'

I told Gunther the story about the rats in Cairo.

This was to be the last day and night on the river. If the diesels kept working, the *Mudimbi* was supposed to arrive in Kisangani the following morning. Wanting to see the river and the forest, from which the daylight was fast ebbing in a luminous tide, I climbed up to the pilothouse. The captain was sitting in his high chair looking out over the river and next to him the pilot was drinking from a bottle of Zaire whiskey.

The captain ordered the pilot to bring me some of the whiskey and I saw that the captain had a glass of it at his right hand. The pilot took a glass from the map table and hurried over, taking little dance steps and grinning. Very formally then, he poured me out half a glass and bowed. The communications officer came in from the other room and he too was drinking.

'Oh, you must drink it,' the officer said.

'Drink it,' the pilot insisted.

'Yes, drink it,' the captain ordered.

Not wanting to spurn their hospitableness and touched by a manic impulse, I took a gulp of the liquor and choked on its fierceness. I took another gulp and it burned. The three men cheered.

I finished the glass and drank another. Outside the big windows of the pilothouse, dry lightning licked along the horizon in untamed counterpoint to the beams from the ship's spotlights. The whole world, the seen and the unseeable, was intoxicated. We needed to shout, to sing, to dance, to procreate, to fill the vast, lush vacancies with illuminating purpose.

I was yet sane enough to refuse a third glass of the pilothouse whiskey and zigzagged down one flight of stairs after another until I got to *La Cave*. I had not gone by the cabin to check on Tim, whom I had left lying in bed with his fever.

I wasn't to be satisfied until I found that imaginary peace I had left behind in Mbandaka, that place in my mind where the narrow confines of life disappeared, where rampant flowers bloomed under an unlimited sky, where surprises were delightful, and where people fell in love with the world every day.

When the barman saw me, his lugubrious expression broke into smiles.

'You were beautiful last night,' he said, having watched my dancing with approval.

I didn't answer. The music was too loud to talk. I danced and drank. Then I wandered out to another bar, and then another. It was the last night and I wanted to miss nothing.

Tim, meanwhile, was back in our cabin, sweating out his fever. But after hours of wondering where I was, he set out to look for me. He searched the boat from end to end. When I finally stumbled into Marie Thérèse, she scolded me for having drunk too much and sent me on my way back to the cabin. Tim, having spent the night sweating in his fever, was sleeping exhaustedly and I collapsed next to him.

TEN

We both woke with fevers that conspired with a light rain to obscure the outlines of things. We had arrived at Kisangani and the *Mudimbi*'s labors had temporarily ceased. The Congo rushed past the docked riverboat, pulling with it a big pirogue paddled by seven standing men making for the far bank.

This was deepest Africa, the geographic center of the continent, equal distance from Cape Town and Cairo, the Atlantic and the Pacific. This was the place I had longed to see.

We were too dizzy to make the effort to say goodbye to any of our fellow passengers and were barely able to carry our assorted equipment off the boat and through the crush of disembarking people to the port gate. There, some boys were huddled in the rain beside their homemade pushcarts, waiting to trundle somebody's stuff somewhere for a dime's worth of zaires. After piling our gear on a cart, we followed the boy away from the river toward the Zaire Palace Hotel, where we hoped to rest and recuperate.

Kisangani is the fourth-largest city in Zaire but it looks abandoned these days. We walked down wide streets with large, broken-down houses set back from the street behind yards that had given way to weeds and bare dirt, worn by the rooting, grazing, and pecking of pigs, goats, and chickens. Squatters had moved into the homes that once belonged to the Belgian colonials. This was the heart of Africa, a place where extremes have surged and ebbed.

Somewhere nearby was the former residence of Captain Rom, an official during King Leopold's rule who decorated his flowerbed with heads chopped from Africans. When it was known as Stanleyville, the settlement here was the farthest outpost of Leopold's Congo Free State, a station that produced many tons of ivory and rubber and levied its share of atrocities upon the people. If the past tumbles onward and affects the future, it is little wonder that this same city became the scene of bloody rebellions that marked Zaire's traumatic birth into independence in the early 1960s.

It was Patrice Lumumba who ushered this city into modernday politics. Lumumba was born in a village in eastern Zaire and as a young man came to Stanleyville where he began popularising the cause of independence from the Belgians. Working as a postal clerk, Lumumba began his political career by joining a government workers' club and rapidly developing a following. People were mightily attracted to the charismatic young man with big ideas about African nationalism. Other political clubs were forming, all of them ostensibly social clubs because Africans in the Belgian colony were not allowed to organise politically. One club back in the capital made much of the former glory of the Kongo Kingdom as a way of re-creating African pride. But Lumumba had a special effect on people, making them believe in his vision of a Congo free of the Belgians and led by Africans, a country where prosperity rather than servitude would be the right of the ordinary citizen.

Leaving the confines of Stanleyville behind, Lumumba took a job as a beer salesman that allowed him to travel and talk up the virtues of both Polar Beer and an independent Congo. Lumumba was not the only proponent of African nationalism but soon enough he became the only man in the country who could claim to have the backing of a nationwide party.

When Belgium abruptly agreed to withdraw from its colony in the face of escalating unrest and freedom protests, elections were organised and Lumumba was voted the first prime minister of the independent Congo in 1960. He began his job brashly by making a scene at independence ceremonies. The Belgian King Baudouin angered Lumumba by delivering a clumsily conceived speech in which he praised King Leopold, the great scourge of the Congolese people. Lumumba responded with a furious rejoinder about the Belgians' narrow-minded arrogance and their cruelty toward the people they had ruled.

'From today we are no longer your monkeys!' he declared.

From then on, almost nothing ran smoothly in Lumumba's Congo, which was hardly a nation but rather a colonial amalgamation of tribes whose people were mostly peasant farmers or forest hunters. Rioting broke out and spread through the interior. One crisis fed another.

Most of the Belgian civil servants deserted the country and the unschooled, untrained Africans could not keep the government bureaucracies functioning. Workers did not get paid, strikes were called, and soldiers in the national army mutinied and rampaged, demanding higher pay and immediate dismissal of their remaining Belgian officers. Violence spread. Fighting broke out between tribes and Africans attacked Europeans. Thousands of Belgians who had established businesses also fled. Before the month was out, the southern province, which was called Katanga then but has been renamed Shaba and is the location of most of the country's mineral wealth, seceded. Lumumba called for help from the United Nations, which sent in peacekeeping troops.

The trouble was exacerbated by the Americans and Soviets, who were vying for influence over the newly independent black African countries. As Prime Minister Lumumba made his political debut, the Soviets were trying to win him to their side while policymakers in the United States were deciding that he was unreliable. Whoever mastered Zaire stood to gain a strategic chunk of land right in the middle of Africa. Zaire also possessed reserves of such important minerals as cobalt, which is crucial for the manufacture of jet engines, and uranium, some of which had already been employed by the Americans to develop the atomic bomb during World War II. The Congo was being used as a stage for the larger world's argument, much as the whole continent had been at the time of the Berlin conference.

From the American perspective, serious trouble started in the Congo only two weeks after the June 30 independence

date, when Lumumba appealed to the Soviet Union for possible
military assistance in dealing with Belgian troops that had
moved in to repress the mutiny in the Congolese army.
Although he had not intended it, Lumumba had stepped into
the middle of the larger East-West confrontation. A month
later, Lumumba was threatening to expel the United Nations
peacekeeping force for refusing to help him stop the Katanga
rebellion, which was backed by Belgian troops and businesses
as well as contingents of white mercenary soldiers hired by
Moise Tshombe, the leader of the secession. The Belgians
favored the conservative Tshombe because they wanted to
keep what they had invested in the rich Katangan mines.

The worry back in Washington at Central Intelligence Agency
headquarters and the Department of State was that Lumumba
would give the Soviets free run of his country. Lumumba,
however, was a disciple not of the Soviets but of Kwame
Nkrumah, the rising Ghanaian politician who preached an end
to intervention and profiteering on the African continent. At
the center of Lumumba's political philosophy was a fervent
nationalism attended by vague socialist ideals.

In his public remarks, Lumumba outlined a policy of neutrality
that would keep the new nation independent of both super-
powers. 'Africa is neither Communist, American, nor French.
Africa is Africa,' he said at a press conference in Washington
where he had gone to try to curry favor at the outset of the
Congo crisis.

But American leaders were freshly traumatised by Fidel
Castro's revolution in Cuba the year before. Cables being
sent back to CIA headquarters in Washington from Lawrence
Devlin, the CIA station chief in the Congo, fed the worry. In
one, he advised:

'Embassy and station believe Congo experiencing classic
Communist effort take over government. Many forces at work
here: Soviets . . . Communist party, etc. Although difficult
determine major influencing factors to predict outcome struggle
for power, decisive period not far off. Whether or not Lumumba
actually Commie or just playing Commie game to assist his
solidifying power, anti-West forces rapidly increasing power

Congo and there may be little time left in which take action avoid another Cuba.'

Based on the information reaching him from the Congo, President Eisenhower decided that Lumumba was a threat to world peace, even though the prime minister had done nothing more aggressive than try to quiet the uproar in his own country. Allen Dulles, the CIA director, ordered Lumumba killed and the agency soon proceeded with an assassination effort. With Lumumba out of the picture, power in the Congo could devolve to some acceptably pro-Western figure, such as General Joseph Mobutu, the young noncommissioned officer Lumumba had promoted to command the army.

Mobutu had come far from his beginnings on the banks of the Congo. After being expelled from a missionary secondary school in Mbandaka, he had been conscripted into the Belgian colonial army. By the time he was discharged, he had risen to the rank of sergeant major in, ironically enough, the army's accounting section. In the remaining four years before the country gained its independence from Belgium, Mobutu worked as a journalist in Kinshasa and then in Brussels as an apprentice at the colonial propaganda agency. While in Belgium he made contacts with Zairians and with the CIA's Devlin that would stand him in good stead on his rise to power. By independence day, Mobutu had made his way back to the top of the army, having befriended Lumumba even as he was cooperating with the CIA.

By September, Mobutu was able to use his army command to arrest Lumumba and temporarily take over the government, with the quiet assent of the United States. Lumumba's arrest ignited more trouble. His followers announced that Stanleyville and the eastern region were seceding from the country. A Soviet plane touched down in Stanleyville, carrying aid to the rebels. Throughout the Congo Basin, meanwhile, intertribal fighting escalated into savagery and massacres.

That same month, slightly more than two months after Lumumba took office, the CIA's top scientist arrived in Kinshasa carrying a deadly poison. The biochemist's assignment was to sneak the poison into Lumumba's food or even inject it into his toothpaste.

But Lumumba remained the most popular politician in the Congo, he was well guarded by United Nations troops, and the CIA plotters could not get anyone near him with the poison. Devlin kept at the assassination mission, though, and had CIA headquarters smuggle a high-powered rifle with a telescopic scope and silencer to him through the diplomatic pouch. So armed, a CIA agent might be able to eliminate Lumumba from a comfortable distance.

The rifle never had to be used. Lumumba tried in late November to flee by car across the breadth of the country to Stanleyville, where he could have rallied support among his staunchest followers for a political comeback.

With the CIA helping, General Mobutu's government set up roadblocks and caught Lumumba at a ferry crossing. The general held Lumumba at a military camp for a little more than a month and then sent him to his death. He was flown to Katanga Province and delivered into the hands of his bitter enemy, Tshombe. Lumumba was beaten on the plane, viciously beaten again at the Katanga airport, and murdered sometime within the next two days. Lumumba's political foes finally did what the CIA had been encouraging them to do for months. How much the CIA may have been involved in the actual murder is not known.

'Thanks for Patrice,' a CIA operative with a nasty sense of humor had wired from Katanga to Kinshasa. 'If we had known he was coming, we would have baked a snake.'

Lumumba was killed at the age of thirty-six, less than a year after his election. He had ruled the country for a mere ten weeks. The United States had assisted in implementing the first coup in postcolonial Africa and the first political assassination, bringing to an end one of the first African democracies. It had helped destroy the infant Congolese democracy in the name of making the world safe for democracy.

Back in the United States, the Republican administration had been succeeded by a shiny new Democratic one headed by President Kennedy. But the basic attitude toward the Congo did not change.

(The extent of the American role in shaping these events in

the Congo was not revealed publicly until 1975 when the Senate held exhaustive closed hearings into the covert activities of the American intelligence community. The revelation that the CIA had been hatching plots to assassinate several foreign leaders, including Fidel Castro as well as Patrice Lumumba, led to the establishment of congressional oversight committees to keep the agency in check. The hearings also disclosed that the project to murder Lumumba was approved at very high levels of government, perhaps even by President Eisenhower himself.)

Turning a sudden corner before getting to the hotel, we heard what sounded like a brass band trumpeting out the opening bars of some triumphal tune. As we got nearer, we saw that it was a military band in ceremonial uniform. A polished car drew up to its front doors and a fat man in a Mobutu suit got out from the back seat. As soon as he had made his way inside with the waddling strut of someone accustomed to others getting out of his path, the band stopped playing in mid-tune. The rousing welcome was not for us, two worn out, fever-ridden travelers, our clothes only half clean from washings in river water, trailing a push cart heaped with canvas bags and topped by our plastic water container with the remnant of our purified water sloshing in its bottom. We got closer to the hotel door and saw another car drive up, delivering another dignitary and provoking a repeat performance of the truncated tune. Rain droplets beaded on the polished finish of the car.

The Zaire Palace Hotel was newer than the buildings around it and rose several stories high, but it, too, had known more prosperous times. Our room was at the end of a carpeted hallway ventilated by a window with a large broken pane. A warm breeze came whispering through the tops of some palms and down the hallway.

Once inside the room, we discovered not cockroaches but, when we pulled back the bedspread, a swarm of ants. What we wanted most was to wash in hot water, so Tim went to twirl the hot-water faucet on the bathtub. He jumped back as water came shooting out of a makeshift pipe in the bathroom wall, dismayingly cold water to boot. Still, this big room, with palm trees waving outside and with no thrumming diesels or riverboat clamor, was luxury compared to the *cabine de luxe*.

We slept the day away, getting up in the evening to look for food, feeling feverish and odd. We did not have the strength to look beyond the hotel dining room, an expansive collonaded place with crisply uniformed waiters and a subjungle of potted plants. The elaborate menu offered cream of celery soup for openers, like the marching band not what we had expected to find in the heart of darkest Africa.

When the soup came, we discovered it was peppered with little black gnats, dead and thoroughly cooked. I picked out many of them with my spoon and ate the ones I missed.

I slept fitfully that night. My overheated mind saw catfish wallowing through some muddy depth. I was assaulted with whirlpools of mud and struck with streamers of light that shot down from the surface and destroyed the smooth dim peace of repose.

Whatever it was that laid us down – we had been dosing ourselves with a broad-range antibiotic with no seeming effect – broke the next day. The fevers subsided and the fabulous images sank down into the invisible underworld where fantasies normally stay.

As soon as we were able to move on, we discovered it was impossible to go on, at least for the moment. This was fine with me, for I was in no hurry, but it was not with Tim, who was. He had promised to be back to his editing job in Baltimore by an exact date, and his colleagues were counting on him. Unlike Tim, I had no compelling reason to get back; in fact, I had every reason to welcome delay, since I would be returning to a reporting job in Washington under an editor whom I disliked. My choice was between a cold winter among politicians or a warm season among Zairians, and it was no contest as far as I was concerned. My worry was that I would be forced to give up the journey and fly back to Kinshasa to meet Tim's deadline. We were on the brink now of really getting somewhere.

Our direct path upriver was blocked, as we had known it would be, by the series of rapids around which Stanley had portaged. But there was a narrow-gauge railway built by the colonial Belgians that circumvented the cataracts as far as Ubundu, where we might be able to pick up a primitive riverboat to carry us along the Congo's upper stream. In Kinshasa we had heard conflicting accounts of whether or not the old wood-burning train still ran. We were pleased, after we sought out the local office of the national railroad agency, to find that '*en principe*' the train was in operation, the only problem being that no one seemed to know when it might go.

Besides the railroad, a road ran along the river near the cataracts, but we didn't know much about it except that it was drawn on our map with a white line, which meant that it was liable to flooding. This was not reassuring, since the rainy season had begun. Storm clouds rolled in every afternoon to drench Kisangani and the surrounding forest. An alternate route that would take us away from the river's main course across its northeast watershed and through the Ituri Rain Forest did not sound particularly promising either. According to the talk going around Kisangani, that road was bogged with mud.

If we were going onward, it was crucial that Tim get a reprieve from his promised return. We had to get word back to Baltimore saying we needed more time, and telephoning was impossible. But we did manage to send a message by radiophone to Kinshasa, where it was relayed by messenger to Wes Fenhagen, who was supposed to telex it to the State Department in Washington, where someone was supposed to telephone the information to Baltimore. We had no way of knowing if the message would successfully travel through the various interchanges and arrive in Baltimore, or if it did, whether the reply would survive the intricate return to us.

In our search for some means of getting upriver, we paid a visit to Kisangani's Catholic mission down by the river, which has a large compound dominated by a cathedral and serves as headquarters for the network of Catholic operations across the whole of Zaire's northeast region. The mission ships supplies to all the lesser Catholic stations north and east of Kisangani, those isolated deep in the rain forest and farther away in the upland savannas that sweep eastward toward the Indian Ocean coast, an area that covers almost a third of Zaire. We had the name of the Catholic in charge of these supply operations, an American called Brother Jerry Selenke.

A watchman at the main gate of the tidy mission compound directed us around a building toward Brother Jerry's office. Just at the building's corner, we ran directly into a fellow wearing pointy-toed cowboy boots and black jeans.

'*Bonjour. Nous cherchons Frère Jerry,*' I explained to the man in French.

'*Oh, bonjour,*' he answered, blending a drawl and a twang into his French. '*Je suis Frère Jerry. Qu'est-ce que vous voulez?*'

We switched into English, which he spoke with the same exaggerated accent of the native Kansan that he was. Friendly and open as anyone you might meet on the main street of a Great Plains farm town, he waved us into his roomy and air-conditioned office.

'Beer, whiskey, gin? Whaddya want to drink? Plenty of beer in the fridge, if that's what you want. Go ahead. Help yourself. So what can I do for you?'

Brother Jerry, tanned, his hair handsomely tousled, looked like one of those men who pose for the Marlboro ads. He smoked Marlboros, too, and constantly, so that his teeth were yellowed with tobacco stain.

We explained that we were looking for some way, other than the unpredictable railroad, to get further upriver or deeper into the Congo watershed. He told us what we already suspected, that our best chances might lie in striking out overland to the northeast, through the Ituri and up into the highlands that rise from the forest to form the eastern edge of the watershed.

'Only problem with going that way is that there's only one road, and from what I'm hearing there's one hell of a spot where everybody's getting stuck in bad mud. A hundred, maybe two hundred trucks are stuck up there,' Brother Jerry said.

He explained that two of his mission trucks were mired there, too, one with a broken axle. He might be sending someone up with some spare parts to get the broken truck going, he told us, but he didn't know when. If he did decide to send out a rescue vehicle, we could get a ride, if we didn't mind the uncertainty of being dropped off in whatever quagmire the broken truck was bogged down in.

We asked about going upriver by road.

'There's only one way that way and people are saying it's flooded. The water might go down, you never know. I'm not sure what would be the best way to go. You basically have a choice of mud or floods. Think it over,' he said.

We had time to think and time left over to explore this city where Africa has played out some of its anger.

Kisangani focuses around the port, some half functioning European-style shops, the post office, the mission, and the Zaire Palace Hotel. The sidewalk in front of the hotel was largely intact, but as we walked toward the edges of the city, the sidewalks crumbled into dirty sand and then disappeared altogether. We ended up walking in the streets, dodging the occasional bus or car. The old buses rattled by leaving clouds of unfiltered exhaust in their wakes. Farther out, where commercial buildings with small shops and bakeries gave way to an architecture of poverty – cinderblock houses, sewer ditches, sun-baked mud shanties, dirt streets, and bare dirt lots – an occasional flowering vine strove to relieve the landscape of its misery.

Up the street from the Zaire Palace Hotel was another hotel with a fine dining terrace that overlooked the street and was usually deserted. When we stopped by there, a beggar woman was pleading for money from a few diners. She gestured silently

across the terrace wall, never talking but persisting until they
gave her some money and a piece of bread. She then withdrew
to the gutter across the street and lit a fire from bits of trash.

We did not begin to get a good idea of what went on beneath
the surface of Kisangani until we stopped by the Transit Bar
one evening to rest our legs after a walk and slake our thirst.
The bar was nothing more elaborate than groupings of tables
and chairs set out in the friendly warmth of the tropical evening.
The motif of the place was travel. A blackboard purported to
track the arrivals and departures of the big riverboats, but the
entries were months out-of-date. Maybe, I thought they will
know here about the train. Maybe we've inadvertently come
to the right place.

Tim scoffed at that hope, but I persisted in questioning the
waiter.

'Can you tell us when the train runs to Ubundu or when it
comes from Ubundu to Kisangani, please?'

The waiter stepped back and stared at me as if I were talking
nonsense.

'*N'importe*, it doesn't matter,' I said, and he went off to get
the beers we had ordered.

A man who was sitting with some companions around a
table next to us leaned toward us and explained that no one
in the whole city could predict the train's utterly erratic
schedule.

We ended up talking to the man for hours, and forgetting
dinner and the plans we had made to catch up on our notetaking.
We bought a few bags of chewy peanuts from a street vendor,
eating them with the beer as we listened. His name was Gabriel
and his face was unforgettable, centered around a flaring nose
and eyes that were never still. He was a science professor at
the Kisangani branch of the national university, having studied
in France and earned a doctorate in physics.

When we asked why he had chosen such an esoteric field
when Zaire needed more essential professionals like road

builders, bridge engineers, and public health administrators, he began to tell us his story.

'I studied physics, you must understand, because I was afraid to go too close to politics. I was afraid I would be killed and then my children would be left without a father.'

As he spoke, he tipped his head back and looked at us from the height of his nose. When he had something to emphasise or to make a joke about, he tipped his head sideways and looked out of the quick, dark corners of his eyes.

'Most of the others I know who educated themselves in France studied political science or social science. Then they come back to Zaire and join the government and corrupt themselves, totally, like philosophers who lie about the meaning of life. Or else they go into some kind of opposition against the government, whether they speak against it openly or not. These ones keep their honesty, but they are all candidates for the security police, for torture, for humiliation, for death. The soldiers here are bandits, the doctors are thieves, the teachers are paupers. So I try to stay away from talking about these things, because my opinions are too strong.'

He told us about the robbery that goes on in the night streets of Kisangani. A battalion of commandos stationed across the river on the left bank preys on the city's residents, robbing them in the dark of cash and belongings, whatever they could get to supplement their meager wages.

A junior professor who had accompanied Gabriel to the bar and had been listening to the conversation, told us what had happened to him.

'I was robbed last week at night in the street that runs by my house. They went through my pockets, they took some money, they ripped my watch off my arm,' he told us, and showed us a healing gash underneath his wrist where the metal watch strap had torn into his skin. 'They even took my handkerchief out of my coat pocket. But what could I do? Complain to the magistrate? The magistrate knows about the gendarmes, but what can he do? He can hope they don't catch him out at night and rob him, too.'

Gabriel laughed at this bitterly, rolling his eyes. His laugh was unforgettable, building from a chuckle to a musical chortle, and it was frequent.

Gabriel had a worse story, one of near cannibalism, for which there was no proof but which we did not absolutely disbelieve. He said a group of soldiers had stolen and eaten a placenta. The soldiers, as the story went, mistook it for animal meat when they stopped a peasant carrying the afterbirth back to his village for a ritual. Having seen the way logic and humanity have been abused in Zaire, we were prepared to believe this grotesque story, but we never were able to confirm its truth.

Gabriel was raised in the midst of political turmoil. He came from a smaller town off to the south of Kisangani, a large village really, where his great-grandfather and his grandfather were chiefs. Both his grandparents had died violently, his father's father killed in a rebellion against the Belgian army and his mother's father by the authorities as punishment for hunting a hippopotamus. By the time his father, the oldest son, was of age to inherit the village leadership, the chieftancy was meaningless, because the Belgians controlled everything. They regulated what the villagers could grow and where they could live, exacted army duty, levied taxes on the heads of all rural households, and promoted Catholicism.

The Belgian colonialists were not as brutal as King Leopold, and by some measures, the Congo had flourished. The Belgians oversaw the construction of roads and railroads, established schools, expanded the trading stations into towns, built mining complexes to exploit the country's mineral wealth, and installed an efficient colonial administration. In the years before independence, it was possible to drive from Kinshasa to Kisangani in a regular sedan, a trip that now is practically impossible in even the most rugged four-wheel-drive vehicles.

But the colonial government was far from beneficent. It ran the Congo for the profit of Belgium, the foreign landowners who were running plantations in the tropical highlands, and the European companies that were mining the colony's minerals.

The copper coming from the Congo was in great demand in the West for making the motors, generators, telephones, power lines, and radios that had come into being with the advance of the electrical age.

Forced labor did not disappear with Leopold. The people were made to work on the roads of the colony without pay and also to maintain the houses of the Belgian officials. Perhaps the most vexing of the Belgian tasks was the mandatory transport of colonial officials, who had to be carried from place to place in hammocks along with their baggage.

All the while, the Belgians were consummately patronising. One of their colonial laws imposed fines or imprisonment on any African who dared a disrespectful word act or gesture. They saw the Africans as children needing to be Christianised, taught, led, and overseen. Africans were not allowed to take meaningful positions in the government or businesses of the Belgian Congo but were trained as servants, laborers, order-lies, clerks, and technicians. The people were ill-prepared to take charge of their country. When Lumumba and others were pressing for independence, about one hundred thousand foreigners possessed most of the colony's wealth and privilege.

After Lumumba's death, chaos continued to plague the Congo. The central government in Kinshasa, which General Mobutu had returned to the hands of pro-Western civilians, was weak and unable to stem a series of rebellions that swept the country. The rebellions were fueled by profound frustrations that had been felt for years by people subjugated by Belgians and then by an unpopular African government. They began in the east near Kinshasa and spread across the country through Lumumba's old territory until nearly two thirds of the country had revolted. The Lumumbists in Stanleyville believed for a time that their cause, their pre-independence dreams of a more just society, were being revived. But the rebels' discipline fell apart, and what had started out as a visionary political movement went awry as the Simbas took over.

The Simbas were a faction of warriors who took their name from the Swahili word for lion. Inspired by drugs and by witch doctors to think they were immune to bullets, the Simbas were terrifying. They wore headdresses made of feathers and monkey skins that shook like the manes of lions. They went on the attack yelling '*Mai*,' a word meaning 'water' that magically was supposed to protect them. The soldiers of the Congolese government army dissolved before them and the United Nations was no longer around to help. After helping to quell the Katangan secession, the UN had pulled out its troops.

The Simbas overran the whole northeast region of the Congo's watershed in 1964, committing wholesale murder along the way. They were unstoppable until they were confronted by an equally bloodthirsty army of white mercenaries, who had been recruited by the central government.

The mercenaries, some of them Belgians or ex-Nazis, but most of them from the racist countries of Rhodesia and South Africa, marched up the Congo, supported by American advisers and accompanied by anti-Castro Cubans who were flying American bombers. The mercenaries looted, raped and murdered as they went, their manner reminiscent of Leopold's rubber agents. The lineup of combatants became more complex when Castro's righthand man, Che Guevara, leading a band of about a hundred Cuban guerrillas, briefly joined the side of the rebels.

The mercenaries, backed by government soldiers, moved on toward the rebels' Stanleyville base, where the Simbas captured world attention by taking 1300 Europeans and Americans hostage. They threatened to execute the whites if the mercenaries kept advancing, vowing in their newspaper: 'We shall cut out the hearts of the Americans and Belgians and we shall wear them as fetishes. We shall dress ourselves in the skins of the Americans and Belgians.'

While the fate of the whites concerned the West, the Simbas were executing Congolese residents of Stanleyville in a public square. The Simbas went after those who had cooperated with the Belgians and those suspected of being intellectuals, which could mean anyone who had finished primary school, because education represented the values of the foreigners who had so ravaged their country. Stanleyville was finally taken by a combined force of mercenaries and Belgian paratroopers dropped from US Air Force transport planes. The Simbas gunned down fifty-one of their white hostages in the course of the fighting.

The rebels and anyone thought to have sympathised with the various rebellions against the central government became the next victims of horror. Thousands of people were rounded up by government soldiers and tried during scenes of mass hysteria at Stanleyville's stadium, where each prisoner was led in front of a fierce crowd incited by the memories of relatives and friends they had lost during the rebellion. If the crowd in the stadium jeered, the suspected rebel was taken out and shot.

In late 1965, General Mobutu decided to throw away the pretense that the Congo was being run on a Western model of parliamentary democracy. He staged his coup and made himself ruler of the Congo at the age of thirty-five. Within several years, he had succeeded in getting a strong grip on the tribally divided and politically fractious country. In the troublesome regions, he waged bloody but successful wars against the rebels and installed loyal military officers and governors. All told, as many as 200,000 Africans and hundreds of whites, including many missionaries, died in the fighting.

Amid the ensuing confusions and rebellions large and small, Lumumba's supporters found themselves suspect in their own country. Gabriel's father fled with his family north to the Central African Empire and others hid in the forests for months.

'Lumumba is a folk hero in Kisangani. He is seen as a political martyr,' Gabriel told us that night at the bar. 'It doesn't matter whether he would have been a good leader or a bad one. That cannot be answered because he was not here long enough, because people never had time to become disillusioned with him. So now, the worse things get, the better the dead Lumumba looks, and the worse Mobutu looks, and the worse his circle of important men, his relatives, his allies, all the big men.'

Gabriel decided to teach us what he could of the life of his city. He wanted to show us the state of Kisangani's schools and hospitals, a good measure of any society's health, and also show us how most of the city's residents lived. For him, this was a chance to funnel a piece of truth to the outside world through our notebooks, despite the risk that agents of Mobutu's security police would discover what he was doing.

Bidding Gabriel good night, we headed back to the Zaire Palace Hotel. On the way, we saw an old watchman determinedly sweeping a piece of buckled sidewalk. He was using a broom whose straws were worn to a stubble.

With each passing day, Tim grew more anxious about time and transport. Tim's frustration was made worse by Wolfgang's and Gunther's departure. The Germans roared off one morning on their motorcycles, heading back for Rwanda with their orphaned chimpanzee in a large covered wicker basket lashed to the back of Gunther's Honda. Gunther had big plans for the chimp, whose intelligence was becoming more obvious each day. He wanted the chimp to learn to ride behind him on the motorcycle and accompany him on his recreational excursions to Bujumbura, the capital city of neighboring Burundi.

'We'll walk into the bar and sit down, just like we're friends out for an evening on the town. Then, I'll say to the bartender, "One beer, please, and two glasses."' We all laughed, and they left.

That same morning Gabriel arrived at the hotel, ready to escort us around the city. We set off on foot, Tim and I hurrying to keep up with the tall and energetically striding Gabriel and then hurrying faster when a drizzly rain began to fall. He was taking us across town to see a government school, and had no intention of letting a little rain delay his project. His enthusiasm was enough to carry us along in his wake, our notebooks tucked up under our shirts to keep them dry. We had not brought along jackets because we had been counting on the afternoon regularity of the rains, but we should have known better than to count on anything in Zaire.

'It's raining. It's raining, but all the rain in this great rain forest, all the rain in this great forest is not enough to wash the streets, is not enough to wash the streets of Kisangani clean,' Gabriel chanted, merrily making up verses as we went along.

The school was cheerless in the rain. Seven or eight rough cinderblock buildings edged the school compound and inside each were a couple of classrooms. This was a primary school. Those pupils who had carried stools to school with them, the way American children carry gym clothes, had seats, and the rest sat on the broken cement floors of the narrow rooms. We saw neither desks nor textbooks. The children were reciting lessons read out by their teachers or written on blackboards, which they had to strain to see in the dim light coming in from high windows. In some classrooms, the pupils were sitting without teachers, without anything to do. Gabriel had one of these children show us a page from his assignment notebook and we saw the teacher had been absent most of the week.

We had heard teacher absenteeism was common across the country, but that didn't make the scene any less pitiful, a roomful of would-be students waiting vainly for their teacher while time washed by meaninglessly, watering the country's ignorance. A government primary school teacher earned about ten dollars a month, so that many teachers took other jobs to survive and did not show up at school. Some teachers survived, at least in part, by taking bribes from their students. Teachers sometimes were not paid anything for months when the money for a regional payroll was stolen by corrupt officials.

Our tour of the school did not take very long, so we stood under an overhanging roof to wait for the rain, which had increased to a drenching intensity, to pass. The rain raised a smell of urine from a ditch in which the boys peed on their way to and from the school.

'The great fault of the government is that it does not teach the children,' Gabriel said. 'A child may be going to school, but he may be learning nothing. His teacher may not be there, he may have no books, he may have no pencil, he may have to study at night under the light of a streetlamp.'

Some idle girls gathered around us under the eaves, curious

about us, giggling when we looked back at them. They tired of us after a while and started a hand-clapping and skipping game that sent them dancing about in a circle.

When the rain let up, the girls went leaping barefoot over the puddles that had formed in the dirt schoolyard and Gabriel set off again at an ambitious pace, this time for the city's hospital. We arrived breathless at the hospital's door and rested on a bench in the lobby. A torn canvas stretcher leaned against a wall and dereliction hung in the air, a feeling particularly strong in contrast to our concept of a hospital as an efficient institution, clean and committed to healing.

When we started out along a passageway that led to the surgical wing, we came upon a girl lying on a wooden bench and writhing in pain. She clutched at her abdomen and sobbed until she ran out of breath. When she caught her breath, she began sobbing anew. She was about twelve years old and her father was holding her hands and trying to calm her. He told us that she needed to be operated on for appendicitis, but the hospital did not have the surgical supplies for the operation. His brother, the girl's uncle, was in town going from pharmacy to pharmacy, hurrying to buy what the surgeon had said was necessary, a list of supplies that ran all the way from surgical cotton to scalpel blades to anesthetic drugs. Her father could do nothing except promise over and over that her uncle would be back soon with the medicine.

The hospital pharmacy was in the basement, down a flight of stairs and along a corridor wet from dripping pipes. Once secured by a grillwork door that no one bothered to close and lock any longer, the pharmacy had been looted. On the shelves lining the walls of the room were three or four dusty vials and some disordered and yellowed papers. No one sat behind the old desk lit by a lightbulb hanging unshaded from the ceiling. Neither common thieves nor underpaid gendarmes had done this work. The hospital doctors themselves had stolen the medicine.

Gabriel told us how this worked. The doctors, who were paid better than teachers but still not enough to live decently, raided the inventories of government-supplied medicines. They would resell the medical supplies to pharmacies or private clinics.

The beds we saw in the rooms and wards of the hospital were torn and blotched with filth. What was most shocking about Kisangani's hospital, though, was not its dirtiness and disrepair, but rather that it was partly empty – a strange sight on this continent where hospitals are scarce and usually terribly overcrowded. When I was a teacher in Ethiopia a decade ago and a student of mine fell seriously ill or was badly wounded, I would go with the child down to the government hospital and use my status to get quick treatment. Otherwise, the child, bleeding or not, would have stood in line with dozens of others, waiting out the day and maybe the next.

But in Kisangani, Gabriel said, 'Average citizens cannot afford to come here. They have to pay for everything – the medicines, bribes for the doctors and the nurses and the orderlies – and they haven't the money.'

If the ninety miles of rapids above Kisangani had not been so unnavigable, Kisangani would never have grown so large. The series of cataracts that had given Stanley so much trouble blocked upriver traffic and forced travelers and traders to stop. Kisangani had a large outdoor market about the size of a New York City block, where hundreds of vendors had stands of gray, weathered planks from which they marketed many of the necessities of life and a few of the luxuries. They sold fresh meat, vegetables, and fruit, smoked snakes pressed between wickerwork panels, used clothes hung out on sticks, thread, secondhand records, salt, earth-colored spices, fresh fish and dried fish, whatever could possibly bring in a few zaires.

Some beggars lingered on the dirt pathways between the stalls, most of them polio victims, their legs shriveled and twisted irrevocably by the disease. One or two of them rode handmade, hand-pedaled scooters and the rest hopped along as best they could. One of them had shod his hands with flipflops and came flinging himself along the dirty ground, swinging his hands forward and then pivoting his shrunken torso and legs with a lurch of his shoulders, making a short bound, a human hop with a near inhuman effort. His legs curled, crossing over each other, and his feet were upturned on his thighs, paralysed in misery's imitation of the Buddha.

The result of untreated polio was something I had seen many times before in other countries. The sight of a leper with half his face eaten away by leprosy and his fingers eaten back to the knuckles, the sight of a child with pus-filled, blinded eyes, or the sight of a polio victim dragging through the dirt, always shocks me, but never as much as the idea that these diseases could be prevented or at least mitigated.

One of the market's sections was devoted to secondhand spare parts, sold by men who sat behind tables, the greasy pieces of metal arranged by function and ranked by size. New spare parts were hard to get because they had to be imported and paid for with scarce hard currency. One man sold nothing but ball bearings that he prevented from rolling with slats of wood. Another sold piston parts and another gear rings. The mechanic in Zaire is a true artisan, having to find the appropriate part for a repair not by brand and by year, but by shape, size, heft, guesswork, and luck. Sheer ingenuity has kept many engines running in Africa.

Off to one side beneath a leafy stand of bamboo were the market's barbers. In the comfort of the scattering green shade, their customers sat on folding chairs in front of small tables on which mirrors were propped while the barbers clipped and shaved them.

We took a few pictures of the merchants, an innocent enough subject we thought. But we were abruptly ordered to stop by an emphatic young man who did not explain his reasons. He may have been a member of Mobutu's youth movement, vigilantes who patrol the streets and the cafés to ensure adherence to the party line. We left the market quickly, fearful that he would bring the security police. Thereafter, we used our cameras furtively, always afraid they would attract attention from the authorities and expose us as more than recreational travelers. In the minds of the police, journalists were simply spies.

If you could not find what you needed or wanted at Kisangani's market, your best bet might be to go to Brother Jerry. Beneath his amiability, he was one of the most powerful characters in all of northeastern Zaire because of his job as 'procurer' for the Catholic missions. The procurer dealt in just about everything from vehicles and cement to beer and Bibles, running a fleet of trucks and jeeps to mission stations throughout a region chronically short of most supplies. As the procurer, Brother Jerry also served as unofficial travel agency for the entire Catholic community, commodity broker, organiser, and communications chief. He had the most efficient business around, except perhaps for the beer company, without whose products Zaire would be far tenser, for there is nothing like a large beer on a hot afternoon in the tropics to cool frustration.

The Catholic mission's rectangular compound was bordered by the cathedral, classrooms, offices, storerooms, a printing workshop, and sleeping quarters for the residents and for any traveling Catholics. Pope John Paul II himself spent a night there during his tour in Africa in 1980. The mission was more prosperous than most Zairian establishments, yet not even it was entirely spared at the time of the rebellions: If you look closely, you can see bullet pockmarks in the stonework of the cathedral's facade.

Brother Jerry had been operating with such energy that he was making money for the Kisangani mission. He was inundated with cash, not that Zairian cash is worth all that much. He had packed bunches of paper currency, bricks as they are called, into several big blue file drawers at the mission.

'It's like toilet paper,' he had said of the money when he was going through his drawers looking for something else during another visit we made to his office.

It was then that Brother Jerry suggested how we might get out of Kisangani on the road heading up the river.

'Come to think of it,' he said, 'you could deliver a Land Rover for me. I've got to have one driven to a mission up that way. The only problem is that it hasn't arrived here yet. I've got two new ones coming up on a barge. Might arrive any day now, might not.

'The rule you learn to go by is, don't count on it until you actually see it. Take cement. It's heavy, hard to transport, and hard to get hold of. It's a very valuable commodity around here. Well, I had eight thousand pounds of it shipped out of Kinshasa upriver to here. First two weeks went by, no cement, then a month, then two months, three, four, five . . . It took six months to get here. The barge had engine trouble,' he said.

There was no way for us to tell what would happen first, the recession of the flood waters, the departure of the little train, the arrival of the Land Rovers, the departure of the spare parts for the mission truck, or the arrival of a reply from Baltimore.

That night we went with Brother Jerry to an outdoor restaurant in the courtyard of a small hotel over by the market. Tropical plants grew in the corners and two forest parrots in a tall cage sang and squawked, improvising an accompaniment to the fractured melody of the diners and dishes. One of the birds, though, had had some musical training and periodically broke into a whistled version of 'When the Saints Come Marching In.'

Brother Jerry was not your average missionary. Having dressed for the occasion in a cowboy shirt with pearl buttons, he ordered a beer with us, lit up a cigarette, leaned back, and, in his prairie twang, told us some more about himself.

His religious colleagues at the mission were Zairians or Belgians and far more orthodox in their conduct, but they tolerated his habits, which included sleeping late and missing morning mass. After serving on a mission project in southern Africa, he was dispatched to the Kisangani mission as a high-level fix-it man, to repair generators, engines, radios, and other electronic equipment, but ended up filling the procurer's job as well. He was an electronics expert as well as a licensed pilot and able mechanic.

Brother Jerry was one of the few people we met in Kisangani who was not in awe of the local authorities. The secretary to the provincial governor had stopped by the procurer's office recently with a request for a load of cement for a new house his boss was building. The governor was an important man, responsible directly to President Mobutu, but Brother Jerry, knowing the power of his church, brazenly refused to provide the cement.

Zaire's Catholics, in general, can take the rare liberty of criticising Mobutu's one-party government without fearing retribution, because their church has tremendous influence in the country. About half of all Zairians are Christians, and the majority of those are Catholic. Indeed, if the Pope himself spent the night at your mission, you might assume the papal presence gave you a special dispensation to speak your mind. Zaire's Catholic bishops were counting on their grassroots power when they issued a declaration in 1981 condemning the government.

The bishops wrote about the sorry state of government schools:

Teachers suffer from a loss of social consideration and a sort of persistent erosion of their dignity. Precise facts are at the base of this manner of destabilisation of this sector: insufficient salaries in the face of real expenses, irregularities in the payment of salaries, great delays and even unjustified blockages and nonpayment of a large number. Social dramas follow . . . a traffic in grades, corruption et cetera.

They wrote about health:

From every side complaints are registered regarding the insufficiency of equipment, medicines and medical personnel themselves. In this context the population is not sufficiently protected and defended against all sorts of diseases and epidemics. The most fortunate have evidently the opportunity to be treated outside the country . . . Certain [of the ill-paid medical personnel] end up trafficking in care,

medicine, equipment, for their personal profit. Who is un-
aware that people have sometimes died in emergency rooms
while waiting for their relatives to meet and bring the money
necessary to purchase care?

They wrote about justice:

Well-founded complaints are even formulated against the
courts, institutions of recourse. Has money imposed its law
everywhere? Impurity is for those who know how to pay,
and money permits the authors of crimes to prosper, free
and tranquil, not without arrogance before their humiliated
victims.

When the soup arrived at our table, Brother Jerry took the
bowl of hot-pepper sauce, the ubiquitous condiment in Zaire
for anything from bland manioc to delicate river carp, and
dolloped it in. His taste for the fiery was as highly developed
as an African's.

He told us a story about how villagers on the Congo to the
south of Kisangani had helped him salvage a sunken boat. Full
of Catholic supplies, the boat was too heavy to winch up from
the water, so Brother Jerry decided a dam would have to be
built to keep the water off the wreck while its hull was repaired.
The village people surrounded the boat with a dam of woven
vegetation and clay. They had never built such a thing before,
but they improvised excellently and the dam held until the boat
was fixed and refloated.

'That's basic intelligence of a high order,' Brother Jerry
said.

Next, he recounted a story about a piece of sheer Zairian
cunning. One afternoon, a man came running breathless into
his office and reported that an automobile accident had occurred
on the road leading to the Ituri, several hours away from town,
and that a Catholic seminary student had been killed. A shroud
was needed desperately so the body could be transported back
to Kisangani for burial, the man told Brother Jerry, and asked
him for the money to buy one. Moved by the man's desire to

perform a good deed but mildly suspicious, the procurer sent a mission driver with the man to get the burial cloth. The man disappeared in the marketplace as soon as he could find an excuse to abandon the driver. There had been no mishap and no death, of course, only the creativity of a Zairian who had wanted to bilk him out of the price of an expensive shroud.

'The thing is, it almost worked. I almost believed him. You've got to respect people with that kind of entrepreneurship. It's the spirit that Americans are so proud about. It's what was supposed to have won the West. You know, there's all this talk about reforming the economy and rejuvenating it, but what they need to do is much simpler than that. Just set the *commerçants* free. The people just need an even chance to save themselves. These people are smart. They've got to be or they don't survive.'

For all his resources, Brother Jerry could do little to speed our onward journey. It had continued to rain every day, so much that he was leery of sending any more vehicles out onto the mired northeast road right away. He could do nothing to speed the arrival of the barge carrying the Land Rovers, and he certainly could do nothing to make the train run.

When Tim and I made a second visit to the railway office, we found an officer on duty. He informed us that the train was at the station on the left bank across the river and ready to go, even eager to go, but its departure was being prevented indefinitely. The problem was that it could not leave until the riverboat arrived at Ubundu to connect with it, and no one had any idea where the boat was, only that it was many days late.

'It is not a problem with the train. It is a problem with the boat,' he concluded.

Nothing on the river seemed to be cooperating with us. Tim was going down to the port every morning to look for the Land Rovers and coming back to the hotel more irritated each time. We had heard nothing from Baltimore, and he had started talking about catching a flight back to Kinshasa. He was not any cheerier about the situation after he drove out to the airport one afternoon with Brother Jerry to put one of the Catholics on a flight to Kinshasa. They had arrived with time to spare, only to discover that the flight had left early, contrarily ahead of schedule. If things had been uniformly late, that at least would have been predictable. But no, nothing was turning out to be quite predictable in this country. A week had slipped by and we were no more sure about how we were going to get out of Kisangani than on the fever-fogged morning when we had arrived.

We were getting a good look at Kisangani, though. The next morning we went off with Gabriel, trotting along behind him to have a look at the university campus. We got there in a quick fifteen minutes, with Gabriel chatting as fast as he walked. He began with the Belgian colonials, talking about how they had discouraged Zairians from getting university educations.

'They saw us as too primitive to be able to benefit from the knowledge of Western civilisation. We could work for them and cook for them and be servants in their houses, but we weren't advanced enough to partake of the highest learning with them.'

The Belgians left behind an educationally impoverished citizenry. Among the millions of Africans in the Belgian Congo, at the most two dozen had earned university degrees under a colonial rule that approved of elementary and technical education but discouraged Africans from attaining the higher levels of intellectual accomplishment.

The campus at Kisangani, a branch of the national university and one of Zaire's three seats of higher learning, was part of a massive effort to produce an educated class to run and to lead the country. The campus is large, roomy enough for decades of pedagogical growth. We followed Gabriel across the campus, walking single file when the pathway snaked between shoulder-high weeds. Green reeds sprouted in a swampy area behind a couple of dormitories whose windows were randomly broken.

Gabriel took us to the library, a newer building whose sharp corners were primly out of place against the landscape of rebellious vegetation. It had been built with the help of foreign aid and planned with space to spare for the acquisition of thousands and thousands of new books. The stacks were overwhelmed by the space around them. The books that were there were dated and written in English, a language most university students in the French-speaking country cannot read. Gabriel picked a dusty volume off a shelf and read its title page, 'The Fundamentals of Orthopsychiatry, published in 1960.' He closed the book and gestured with it.

'This is how we are educating our children for the future. They are already twenty years behind,' he said.

The university's courses were being taught without any textbooks, because there were none available. The professors had either to mimeograph information for their students or read them notes in class for copying, a procedure exhausting to both teacher and learner.

'In France, this would not be considered a university. They might not even call it a school,' Gabriel said.

We had lunch that afternoon at a Zairian restaurant down by the Congo. As we walked toward the river, Gabriel told us the story of Kisangani's radio station. It was off the air, having ceased broadcasting abruptly the year before when a band of thieves cut the last guywires that held steady the station's tall broadcasting tower. Thick wires can be resold very profitably in this part of the world for use as towing cables, or for making metal wares, and even for setting snares to trap elephants. One of the thieves scaled the tower in order to snip the final pair of wires. It was his last act; the tower toppled and he was killed.

The restaurant was a group of thatched rondavels in a walled courtyard. A couple of women stirred cast iron pots of manioc and fish stew over wood fires. We sat by ourselves and talked about politics, and corruption.

'A whole generation in this country has grown up feeding on corruption. What they know is a black-market economy; what they understand is bribery. They are practiced in illegality and their government is practiced in ignoring the welfare of its society. How do you reform a whole generation of people?' Gabriel was saying.

He stopped in mid-thought when he saw two men sit down in a neighboring rondavel.

'Those are security police. They are acting like they aren't interested in us, but they are,' he said.

We turned to our fish and hot sauce, managing not to talk about anything more serious than the menu aboard the *Mudimbi*, the state of the road in the Ituri Forest, and whether the train would ever go to Ubundu.

'Tonight, I will take you somewhere where only my friends will know you,' Gabriel said quietly. 'I will take you out to Tshopo.'

Tshopo is one of the slums that encircle central Kisangani. Recorded rock music from mud-walled bars blended with the croaking of frogs that bred by the thousands in the big puddles that pock Tshopo's dirt streets. We kept splashing into these puddles, which the residents seemed to be able to avoid with some sixth sense. People emerged from shadowy huts to talk in shifting groups or to haggle with the women selling food at candlelit stalls along the streets. In the light of a flickering cooking fire, a group of boys mimicked an electric band, pantomiming an accompaniment with imaginary guitars to the singer who used a length of rubber hose for a microphone.

'People live on the dirt. Dirt is not good for the health, but Zairians are used to it. They are accustomed to death,' Gabriel said as he led us up through the streets.

I hadn't the slightest idea of where we were when we arrived at a bar, a relatively prosperous one, run by a friend of

Gabriel's. It was built of cinderblocks rather than mud, and decorated with cheerful strings of multicolored Christmas tree lights. The proprietor was a Nigerian who had come to Kisangani to teach economics at the university but found he could make more money as a bartender than as an academic. We fell into a discussion about the devaluation, which the bar owner predicted would dampen the black market only temporarily.

'You can't cool off the black market like that. You can't stop corruption with a decree from Kinshasa. This economy is overheated. It's falling apart. You can't just make a law to prevent that, not if the people who are setting the prices don't trust you,' he said.

We told him how we had been tracking the rising price of beer since we had been in Kisangani. It had cost about thirty cents a bottle the day after we disembarked and now, seven days later, it had risen to fifty-five cents. Before we finally left town, the price had risen another ten cents. We were marveling at how the beer prices had increased almost one hundred percent in one week.

He shrugged and said, 'I've been playing the same game, but I've been playing it for years. By my calculations the price of beer has gone up fifteen thousand percent since 1965.'

After leaving the Nigerian's bar, we walked until we came to the Tshopo Bridge, where many people were massacred during the turmoil of the 1960s. The bridge is an ideal spot for efficient and unmessy executions, for it spans a tributary of the Congo just where the waters plunge down into a short but vicious set of waterfalls and rapids. The bridge was a favorite execution spot of the Simbas, who simply threw their victims off it.

Kisangani has never recovered from the rebellion years, physically, psychologically, or politically. Even those towns-people who have prospered during Mobutu's rule carry deep grudges.

We talked to a well-to-do businessman at the former Belgian tennis club where the city's elite still play on clay courts. The businessman's father was a high-level member of Mobutu's government and his son had profited from political connections. But sitting at the tennis club, sweating after his match, a drink at his elbow, the man's conversation circled from discontent to grievance. Other members of the club – university professors, expatriates, and successful merchants – continued to play their tennis in the brilliant afternoon sunlight of central Africa, imitating the days before colonial values were challenged. Urchins chased after the tennis balls. The businessman complained that the central government was systematically short-changing the Kisangani region in long-term retribution for the Lumumbist rebellions, failing to invest in new buildings or useful highways.

'This is one of Zaire's largest cities, but you would never be able to tell that by the way it is treated,' he said.

It was an ominous sign for Zaire's future that the regional feelings have continued to simmer. A centrifugal force has been pulling Zaire into separate economic pieces, divided by deteriorating transportation, crumbling institutions, and unforgiven feuds.

Ten days passed in all before we got out of Kisangani. The train had refused to budge and the river barge had failed to come, so when Brother Jerry told us he was going to send spare parts to his disabled truck in the Ituri on one of his Land Rovers and we could hitch a ride, we leaped at the opportunity. We were more than ready to pack up and leave the Zaire Palace Hotel, with its gnat-seasoned soup and windowless windows, although it was difficult to take our leave of Gabriel, who had taught us so much.

The Land Rover had to haul the spare parts more than 250 miles through the forest and mud to reach the disabled truck. We did not know what we would do when we got there and we did not know if we would make it even that far. The reports coming back to Kisangani were that the road had turned into a slough of mud somewhere deep in the forest.

ELEVEN

There was not much room left in the back of the Land Rover once the spare parts were loaded. We heaved our stuff on top of a truck-sized shock absorber and got in front with Amisi, a Zairian driver who worked for the Catholic mission. Brother Jerry, who had gotten up earlier than usual to see us off at dawn, waved us out of the mission gate.

'Watch out for the mud,' he yelled.

Amisi drove slowly and cautiously through the streets of the waking city. He was a wiry man, not tall, looking dwarfed at the wheel of the safari car. Even at the speed he set, we were soon out of the city on a single-lane dirt highway heading into the rain forest. At first, the road ran through cleared areas where peasant farmers planted corn, manioc, and papayas on small plots of land. They built their homes close by the road and struggled to keep the greenery hacked back from their patches of ground. The farmers supplemented their crops with the meat of forest beasts that had ventured out to the man-made peripheries of the forest. Porcupines were strung up for sale along the road, trussed to stakes by their hind legs so that their yellow quills hung down around their elongated bodies like primitive skirts. Porcupine is a much favored and sweet meat.

Dozens of large butterflies with varicolored markings fluttered at the sunlit edges of the road, feeding on the nectar of flowers that burst blooming into the strip of light that the highway sliced through the forest's shaded gloom. Amisi told us the road always attracted myriad butterflies no matter what the season, but he did not share in our delight at the lepidopteran display. He paid no more attention to the forest landscape than we would have to the glossy billboards and illuminated gas station signs of American highways.

Amisi had traveled this road many times before. He had worked as a driver since the 1950s, before independence. The forest has not changed much since then, but the road has. He used to be able to drive from Kisangani to the Ugandan border, a distance of about 400 miles, in one long day. We were hoping that with determination and luck we could get that far in three or four days. The road was no longer maintained by gangs of African men performing their colonial quota of forced labor and it was hardly kept up by Mobutu's officials.

The forest vegetation grew so vigorously in places that it closed in an arc over the road, giving the impression we were traveling down a long, luminescent green tunnel floored with a narrow strip of red-dirt roadway.

It was not mid-morning when Amisi braked the Land Rover to a halt behind a cargo truck, which was pulled up behind another truck and another, and so on down to the bottom of a long slope where a good-sized stream cut across the road. A similar line of trucks faced us, lined all the way up the opposite hill in mimicry of our own plight. Once we got out of the Land Rover and slogged down the hill, we learned the reason for the holdup. The stream was swollen high in its bed in the aftermath of a heavy rainstorm. The water had torn away whole sections of the stream's bank and also collapsed an aged stone culvert that had bridged the stream.

A road repair crew was hard at work, but that did not mean the culvert would be soon repaired. Five laborers equipped with pickaxes and shovels were taking turns pounding and prying at the ruined stonework. They were preparing for a new corrugated metal culvert, which was already delivered and lay across the width of the road, creating another barrier to onward travel. Amisi stood barefoot in the road, having taken off his driving sneakers as he did every time he got out of the Land Rover in order to preserve them. Shaking his head and hunching his shoulders, he predicted a whole day's wait, maybe two, before the new culvert was in place and ready for traffic.

Tim was thinking about turning back. He was worried about

time, because we had left Kisangani without hearing from Baltimore. I was worried about Tim's worry.

We had not gone sixty kilometers yet, less than forty miles, but an African kilometer can turn out longer in terms of time and events than an American mile clicked off on a well-paved road without potholes, animal herds, or broken culverts. This highway through the Ituri was not an unusually rugged or neglected stretch of road. It was typical of most of the road system, which we knew had been steadily deteriorating since independence, making the kilometers grow longer, slowing down the movement of goods, and strangling the economy. In 1960, Zaire could boast 90,000 miles of passable highway. Now the country is struggling to maintain 6000 miles of dependable roads, mostly of dirt that turn to mud in the rains.

At the outset of Mobutu's rule, things were not so bad. To remove the political pall left by Lumumba's assassination, Mobutu elevated him to the status of national hero and, with tactical brilliance, gradually replaced portraits and symbols of Lumumba with his own.

The economy was buoyed by a boom in copper, the country's biggest export. Copper was bringing record prices on the world market and the mines in Shaba Province were shipping out as much as they could. Mobutu had money to spend, but rather than tend to necessities like maintaining provincial roads, repairing damages from the rebellions, expanding sewer systems to the outlying districts of the growing cities, supporting broad economic development, or improving the lot of peasant farmers, Mobutu tried to buy modernity wholesale. He built himself grand houses and four-lane highways around the capital, a huge new stadium and, after a trip to New York City, a scaled-down imitation of the World Trade Center, the building back in Kinshasa that was losing its tenants. More money went into an extravagantly sophisticated telecommunications and radio building, into limousines and Mercedes Benz sedans to ferry the president and his high-level underlings around the capital. He hosted the 1974 world heavyweight boxing championship in Kinshasa, featuring Muhammad Ali and George Foreman, at a cost of $15 million. A billboard outside the fight stadium boasted: 'A fight between two blacks, in a black nation, organised by blacks and seen by the whole world, that is a victory of Mobutism.' The boxers and prominent guests were treated like royalty and Ali was impressed.

'Zaire's got to be great. I've never seen so many Mercedes,' he said. As long as prices stayed high for copper, the economy was able to absorb Mobutu's extravagances and support the huge amounts of graft that went to ensure the loyalty of his political entourage. But the economy did not survive.

To erase the stamp left on the Congo by the Belgian colonials, Mobutu instituted an 'authenticity' campaign, a commendable enough effort to revive the indigenous spirit of a territory so abused by foreigners. Besides renaming himself and the country, he ordered all citizens to throw away their Western Christian names and adopt African ones. It would take more than these cosmetic measures to alter the dark effects of colonial history and the European economic dominance that had characterised it.

Going further, Mobutu ordered a sweeping nationalisation of foreign-owned enterprises, declaring that he was going to end the condition of Zaire's being 'the most heavily exploited [country] in the world.' In 1974, Mobutu expropriated $500 million worth of plantations, businesses, and stores, from Belgians, Portuguese, Greeks, and other foreigners. More than half of the properties were parceled out to influential politicians, party officials, businessmen, and Mobutu's friends and relatives from Equateur. Many of the new proprietors simply sold what they could of their sudden acquisitions before abandoning the businesses altogether; others tried to run their new businesses but didn't know how. Most of the dispossessed foreigners fled the country, taking with them their still-needed business skills.

While shortages caused by failing businesses afflicted most Zairians, a few profited immensely from the nationalisations. Imports of luxury goods surged, signaled by a dramatic increase in the number of Mercedes Benzes Zairians were purchasing. Costing $50,000 a piece, Mercedeses were the ultimate status symbol. On the anniversary of the nationalisation initiative, Mobutu, knowing how the economy had been suffering, announced bitterly that Zaire had broken all African records for Mercedes imports in the preceding year.

One of Mobutu's talents is his ability to recognise corruption, voice his outrage and continue to participate in the very thing he has denounced. He didn't cut himself out of the looting of foreign holdings, becoming rather the largest beneficiary of all. He, or his wife, took ownership of fourteen plantations that amounted to a virtual rural empire with 25,000 workers, which made it the third largest employer in the country after the government and the mines.

Adding to the trauma caused by the nationalisations, copper prices plummeted in the mid-1970s, pulling the rug out from under the economy. The country fell into debt, and then ever more severe debt, to foreign banks and the International Monetary Fund.

Mobutu's most basic weakness is the unhappiness of the Zairian people who live in economic conditions that would be condemned as inhumane by any Western government. But his counterbalancing strength has been his persistence in holding the country together – no small feat considering the size of Zaire, the difficulty of its topography, and the fractious ethnicities of its tribes. If persuasion does not work, he uses force. His security police punish any dissidents, arresting scores of people each year, holding them without charge, and often torturing them. Would-be presidential assassins are executed and, just in case, Mobutu has bought himself a gold-plated bulletproof vest.

Persuasion often does work, though, since Mobutu is a master tactician when it comes to coopting his enemies. More than one of Mobutu's opponents have returned from exile in Belgium, where they excoriated him from a safe distance, to Zaire, where they meekly rejoin the presidential entourage and again become beneficiaries of the presidential largesse.

Members of the president's inner circle occasionally break

loose, flee the country, and then tell the world what they know about Mobutu's free spending of his country's money, if not about how their own loyalty had previously been bought with it. One of the leading exiled critics of Mobutu in recent years was Nguza Karl-I-Bond, who resigned as prime minister in 1981. Before he went into exile, Nguza had experienced an outlandish mix of political fortune and misfortune prototypical of those who serve Mobutu. Nguza had been foreign minister and director of Mobutu's political party before being charged with, tried for, and convicted of treason. But Mobutu saved Nguza from the firing squad and less than three years later named the convicted traitor prime minister.

Once out of the country, Nguza lambasted Mobutu for his excesses in testimony he gave in Washington, DC, before the House Subcommittee on Africa in the fall of 1981. He described for the congressmen 'one small example of the widespread embezzlement practiced by the Zaire president.' He used information from a parliamentary investigation of Zaire's national bank, which found that Mobutu and several close family members had withdrawn $150 million worth of foreign exchange for themselves between 1977 and 1979. Mobutu was regularly taking money from the bank for deposit in his personal accounts abroad. Mobutu also was acquiring huge sums of money from Sozacom, the state trading company, and Gecamines, the national mining company. He was putting his hands into anything he wanted.

Nguza told the House subcommittee that Mobutu had arranged for the state trading and mining companies to export twenty thousand tons of copper and then sell it for his profit. Quantities of cobalt and diamonds, Nguza did not know how much, were being exported as well on chartered airplanes to Europe, where the money from the sales was deposited into Mobutu's European accounts.

In the meantime the average Zairian was earning only ten percent of what he had at independence. The gap between Mobutu and the people was becoming a chasm. Nguza told the congressmen that the United States was being held responsible for this.

'The people are suffering; we have misery and starvation in the country. The people know that Mobutu is personally responsible for this. And our people know Mobutu was placed in power and remains in power today because of the continued support he is given by the Western nations, particularly by the United States. You must understand that in the eyes of the people in Zaire, the United States is ultimately responsible for the suffering and oppression brought on them by Mobutu.'

As I was speculating about how long the repairs on the culvert would take, an orange jeep came bouncing down the opposite hill, made its way past the stalled trucks, and slammed to a stop at the trench. Lettering on a mud-splashed door proclaimed 'Office des Routes,' the national highway department. A Belgian, his brawn turning into fat but still a man of imposing stature, got out of the passenger seat and stomped to the edge of the trench.

Hands on hips, he yelled in French, 'To hell with this. What in the name of Christ is going on here?' His face was red with anger. 'This is not possible. This is not permissible. I have been five days on the road now, sleeping in the damn forest, sleeping in the damn car, eating damn bananas, and I am not going to spend one more night in this godforsaken wilderness. Tonight, I am going to sleep in a bed in Kisangani. Do you hear me? Do you hear me?' the Belgian was shouting at the crew, bending over the convexity of his stomach to get his mouth as close as he could to their ears.

A smattering of Belgians have continued to hold jobs in the Zairian bureaucracy and some have not changed their attitudes since independence. The Belgian, getting angrier by the minute and hopping from one foot to another, ordered the road crew to shove the new metal culvert off to the side of the road and then build a temporary log bridge across the ditch so that his jeep could pass.

'Go cut down some trees from the forest. Go on, there are plenty of trees, or are you too stupid to do even that. Cut down any damn tree you see, I don't care. But quickly, immediately!' he ordered.

Two hours later, four rather slender tree trunks had been laid across the ditch, two for the right wheel and two for the left, looking barely substantial enough to hold the tires steady above the fifteen-foot drop into the stream. By this time, Tim was slightly optimistic that our journey might proceed. It was raining again, not violently but steadily, when the Belgian climbed back into his jeep and slammed the door as his driver headed onto the makeshift bridge. The driver accelerated and cleared the stream, outrunning the wobble of the logs. Another Land Rover, from our side, was next, the driver bullying his way across the logs with aplomb, a lit cigarette in one hand.

We were next, having persuaded Amisi that the logs were navigable and coaxed him to maneuver the Land Rover down to the front of the line of trucks. Tim and I walked safely over the bridge, having rationalised that our presence in the car would serve to make Amisi more nervous than he already was.

Amisi nosed the front wheels of the Land Rover onto the ends of the logs and stopped. Then he hit the gas pedal and the boxy car lunged halfway across the log bridge, shimmied, and stopped. Down below the brown water surged and chortled. Amisi hit the pedal again, sending the Land Rover at an angle along the logs so that one rear tire spun out over emptiness.

'Oh no. Jesus, he's going to crash!' I thought, not having time to articulate a shout.

The rear tire spun and the front tires slithered. I was certain that the vehicle was going over and so, I think, was Amisi. But, incredibly, he made it to the other side. We rushed to congratulate him for his courage. He was staring through the windshield, his hands clenched on the steering wheel and his elbows locked straight, as if he were not yet aware that he had come to rest safely on the muddy bank of the stream's far side.

After Amisi caught his breath, we continued onward, leaving the cargo trucks, which were too heavy for the improvised bridge. We had covered just a fraction of the distance to our destination, a town called Goma on the shore of Lake Kivu that lay more than 600 miles away. Our hope was to follow the highway northeast and traverse the Ituri Rain Forest, where the Bambuti Pygmies live, and then come up out of the heat of the forest to the highland foothills of the Ruwenzoris, the Mountains of the Moon that rise along Zaire's border with Uganda. We wanted to cross most of the province of Haut Zaire and then cut south through the scenic hills of Zaire's easternmost region, skirting the Great Rift Valley for a stretch before descending the escarpment to the valley floor on our way through Kivu province to Goma. At the airfield there we hoped to get a plane back to Kinshasa. On completing the circuit, we would have seen most of the river's mainstream and the tributaries of its northeast watershed.

We splashed along through the rain without further crisis, and at dusk we were close to the town of Nia Nia, where we hoped to find some kind of shelter at a Catholic mission. The way led up a hill on which the road had been eaten half away by a gully. A truck had tried to squeeze past the gully and was stuck in a ditch on the remaining side of the mud-slick road. Other trucks were stopped at the foot of the hill, for there was only enough room for a jeep or a Land Rover to squeeze between the canted truck and the gully.

Amisi looked more unhappy than ever, as he took off his shoes to climb out of the car and measure the space he would have to drive through. He had about three inches to spare on each side. People climbed down from the cabs and backs of the trucks to watch. We stayed in the Land Rover this time. With his eyes widened in absolute concentration, Amisi kept the Land Rover moving, coming in toward the gully at an angle, straightening, veering toward the ditched truck, his wheels spinning on the mud, slithering, holding, straight, straight, skidding again sideways until, at last, he swiveled past it and gunned up to the crest of the hill. The bystanders cheered and we slapped Amisi on the back. He smiled and reached under the seat to where he kept a small, precious, and carefully watched cache of cigarettes. He managed to light one even though his hands were shaking.

When we pulled up in front of the mission a few minutes

later, we saw a line of nearly forty townspeople carrying jugs, jerrycans, and buckets waiting a turn at the handle of a water pump. Perhaps the only thread holding this part of the country together is the system of Christian missions, most of them Catholic. The mission was the only place these townspeople could get clean water, and it was the only place we knew of to seek shelter, although the reception we got was anything but warm. A stout priest came to the front gate and shrugged disinterestedly. When we told him we needed a safe place to park the Land Rover with its valuable spare parts, he shrugged again but waved us around through a back gate into the mission compound. Amisi was quartered with one of the mission's workers and we were allowed to camp on the lot inside the compound walls.

The mission house, a chapel wall, some spare rooms, and a shed housing machinery and chickens formed the perimeters of the compound. We pegged up our lightweight tent on the gravelly lot. Darkness had fallen and the mission lights had gone off by the time I started to fire up the recalcitrant kerosene stove, which had been giving us trouble the whole trip, refusing to light and then refusing to stay lit. Only after numerous matches and curses did I get it going. For dinner, we treated ourselves to a first meal from our freeze-dried stock, 'Shrimp Cantonese with Long-Grain and Wild Rice.' We were eating the food out of the pot, finding that it tasted like shrimpy cardboard mixed with textureless rice, when rain started coming down hard. We dragged the stove and the pot into the tent, where we mixed up two big mugs of Tang and vodka, whose supply we had replenished in Kisangani. Once our stomachs were full and the immediacy of our worries dissipated by the vodka, we felt pleased for having made it this far, and we slept soundly, snuggled against one another, not waking even though the rain had flooded the floor of the tent by morning.

The rain had stopped by the time we were on our way again and the sun, already hot, was evaporating the water from the orange puddles that mottled the dirt highway as it led us deeper into the Ituri. Grasses the size of bamboo pushed in toward the road. Bamboo itself grew to the size of trees, and trees shot straight up in the air, some going up 150 feet before exploding into great, branchy crowns. The trees were challenged only by the creeping vines, lianas, which grow with a vengeance, killing mighty trees by wrapping around and around them, up and down the trunks in strangleholds, and preempting the sunlight at the airy heights where the trees transpire. Wherever these vines hit the sunlight, they burst into blossoms – purple, blue, yellow, crimson flowers. The dead trees rot into nothingness, leaving hollow pillars of thick, twisted vines that rise from the forest floor to its roof. The same thing happens with huts left vacant. Unchecked by people, the vines can smother an abandoned hut even before the torrential thunderstorms that sweep the forest can wash away its thin thatched roof and mud walls. Vacant huts look like green tents, lacking doors and windows and festooned with flowers.

As Amisi drove further and further into the forest, it seemed that the vegetation was closing in behind us. I could look back and almost see the tendrils uncurling, the roots creeping, and the leaves unfurling as if to heal with greenness the red slash of the road. The forest was forced to yield to occasional clearings or small villages, and each open space marked an heroic endeavor in the unceasing war against the vegetation. So too the road; that it existed at all, seemed a continual feat.

The villages were becoming more primitive, the people poorer, the huts of mud and thatch less well made. Children ran about naked on the packed dirt yards fronting the road. Their mothers squatted over cooking fires outside the huts, stirring food in pots blackened by soot. Worn-out truck tires were employed as furniture and worn-out tire rims as gongs to summon children to school or Christians to church, humble buildings of mud and sticks built at the edges of some of the villages testified to the will to learn and to transcend.

The villagers sold what they could to the truckers. Besides the porcupines, we saw blue-faced monkeys also tied by their hind legs to roadside stakes, and then gray forest antelopes, an occasional flying squirrel and spotted wildcat.

The road provided a market for the villagers, but it also emphasised their poverty. The children from the villages ran out to greet any passing vehicle. They would circle their arms in exuberant waves and then gracefully turn their outstretched hands palms upward in the universal gesture of beggars.

The road was getting worse, wetter and muddier, for we were entering the area of a natural catchment that funneled water toward the Congo. We began encountering mud patches spanning the road, first inches deep and then feet deep. We made it through with little trouble until we came to a patch that extended a good fifteen yards. Amisi went through his ritual shoe removal and waded out into the slough. The mud came midway to his knees. Shaking his head, he told us it was impossible to drive through, impossible. But he was as loyal to his assignment as he was pessimistic about accomplishing it. He was supposed to get to Brother Jerry's crippled truck, and he drove forward.

A minute later, we were all standing in the orange mud, next to the Land Rover, which was mired in mud above its wheel hubs. Taking out a shovel and pickax, Amisi started digging the mud from around the wheels, while Tim and I unloaded the baggage and spare parts in order to lighten the car. When we waded back into the mud to see how Amisi was doing, we found he was not doing well at all. The mud was so wet that it was sliding back around the wheels as fast as he could shovel it away.

Amisi declared the situation hopeless, saying that we would have to wait until help of some kind arrived. Tim suggested that perhaps a jeep or a truck from the Office des Routes might happen along and be able to tow us out.

'Ha,' he responded, summoning his entire stock of negativity. 'Ha. Office des Routes. They never do anything.'

As if we didn't have enough trouble, heavy clouds that had collected in the sky unleashed a thunderstorm, sending the three of us into the forest for shelter. The forest canopy broke the fall of the raindrops and shielded us like an umbrella. Most of the water was stopped far above our heads by the leaves that caught and sucked in the drops before they evaporated. Although we had been traveling many weeks through the forest and had come a thousand miles since we crossed its eastern periphery above Malebo Pool, we had been confined to the riverboat and the riverside towns. We had not yet had a close look at the forest.

Tim and I left Amisi sitting on a log and ventured several hundred yards into the forest. It was like walking through a crepuscular greenhouse of stupendous proportions. Wherever light came dappling through the canopy, luxuriances of greenery climbed upward, ferns, bamboos, shiny-leaved bushes, and red-leaved plants, some with cupped leaves to catch falling forest debris and raindrops. Above the forest floor was a whole other stratum of vegetation, epiphytes living in the trees' crotches and using the water collected there in arboreal pools.

Lianas as thick as a man's arm and other vines threw tangled veils across the cathedral spaces and dim clerestories that rose around the trunks of the big trees to the forest roof. The trunks were like great columns and the shadowy niches around them were like holy alcoves where you might expect to see, if you were patient and pious enough, the shy spirits of the forest looking down from some remote and ancient perspective. The place also had a cathedral quiet, in which the little noises made by men are silenced by the sheer grandeur of the place. Rising out of the floor, stalagmitic and prehuman, were ocher-red termite hills, some ten feet tall and all hard as rock. We tried to chip a piece from one of the hills, without success, and then just stood there, lapsing into a meditative silence.

It was by studying the ecological complexities of the tropical regions and their rain forests that Charles Darwin came to his theory of evolution. As many as five million species of plants, animals, and insects inhabit the rain forests of Africa, Brazil, and the South Pacific, even though these forests cover less than two percent of the surface of the globe. A forest in the temperate zone may have only four species of trees growing on an acre, while a rain-forest acre may support forty to eighty tree species in the same space.

The same superabundance is also true of animals, insects, and plants. One report by the National Academy of Sciences said that as many as 1500 species of flowering plants, 750 species of trees, 125 mammal species, 400 species of birds, 100 of reptiles, 60 of amphibians, and 150 of butterflies could be found in a typical four-square-mile patch of rain forest. If all the insect species in all the world's rain forests were counted, the total might reach thirty million.

No one knows what potential benefits are being destroyed with the forests, but the loss is real. Already the rain forests have produced substances such as rubber, coffee, quinine, and anticancer drugs that have had great effect upon industry, medicine, and agriculture. The loss of whole species of plants and animals is not just a waste; it is also plain sad.

Our meditation in the forest was shattered by a band of monkeys that came screeching and leaping through the high trees, their gleeful acrobatics a taunt to the earthbound, their aerial highway immune to mud. When they saw us standing there in the gloom, our heads tilted back and our bright monkey-like eyes staring up at them, they whistled in warning and chattered in mirth at our ungainliness.

Amisi was still sitting on the log when we got back to the road, looking out glumly at the Land Rover and the orange mud. We had brought the stove and a pot to boil water with us into the shelter of the forest, so we set about making some sweet tea to fortify us against ill fortune. Near where we sat and drank the tea, some old grains of rice had fallen on the ground, having been knocked from a lip or handle of our cooking pot. Within minutes the grains were covered with insects. Beetles, ants, and butterflies were tugging and tearing at the rice there on the floor of the forest where everything is consumed by animals, plants, or the quick forest decay that feeds and re-feeds the rambunctious vegetation.

The rice was gone half an hour later when a group of men came carrying bicycles through the mud slough in which our Land Rover was marooned. They offered to help, automatically and ungrudgingly, the way aid is so often extended to travelers in the African interior. With nine men pushing and Amisi driving, shaking his head at the wheels' churning, the Land Rover was muscled to solid ground.

Underway again, we rejoiced tentatively, splashing through shallow puddles, marveling at the butterflies, laughing back at the monkeys fleeing through the treetops from the sound of the engine. We even dared to speculate that we might be in Goma in two more days, with time enough on our hands to climb one of the volcanoes near there or even to visit the reclusive mountain gorillas.

In the early afternoon, we entered an extravagantly lush section of forest whose canopy closed overhead, filtering a soft green light down onto the roadway. The luxuriance meant only one thing: that the place was wet, wetter than the normal rain-forest wet, and that the road would get muddier. It did. We plowed into a slough so deep that the Land Rover's chassis bellied onto the mud. Its wheels were spinning and its engine was roaring like a disconsolate lion, at the silent regard of the surrounding forest.

We climbed out into the deep mud. I struggled over to the bank of solid ground at the road's edge and sat down, watching Tim and Amisi getting out the pick and shovel, a valiant gesture, but not one that was going to get us out anytime soon. We were far from anywhere and the forest grew so thickly along the edges of the road that we couldn't even pitch a tent.

Tim and Amisi were debating whether it would be more useful to dig under the front or under the rear wheels, when a couple of dogs came bounding out of the forest a few yards from where I sat. The dogs, dun-colored and sharp-eared, were unusually small and close behind the dogs, a band of Pygmies came stepping out of the greenery, two men, two women, and three children. True to their reputation, they were diminutive; the taller of the men reached a little more than four feet. They all had the same unambiguous features –

triangularly wide noses, prominent cheeks, and large, dark eyes accustomed to the gentle, shielded light of the deep forest – and they were full of smiles despite their shyness. The men of this little band waded out into the mud to help while the women, calling the children and whistling to the dogs, retreated down the road.

The men had laid their hunting tools on the bank – nets, which they carry bunched over their shoulders and use to trap animals, and tiny bows, which measure only about two feet and launch poison-tipped arrows at game as large as elephant. The women were carrying deep storage baskets on their backs slung by straps from their foreheads. The men dressed in loin-cloths and the women in simple skirts.

The Pygmies are thought to be the descendants of the original inhabitants of the central African forest. They may have settled in the Congo Basin as long ago as the late Paleolithic period, tens of thousands of years before Europeans came to the African continent. Unlike the villagers who cling to the road and battle the vegetation, the Pygmies do not war against the forest. They gather its fruits, hunt its game, fish its rivers, feast on its dark wild honey, and roam to its most secret corners. They move through the forest, not against it, living still in that time before people built walls to protect themselves and created technologies to harness nature.

With the Pygmies' help and plenty of digging, pushing, and swearing, we got the Land Rover forward onto solid ground. Amisi took two cigarettes from his cache and gave them to the men in thanks. Each stored his cigarette behind an ear and, almost instantly, the entire band had disappeared into the forest.

We were getting an idea just how treacherous the road was. We also realised we had not seen a single car or truck heading the opposite way toward Kisangani, which meant that something major was blocking the road. There should have been traffic since we were not traveling on an out-of-the-way road whose upkeep would be of little consequence to the country's economy. We were headed toward the Ugandan border on the main highway linking Zaire's agriculturally bountiful northeast with Kisangani and the great river. Convinced big trouble lay ahead, Tim argued that we should turn around before we got stuck for good. Amisi said that he had to complete his mission. Reluctantly, Tim agreed to proceed.

He regretted it almost immediately. Leading us downhill and around a bend, the road dumped us at the end of an interminable line of trucks whose beginning was lost somewhere in a series of mudholes ahead. Despite the warnings we had heard about the bad mud, it was worse than we could have imagined before we came around that final bend at kilometer 418, 250 miles out from Kisangani.

The first mudhole was as deep as a truck and as long as six. Ruts at the bottom were brimming with mud. Around the perimeter of the hole men were ganged, cheering encouragement and shouting advice to the driver of a truck wallowing in the bottom. The driver had looped a couple of cables from his truck to a facing truck on solid ground. The second truck heaved into reverse and the paired drivers gunned their engines, the cables strained, the tires threw gouts of mud into the air, the engines screamed, and blue smoke billowed from the exhausts. There being room enough for only one truck to try to move at a time through the mudhole, everyone was intent on seeing it make forward progress. It was like watching a rodeo in the mud.

We had no hope of getting through any time soon. We were stopped at the end of a line of forty trucks waiting to get to the first mudhole. Beyond that, the road dipped down a hill and disappeared. To investigate the future, Tim headed forward on foot, edging around the perimeter of the first hole and then along the edges of the highway, sidling along the narrow spaces left between the waiting trucks and the forest. He did not get back until dusk, bearing an appalling report. More than a hundred trucks were strung out over the next two miles in various stages of negotiating one mudhole after another. Tim counted ten of these holes, some as big as the first. Beyond that, there were probably more trucks and more mudholes, but he was not sure since he hadn't reached the head of the line.

Tim also brought back information about Andrew and Elly, who had set out from Kisangani almost two weeks before us aboard a cargo truck and had spent the intervening time in this morass. They had been having a hard time, running lower than ever on money and scrounging what food they could in the roadside villages. The only good news Tim bore was that of a beer truck bogged down about a quarter mile ahead whose crew was selling off the cargo bottle by bottle.

With the arrival of evening, I was crouching on a shelf of dried mud at road's edge struggling to keep the kerosene stove going under a pot of freeze-dried 'Beef Stroganoff with Long-Grain and Wild Rice.' Amisi had gone looking for bananas and, coming back empty-handed, he dubiously agreed to share our fare. The Stroganoff was bubbling mushily when the truck ahead of us lurched into gear and rumbled forward several yards. Even though it was dark, the truckers, who finally were getting their chances at the first mudhole, were not about to stay put. To preserve our place in line, we could not stay put either. Tim and Amisi hurriedly packed up the Land Rover and drove on, leaving me with the red-hot stove and the half-cooked food. As I was stripping leaves from a forest bush to use for potholders, I knocked my beer over into the mud and my mood was not good by the time I had slogged through the mud to the Land Rover's new position. But I was hungry and busied myself trying to relight the stove. The food was almost hot again when the truck ahead made another forward lurch, leaving me to pick up stove, cooking gear, and congealing food and stumble forward once more in pursuit of the Land Rover. Twice more we stopped and moved, and twice more the beef Stroganoff almost got cooked before we made it to the edge of the hole.

The hole gleamed evilly under the Land Rover's high beams. In between the ruts at the bottom was a mucky hummock over which the big trucks could pass without scraping. The Land Rover was bound to bottom out on this hummock unless Amisi could keep the wheels of one side up on it and the wheels of the other in the rut, scuttling along at an angle that would probably pound the side of the car against the side of the trench. Tim sat up in the front next to Amisi ready to give advice. Amisi hesitated, grimaced, and then coaxed the left wheels onto the hump.

'Good,' Tim said. 'Good. Good. Okay. Stay to the right, over to the right. Keep going. Don't stop. Don't stop.'

The Land Rover tipped to the right, sickeningly, as if it would topple, and the corner of the roof sheered into the righthand wall of mud, slicing into it.

'Good,' Tim yelled. 'That's it. We're okay. Keep going!'

Amisi panicked and yanked the Land Rover toward the left, seeking desperately to level the vehicle but snagging it on the hummock. Other drivers who had been watching from the sides of the pit pelted us with criticism. Eventually, we were winched out by the crew of one of the trucks and resumed our place in the traffic jam.

We went to sleep that night hungry. Amisi, being short, stretched out satisfactorily on the Land Rover's front seat. Tim and I contorted ourselves on top of the luggage and spare parts in the back, making a bed from duffle bags, a pack frame, and the shock absorber and drifting off to sleep to the noise of trucks growling distantly down the line and to the sounds of the Ituri. A million insects ticked and whirred, their noises weaving into a restless blanket that covered the nighttime forest. Twigs snapped, branches popped, and an occasional parrot whistled.

Sometime during the night, our uneasy sleep was shattered by a howling unlike anything either of us had heard before. It rose from an angry murmur to a bloodcurdling scream, sounding as if someone was being murdered off in the forest, except that the victim's screams did not choke away into silence. The howling intensified, as if several people were being murdered quite nearby. The screechings went on without lull. Amisi woke up and heard us, sitting bolt upright, debating the origin of the howls. He told us the noise was made by a monkey.

(Weeks later, we learned that the screams emanated from the throats of tree hyraxes, which are among the oddest animals in the world. The savagery of its call belies its size and timidity. It looks a little like a rabbit without a tail or long ears and lives high in the trees of the African rain forest. The hyrax is seldom seen, being a nocturnal creature that feeds on tender leaves and insects as it moves through the night, communicating with its fellows by its howls. The hyrax belongs to a unique order of mammals. Despite its appearance, it is related to the elephant, having footpads like those of its mammoth kin and having teeth like those of the rhinoceros.

If you can catch a hyrax, it is a highly tamable animal, being both intelligent and affectionate. But the hyrax never loses its gift for howling. A missionary doctor told me she had made one into a delightful pet, except for when it became excited or unhappy. If someone it did not trust entered her house, the hyrax would give a low howl. If she could not calm it down, it would perform its whole terrible scream.

When we woke in the Land Rover after our first hyrax-plagued night, it was early enough that the sun had not yet steamed the dew off the elephant grass. Three Pygmies appeared walking down the edge of the road, all of them smeared head to toe with a white clay. They were wearing stiff straw skirts that stuck out like ballerina's tutus and had wide leaves pasted over their mouths as if to symbolise the muteness of death. They were a grieving widow and her two children on their way to a funereal dance, and they disappeared, as suddenly as they had come, down a narrow path through the tall grass at the road's edge. The sunlight beaded in the dew drops on the blades of grass that rose above their heads.

After our first encounter with the band of Pygmies and their hunting dogs, we had been seeing groups of them all along the road, but never for very long. Before you could take a second look, much less raise a camera to take a photograph, they would be gone, melted into the shadows and the leaves, stepping onto a path invisible to the non-Pygmy, retreating into their green sanctuary.

As a people, the Pygmies are extraordinarily gentle, disinterested in the warfare, ancient and modern, that has episodically swept through central Africa. Starting about the time of Jesus Christ's tribulations and triumphs in another part of the world, Bantu tribes migrated in massive numbers into the Congo Basin where the Pygmies had settled thousands of years earlier. They came planting corn and herding cattle, these tribes with their warrior traditions and iron weapons, but the Pygmies did not try to fight the newcomers. Instead, they moved deeper into the forest. Somewhere between 150,000 and 300,000 Pygmies remain scattered through the Congo's watershed. Concentrated in the Ituri are the BaMbuti, who are the most isolated and traditional of their kind. As hunters and gatherers, they have never acquired some of the simplest of technologies, like the use of matches or flintstones to light fires. Each new fire must be lit from another in a chain of dependency from some original fire, whose site has been long forgotten by the wandering Pygmies and whose flame may be the oldest continuous one in the world. When they move their settlements about the forest, a periodic chore to find fresh hunting grounds, they carry burning coals wrapped in thick green leaves.

Because the villagers fear the deep forest and are ignorant of many of its secrets, they depend on the Pygmies to bring them game and honey in exchange for vegetables and other farm produce. Over the years, the villagers have come to consider the Pygmies as inferiors who are duty-bound to labor in their service, which the Pygmies will do until they choose to return to their secluded settlements in the forest's veridian shadows.

The Pygmies have shunned the highway that bisects their forest and the trucks that venture out on it. The truckers go prepared to fend for themselves. A cargo truck is a moving repair shop, the home of a private road crew, and even a bus if the driver decides to make some extra money transporting passengers. A truck travels equipped with spare tires, an assortment of spare parts, a mechanic, and two or three laborers to get the truck through the worst sections of road. Most trucks also operate with sleeping mats for overnight accommodations, food for the crew, and flexible schedules. A truck arrives when it is able to and does not usually try to haul fresh produce or livestock in the rainy season.

In the tepid shade of one truck stalled in the road and loaded with plastic jerrycans of palm oil, a road-hardened threesome expanded on each other's complaints. The driver of the truck sat on the ground with the knee-high rubber boots he wore pulled up toward him. He was knocking chunks of dried mud off them as he talked.

'How are we supposed to live like this?' he asked. 'We can't live like this,' he answered himself. 'Zaire truckdrivers are the best in the world, but even they can't drive on these roads anymore. The roads get worse. They don't get better. If the big man knows,' he said, referring to President Mobutu, 'he doesn't care anymore.'

The man with the boots had been driving in Haut Zaire for nearly twenty years. He said that the road had deteriorated so much that most trucks no longer tried to carry any foodstuffs other than oil, rice, or other produce amenable to delays.

'How can the country continue like this? Kisangani needs the crops from Kivu. We can't transport anything that will spoil or it will be rotten whenever it gets there.'

A second man, a truck owner, nodded in agreement with the driver. He was a short, bespectacled fellow who stood at the edge of each mudhole and affably coached his crew. Day after day he wore the same T-shirt, one that had a grinning likeness of Mickey Mouse stenciled on it. He did not know what the cartoon mouse signified, but he did know the exact price of every spare part for his battered Mercedes truck and how the rising cost of diesel fuel was threatening to throw his profit equation out of balance.

'When you buy a new truck and you run it on these roads for a year, then you have to start paying out for spare parts. Every trip you make something breaks. The spare parts get more expensive and then you have to decide whether to stay in business.'

The third man, another driver, estimated that 180 trucks were stalled in this series of mudholes. 'Every truck in Haut Zaire must be here,' he said.

'Every truck in Haut Zaire and Kivu,' the other said.

That morning we made tortured advances through several more holes, in each of which Amisi got the Land Rover hung up on the center hummock. Our progress was broken by vacant episodes of waiting during which our chief occupation was walking forward along the edges of the road, slippery with mud, to scout out the sloughs. On one of these reconnoiters, I miscalculated my footing at the edge of a hole, slipped down into the deep mud, and sank until it was above my knees. I was helpless. I could not reach solid ground with my arms and when I tried to bend my legs, the motion only made me sink deeper. Luckily, a couple of truckers saw what was happening and were able to grab me by the arms and pull me back onto solid land, leaving my shoes two feet under in the mud, irretrievably lost. By the time I got back to the Land Rover, the mud had dried, caking on my legs and hanging like curtain weights on the bottom of my dress. I did not want to waste any of our drinking water for washing, so I did what I could to scrape the mud off with leaves and sticks, a technique that was not very effective. By then I had mud in my hair and down my back. For the first time on the journey, I was reaching the limits of my patience, those mental perimeters where curiosity ends and frustration begins. I was getting tired of the mud.

Tim had long since tired of it and his antipathy for tactical bungling was roused by the dearth of any concerted effort to get traffic moving. The crew whose truck was moving through one of the mudholes would be frenetically engaged, shoveling, and shouting, as would the crews from the trucks immediately behind it. But the rest of the drivers and helpers would be sitting around, eating or talking, watching or sleeping, and just waiting. Organised, they could have constituted a small army capable of dragging a truck through the mud by hand.

The bad roads eat into the meager earnings of the peasant farmers, who often have to pay more than half of the price of their crops just to get them transported to market, if they can get transportation at all. It is not surprising that agricultural failures have added to the country's troubles.

At independence, Zaire was a food exporter. Twenty-five years later, it was importing rice, corn, and meat. By some estimates, less than two percent of Zaire's potential farmland has been put to use.

The United States has given Zaire quantities of money over the years, but not enough to stop the country's slide into economic crisis. Since World War II, the United States has given or lent to Zaire more than $700 million in official aid and invested uncounted millions more on the CIA's clandestine projects in central Africa. Meanwhile, in recent years, the Agency for International Development has been concentrating on trying to help Zaire with some of its most fundamental problems. AID has been financing imports, trying to encourage better government administration, aiding small farmers in two regions in growing better crops and getting them to market on repaired roads, and helping improve health care. These efforts, well intentioned though they might be, have not counteracted Mobutu's mistakes or his greed.

During his first years in power, Mobutu launched several ambitious projects, including a steel mill at Maluku near Kinshasa and a hydroelectric complex to harness the power of the Congo River as it plunges down through the Inga Rapids below the capital city. The dams on the rapids were supposed to produce enough cheap electricity to operate the steel mill as well as an entire industrial zone in lower Zaire, an African Ruhr, or so the vision went. Mobutu was not dissuaded by the real problems with this plan. Although Zaire had iron ore, the country was poor in coal and had no great market for steel. When the mill was ready to roll, the iron ore had yet to be mined and it had to use imported scrap metal to feed its furnaces. The mill never operated at anywhere near its capacity and the steel that it did produce cost eight times as much as imported steel, or more. It was producing almost nothing by

1980. The major beneficiaries of the Maluku mill were the Italian and German companies that built it.

The $250 million steel project was a tiny investment compared to the hydroelectric scheme, which came to include the world's longest and most ludicrous transmission line. Built largely by American companies, the line is an engineering feat, running a thousand miles from Kinshasa to the Kolwezi copper-mining operations in Shaba Province and passing through the terribly difficult terrain of the rain forest. The cost of the whole project soared to $2 billion, accounting for nearly a quarter of Zaire's foreign debt.

If the Inga power were needed, the project would have been less absurd. But the idea of attracting big energy users like aluminum companies to the lower Congo fizzled. The second idea of supplying Shaba with electricity was truly grandiose but it was extremely appealing for political reasons. If Mobutu could control the main source of power for Shaba's mining operations, the rebellious province could be brought to heel by the flipping of a few switches in Kinshasa. The American embassy liked the idea of the Inga-Shaba project, too, and energetically promoted an American contractor to build the power line. A unit of Morrison-Knudsen, a company based in Idaho, ended up doing most of the work on the line. The loans to pay for it came almost entirely from American banks and were guaranteed by American taxpayers through the Export-Import Bank.

Inga-Shaba has turned out to be one of the biggest white elephants ever. Since its completion in mid-1983, the line has been operating at only about one-third of its capacity. Its main client, the Gecamines company, still gets two thirds of its energy from smaller, far closer and cheaper hydroelectric stations on the upper reaches of the Congo. Making matters worse, most of the huge region between Inga and Shaba is without electricity. The people living near the line have been retaliating in their own way by scavenging metal bars from the line's pylons to use for roofbeams, bed frames, and anything else village blacksmiths can turn them into.

More modest and more routine economic and military aid

from the United States has run into trouble, too. One of the bitterest critics of the way American aid was appropriated was Nguza Karl-I-Bond, who compared foreign aid to water being poured into a leaking barrel.

'There is a hole in the bottom, so you put in the water, but there is no water. It is gone.'

This is true, too, of military assistance, Nguza testified, using as an example the treatment Mobutu was giving to Hercules C-130 transport planes provided by the United States.

'You will see that the C-130 aircraft, the Zairian C-130 for which you are paying the spare parts, [has been misused]. One of the C-130s is the personal property of President Mobutu; [it] has become his personal property. It is a presidential plane for him and his family. And the other, instead of transporting troops, because it is a military plane, it is bringing ivory and coffee fraudulently to Mombasa [Kenya] or to Brussels.' Other Congressional reports recount that Mobutu has used the military transports for carrying cattle to his ranches in Zaire's interior in order to improve the quality of the presidential herd.

Even with all the information about Mobutu's antidemocratic and corrupt ways, successive American administrations have stuck by their ally in central Africa. Some have done so less enthusiastically than others, but none has drawn the line and stopped sending economic and military aid.

Within the first year of Ronald Reagan's election, Mobutu paid a call on Washington and in August 1983, Mobutu paid a second visit to President Reagan at the White House. After that meeting, President Reagan announced to the public that 'close relations between our two countries, based on shared interest and perceptions, will advance the cause of peace and development in Africa.'

Less than six months earlier, Crawford Young, the leading American scholar on Zairian politics, had testified before Congress in a very different vein.

'But for the overwhelming majority [of Zairians], life is a daily struggle for survival, and their desperate circumstances are blamed on the regime and its external supporters,' Young said.

Coming from Young, a careful academic with an immense knowledge of Zaire who had refrained for many years from harshly criticising Mobutu, the warning was significant, even though it went largely unheeded.

By early afternoon, we were stuck on the Ituri road near a poor village. Some of the village children were malnourished, their hair having turned that strangely sick orange symptomatic of extreme hunger and their bellies having swollen with emptiness.

A bunch of the children climbed up a tree by the road and made a great game out of watching us and laughing at our foreign whiteness. After enduring their attention for a while, I walked over toward the tree to see if I could get them to talk to me. They leaped down and, shrieking, ran away. A trucker who saw this said that they were afraid I wanted to eat them.

Just as the European explorers and slave traders concocted wild stories about the uncivilised behavior of the Africans of the interior, the Africans believed that the Europeans who traded on the distant coast were not normal humans at all. By one account, they were spirits of the dead who had come back to do their business and lived on the bottom of the sea. In turn, old Portuguese chronicles describe the dangers of journeying beyond the coastal cataracts into the inland regions because the rays of the moon supposedly would cause a traveler's head to swell up. One of the commonest of African stories was that the white traders were buying up slaves to ship home for food, not such an illogical idea given the European's practice of holy communion in which they symbolically ate the flesh of their god.

In the backlog of cargo trucks along with the rest of us was an Office des Routes jeep, seemingly as helpless as we were to do anything constructive. The two Zairians in the jeep had come up from Nia Nia to make a report on the road's conditions.

'The problem is that we can't get through to report,' one of them said.

'When we do get through to report, the office does not have enough equipment or enough gasoline to do what needs to be done,' the other said.

I was becoming obsessed by the Office des Routes, whose performance was so indicative of the rottenness of Mobutu's Zaire. Zairians cynically called it the 'Office des Troues,' meaning 'the Office of Potholes.' I counted the number of times Office des Routes crews and machinery coincided with actual mudholes. Including the fellows in the jeep, we encountered the Office des Routes on the job a total of three times during our overland journey that took us through at least three dozen mudholes. I did not include the times we spotted Office des Routes crews busy with something other than road work. Several times we saw dumptrucks, which were donated to the road office through German aid, being used to ferry paying passengers and their merchandise back and forth between towns and villages.

Perhaps the most pathetic sight on the road was an open-backed truck carrying forty seminary students down to study at the Catholic mission in Kisangani. It had been seven days in the mud, when we saw it coming the other way. Standing and sitting in the back of the truck, the students were crowded, tired, hot, and impatient. The truck had just ground its way up out of a hole and the driver paused for a couple of minutes to collect himself. One of the seminarians shouted in anguish, 'Hurry up, the sun is drying us out. Please hurry up.'

We were relatively fortunate. On our third morning in the mud, the trucks ahead budged, budged again, and we advanced to another penurious village at the foot of a muddy slope at kilometer 436. We waited six hours in that village, which was strung along a denuded, eroded slope. Two derelict road maintenance machines crowned the village slope, the remains of a grader and the hulk of a steamroller. Goats, fond of vantage points, climbed nimble-footed on the machines. At the end of the day, we made it up the slope. In three days, we had gone from kilometer 418 to kilometer 436, about eleven miles.

Just beyond the top of the hill was the Catholic mission's truck. It meant the end of the ride for us and the end of a long wait for the driver, who came rushing out from where he had been hunkering in the shade of a large bush awaiting the spare parts. He told us he had been there more than three weeks, eating corn and bananas, unable to venture afield for fear that someone would steel the wheels off the truck.

We tried to convince Amisi that he should proceed with us to the next sizable town where he could get some rest as well as a new supply of cigarettes and patches for the Land Rover's tires. Two of them had blown out on the way, leaving Amisi with no spares. Amisi, though, was adamant about following a strict interpretation of his orders to deliver the parts and return. He was as unsure about making it back to Kisangani as he had been about getting to the truck. But within half an hour of having delivered the parts, this small man whose pessimism was matched by his stoicism turned around and headed again into the mud.

TWELVE

After ‚four days of being mired in the mud, we slept well stretched in the comfort of a tent pitched on solid ground. We were camping on the banks of the rushing Epulu River, a tributary of the Congo that rises from the heart of the Pygmies' homeland.

We had gotten here aboard what must have been the strangest vehicle in the forest, a tourist truck. After Amisi turned back, we hitched a ride on this high-sprung, orange, four-wheel-drive truck belonging to an outfit in London that runs trips across the Sahara, through central Africa and on down to South Africa. Fourteen young tourists – Europeans, Australians, and New Zealanders – were in this truck, which had been outfitted to provide the best in rough comfort. They rode on two rows of upholstered seats bolted into the back of the truck, which was protected from the sun and the rain by adjustable awnings.

As they traveled, they stared backward over the end of the truck and a cart full of luggage and tents that trundled at the rear. They were seeing Africa as they left it behind, pressing forward with little time to discover where they had been. But Tim and I were delighted at this comfortable ride that took us to the banks of the river where the expedition leader had called a halt.

The next morning, sunlight streamed through the tops of the trees, but the forest floor retained a cool gloom. The Epulu was the color of Coca-Cola, coursing swiftly, its currents rushing to be subsumed and transmuted in greater rivers, the Ituri and then the Congo.

We had gotten up early because we hoped to bargain a ride

on a truck heading east. In the muddy village up the road, we found a big, blue-painted truck loaded and ready to go, except that the mechanic and three helpers were underneath the cab working on something near the front axle. The crew was Ugandan. The driver, a lanky fellow who wore the embroidered cloth hat of a Moslem, spoke a basic English and good Swahili that I could understand. Having neared the eastern side of the continent, we found more and more people who could speak Swahili, the part Bantu and part Arabic language that was first used by traders on East Africa's coast and gradually spread toward the continent's interior. With the driver, we struck what sounded like the ideal deal – for twenty dollars, we could ride the truck the whole of the remaining 400 miles to Goma.

'It will be three days to Goma. The roads will be better now,' Mohammed, the driver, promised. *'Twende, twende,'* he shouted at the crew in Swahili. 'Let's go.'

We were so pleased at the prospect of making it through in one long, smooth haul to Goma that we did not worry about what the crew had been doing underneath the truck. They helped us haul our bags to the top of the load in the back, settled me in the cab with the mechanic and the driver, and told Tim to scramble up with them and hold on however he could as the truck moved off, swaying on the uneven road. The day was not yet hot and we felt festive, free of the worst of the mud and washed somewhat clean in the waters of the chill Epulu. We were making time.

Up top, Tim sat on our gear, ducking flat onto his back when the truck's high load brushed branches overhanging the road.

'Hatari! Hatari! Danger! Danger!' the helpers yelled at him as the branches shot into view from around a curve or over a hill.

Mohammed, meanwhile, was telling stories about roads in eastern Zaire he had traveled since fleeing political bloodshed in Uganda. He understood how a good story could make a long trip seem shorter.

'It was the time of the rains last year, when we were on this same road, near to Nia Nia, when we saw this hole, the biggest hole in any road I have seen in my life.'

Mohammed paused and attempted to shift up a gear. He cursed. The mechanic reached over, grabbed the shaft of the gearshift with both hands and wrenched it into third gear. Down in the bowels of the mechanism, something banged. The gearbox ground, the truck lurched and then picked up speed. Mohammed went on with his story.

'This hole was deep, too deep, because a truck got down there and did not get out. We have taken boards, put the boards on the roof and we went over it like a bridge.'

I asked how the roads in Uganda compared.

'Uganda – Uganda is a lost country. Also Zaire is lost, maybe more lost. Even if you can follow the road in Zaire, you get lost in the holes. In Uganda, you kill people. In Zaire, you kill trucks.'

We laughed, at the humor and the truth in what had been said, on a road where laughter and stoicism are ingredients of survival. It was mid-morning by then and the day was getting decidedly hot. The cab of the truck was becoming stifling, heating from bearably to intolerably, pantingly hot. The sun beat down on the roof of the cab and heat radiated up from the engine and grinding gearbox. It was becoming painfully evident that the truck was not going fast enough to create much of a cooling breeze. The gears were getting harder to shift so that the mechanic was reduced to kicking the stickshift, first with one foot, then with the other, and then both. Mohammed ordered a stop to deal with the problem. Tim climbed down gratefully, for he had been broiling away up on top of the load under the sun's glare. The mechanic and crew crawled back under the cab to stuff rags into a seam that was leaking oil.

While this was going on, Tim and I decided to take shelter from the sun in a schoolhouse by the road, a one-room building of poles and thatch. School was not in session but we startled several Pygmies who were taking a rest in the small room furnished with a homemade blackboard and logs for benches. They tried to hide their shyness, pretending not to be surprised by the sudden entrance of two sweating foreigners. I tried to chat with them in Swahili, but they either did not understand or did not want to talk, for they quickly gathered up their bundles and weapons and left. Their bare feet raised puffs of dust as they walked away in the two shallow, dry ruts of the road that ran parallel into the green distance. From what we could gather, they were on their way by foot to Mambasa, a town forty-five miles distant. One of the Pygmies, an elderly man carrying arrows and a bow, trudged out ahead, cocking his head from side to side, looking for monkeys in the treetops to shoot down for food.

When we got underway again, Tim and I switched places in order to give him a break from the sun. The truck went no faster. The forest was monotonous; the vegetation on both sides leaned toward the road, wanting to usurp its slender space. Time seemed hypnotised by the heat and the labored rolling of the truck. I was able to rig a shelter from a length of cloth and in the heated shade I dozed until a whump, whump, whump, whomp, whomp, wang shattered the monotony, followed by a grrRRTTT, grrRRRTTT, wamp, wamp, KALUNNKKK. It sounded like the midnight murder of a mechanical hyrax.

The gearbox was still steaming hot when the crew pulled it to the side of the road, even though dissecting it from the bowels of the truck had taken more than an hour. Dripping lubrication oil had burned welts on their hands. They pried the heavy lid off the box and we all gathered around it solemnly, peering at a hunk of greasy black metal bathed in dirty oil. Bright silver notches in the metal, newly torn, announced that the gears were stripped.

'*Mbaya sana*,' Mohammed said. 'Very bad.'

The problem was not simply that a major repair was going to be necessary. The town of Goma, still hundreds of kilometers distant, was the nearest place to obtain a replacement for the ruined gearbox.

The mechanic started walking the remaining miles to Mambasa, the helpers went off looking for food at a disheveled hovel back down the road, and Mohammed dragged a reed mat under the eviscerated truck and went to sleep. He had nothing more to say. Our relief at being underway, making progress toward Goma and the airfield, was destroyed.

Hoping for an easy solution to our predicament, we listened for another truck to come grinding along the road, one with room enough so that we could hop aboard. But all we heard was the buzzing and ticking of insects that inhabited the elephant grass beside the road. More anxious than ever about being delayed, Tim volunteered to walk into town to get help, since we were not able to carry our assortment of gear that far. The afternoon was well on the way toward its torpid conclusion, though, and we calculated that it was too late for him to make it there before nightfall. Deciding to stay with the truck and having nothing better to do, we pulled out the by now banged-up stove to brew a cup of tea in the shade beneath the truck.

Having run out of sugar, we were sipping on bitter tea when a man huffed up, pushing a heavy old bicycle, wearing patched pants and an upside-down, pale-blue tin bowl on his head with the poise of a British gentleman wearing a bowler. Our bemusement was mutual. But he took the tea we offered and we learned that he was a teacher in a nearby hamlet and told him whence we had come, describing the sloughs at kilometer 418. He shook his head and raised his eyebrows in distress so that they blended into the shadow thrown by the rim of his headgear.

'This is an embarrassment to my country,' he said.

He took the bowl off his head and held it in his hands, twisting it around and staring at it absently as a man might stare distractedly into his hat.

'International travelers come to see the country and they see the roads and they must think that Zaire is just a civilisation in the mud,' he said.

Finishing his tea, he was on his way, thanking us and tipping his bowl. We had not asked him whether he wore it as a substitute hat or just carried it on his head for the sake of convenience.

Still there was no traffic on the road; the rest of the convoy that had made it through the mud had left Epulu before us, and apparently nothing else was getting through. Unhappy at the thought of another night stranded, Tim devised a plan. We waved down a youthful bicyclist headed toward Mambasa and paid him to carry a rescue note to Père Carlo, a Belgian priest who ran the Catholic mission outside the town. Brother Jerry had told us before we left Kisangani that he would radio the Mambasa mission and ask the priest, who had been at the Catholic outpost in the forest for many years, to extend us hospitality. We hoped the procurer's clout would get us rescued.

We waited and the sky began to darken. Our note might not have been been delivered, or the plea ignored, so we prepared for another night on the road. We cut armloads of elephant grass, slicing our fingers on the sharp edges of the blades and trying to ignore the pain, and piled it under the truck. By spreading clothes on top we made an uncomfortable bed. Gray clouds were massing off to a side of the sky, warning of the likelihood of a downpour that would turn the road into a sluice and the approaching night into a misery.

Tim insisted on delaying dinner, maintaining for the sake of argument that help would come. I was dubious and, not wanting to add unfulfilled anticipation to our difficulties, went ahead with the cooking. We were eating another pot of freeze-dried mush when the first rain came, splattering down through the deepening evening. The raindrops sizzled on the red coals of the fire that Mohammed had built to cook a pan of potatoes. We resigned ourselves to getting wet, summoning that acceptance of the rigors of existence that is also one of the basics of getting along in Africa.

The rain was coming down hard when we heard the growl of an approaching motor and a white Land Rover pulled up like something from another world. Père Carlo had come through, having dispatched his driver to collect us. His Land Rover was not only white, it was clean, immaculately clean, oddly clean given the rain and the mud. It made us notice how dirty we were, with mud dried on our clothes and with dust rubbed into our skin and grating between our teeth. After five days in the rain forest, we were looking forward to the pleasures that would be available at the mission, such as a good meal, a bed, and a shower. We imagined we would be met by a kindly old priest with a mind mellowed by the years of working under the auspices of divine love and among the gracious Pygmies.

We were wrong. Père Carlo was a short, wiry man who exuded intensity. Immediately upon our arrival at the mission, he led us to the dining table, where leftovers were waiting, cold but delicious. Fresh cauliflower, roasted meat, bread and butter were laid out for us. Père Carlo carried in beer from a refrigerator, poured it for us, and sat down at the end of the table. He unfolded our note and smoothed it open against the tablecloth. Each motion was precise, exacting.

'Ordinarily, I do not send my vehicle out to pick up travelers from the road,' he said.

Then he asked, 'So, who are you?' He paused, but not long enough for either of us to attempt an answer. 'In this note you wrote you are Americans, journalists. Two American journalists. How long have you been friends with Brother Jerry?'

He found out we had known the procurer for less than two weeks.

'So,' he said. 'So, he is not really your friend. How do you really know who he is? And how do I know who you are?'

The priest stared at us, his angular face concentrated and his crown of gray hair unruly. His face was weathered by the equatorial sun, but it was not wrinkled as much as it was creased by deep lines that met his features in sharp, unforgiving angles.

'So,' he said again. We kept eating.

'Then you are CIA,' he concluded, speaking in French but spelling out the acronym in heavily accented English.

We both denied it. Accused of being spies, we were thrown into an impossible fix. The more forcefully we objected to the charge, which was not so wild since the CIA used to employ journalists as informants, the more guilty we must have seemed.

Père Carlo looked at us, from one to the other, and said, 'People wear masks over their true faces. When I look at you, I do not know what I am seeing. If I am seeing masks, then I do not know their meaning or their purpose.'

Trying to soothe him, I hastened to explain who we were

and why we were making this journey, but the little priest did not warm up. He told us where to find a cold shower and a room in one of the mission buildings where we could sleep.

Père Carlo continued with what he had been doing before our arrival. With a pair of Catholics visiting from another mission, he had been watching a cassette-recording of Zeffirelli's *Jesus of Nazareth*, a modern-day and unsanctimonious film about Christ's life that finicky Christians considered sacrilegious. They were watching it on a wall of the living room in the mission's central building.

Even though the shower was cold, we reveled in it. Getting rid of a week's worth of dirt, we experienced that pleasure of washing that is known only to the truly dirty. Similarly, the austere, concrete-floored room where we were to sleep struck us as luxurious. It was furnished with two metal beds, a table, and a cross that hung on the wall. The unshaded lightbulb that lit the room went out abruptly at nine o'clock, plunging us into darkness and notifying us that the mission generator was shut down for the night.

The chattering of monkeys awoke us next morning. It came from a wire cage at the edge of the mission lawn where Père Carlo kept a troop of monkeys. Their cage was close enough to the mission house so that their noise was heard all day long, a continual reminder of the encircling forest that had bred them. A hundred yards from the tidily kept mission lawn, the line of trees loomed, and beyond it, the separate order of the forest reigned.

Many Pygmies lived in this section of the Ituri forest, but few came to the mission. Père Carlo had been able to stop the forest from encroaching on the mission grounds, but he was not able to tame it. The Catholic missionaries, like others who came to the Ituri Rain Forest before them, have had negligible success in proselytising the forest people and bringing them into the corrals of Western thought. The Pygmies have never absorbed Christianity and continue rather to believe in the holiness of the forest itself, its trees and its rivers, its animals and its fruits, all that endows them with life. In a celebratory ritual, they speak to the forest and sing to it, while it answers back in the form of selected Pygmies blowing on a holy trumpet that sends its sound soaring through the forest nights. They all know who is behind the trumpeting, but that fact does not really matter.

Out on the lawn that morning, two young Zairian men were cleaning the priest's Land Rover as meticulously as if performing a sacerdotal act, polishing its white sides and scrubbing the hardened mud from beneath its chassis. Cleaning the underside of a vehicle that runs on muddy roads was a task devised by someone touched by fanaticism.

Over by a shed stood Père Carlo, his short figure tensed with anger.

'No! No! No! Not there. You don't learn any better than the monkeys. *Comme les macaques*. Like the monkeys,' he was yelling at two more mission workers who were shoveling gravel from the back of a truck.

The priest did not appear pleased to see us and we were not pleased to hear what he had to say. He told us that if we had risen earlier, we might have been able to get a ride onward with the two Catholic brothers who had been visiting. As it was, they were gone and we would have to try our luck on Mambasa's main street, where a passing truck might be waved down.

We spent the day in Mambasa, sitting near the town's main street, a dirt continuation of the forest highway. Over on the other side of the street, in the shade of a shop's overhanging roof, we spotted the mechanic from the Ugandans' truck. He was sitting morosely on a bench and, although it was well before noon, drinking beer. It was the only thing available to palliate the boredom that accumulated with each hour like clouds gathering before a storm that never comes to relieve them of their burden of rain. We began drinking at midday at one of Mambasa's three little thatch-roofed bars, two that sold warm beer and one that sold refrigerated beer at double the price.

Mambasa was a truck-stop town. Its main street boasted several shops selling the same selections – soap, tinned food, matches, sugar, and plastic sandals – and an abandoned gas station. That day the town served no trucks. The reason, according to rumors that floated up and down the empty street and settled languidly among the empty beer bottles, was that the highway was closed completely now. Affirming the rumors, a rooster strutted, unruffled by any traffic, down the center of the street.

The Catholic mission was about half a mile from town across a stream where women beat clothes clean on boulders and children splashed in the water turned a glaucous green by the washing soap. A roadway led from near the stream up through a village of mud houses and then rose toward the mission and its big brick church, built on what would have been the site of the lord's manor if this had been feudal Europe. A school also had been built and a coffee plantation won from the forest.

Truckless by the time evening began its quick descent, we walked back to the mission to find the priest in an expansive mood, a changed humor from his morning misanthropy. He and the two Catholic brothers who staffed the mission were waiting for their cook to serve dinner. As soon as we sat down, Père Carlo dispensed with grace, leaned forward and folded his arms so that his elbows pressed down on each side of his plate. He stared at us and deep in his blue eyes something flashed, an ambiguous scintillation, whether friendly or hostile I could not judge.

'You have come from Kisangani. You have seen the forest and you have seen its beauty,' he said.

Hoping to find some grounds on which to agree with the priest, we made some remarks about the forest's aesthetics, about the luxuriance of the vegetation, the brilliance of its butterflies, the luminosity of its green.

'I want to know if you have also felt its power,' Père Carlo continued as if he had not been listening. 'It is very powerful. You see, the reason I explain this is that the forest has kept me here. I have learned to walk in the forest and understand its nature.'

He had spoken with such conviction that neither of us tried to address his statement. Instead, I told him we were curious about what he thought of the Pygmies, near whom he had lived for so many years. His reaction was abrupt.

'Pah,' the priest said. His eyes burned with intensity. 'They are nothing. They are like infants. Look at the houses they build. They make children's houses. They exist at a point on the scale of life between humans and animals. They cannot learn to live like people and they do not understand God.'

We tried to disagree, arguing in favor of the Pygmies' keeping their own gods, those divinities who dwelt in the forest rather than in some foreigner's description of heaven. The priest was hardly listening, however, as if he had made up his mind a long time ago.

After the cook cleared away the dinner dishes, Père Carlo kept at us.

'The Americans are going to destroy the world. They are everywhere. They are in Zaire. They are in China. They are in South Africa. They are trying to control all the world's resources for themselves. If they want to, they send in their CIA to carry out their secret crimes. If they want to, they threaten to blow up earth and even heaven with their bombs. They are the new colonialists of the world.' He spoke with absolute conviction. 'This is you.'

There was truth to his goadings. We were more than aware of the American role around the world but the priest had aggravated us into counterattacking. Starting with King Leopold, we mentioned some of the low points of the Belgian role in central Africa. How, we wanted to know, could the king of any country that considered itself civilised do what Leopold had done to the people of the Congo? Wasn't it Leopold's Belgian agents who received and counted the hands taken during rubber-gathering forays?

The priest was not swayed. He said that we were wrong, that Leopold had been a great civiliser, that without Leopold's intervention the Congo would be a wilderness today. He argued that some cruelties under Leopold, if there had been any, were understandable.

'Back then, in the nineteenth century, it was not believed that Africans had souls,' he said. 'How do you do wrong to someone who does not have a soul?' he asked.

Later, as we were retiring for bed, he asked, 'Do you think these Pygmies of yours have souls?'

The next morning at the mission, we woke to a hum of domestic activity. One of the Catholic brothers was cleaning out the kitchen, organising cupboards and shelves. He was shaking dust, bugs, and other culinary detritus out of drawers and pans onto the flagstone porch outside the kitchen door. A chicken was on guard there, pecking madly at dozens of large black beetles being thrown from their dark haunts into sudden light and sudden death.

Père Carlo came by, hand-in-hand with a pet chimpanzee. The pair elicited a hooting outburst from the caged monkeys.

'We have been walking in the forest,' the priest said, smiling, beaming, grabbing the chimp by both hands and swinging it in a playful circle.

We hauled our gear back into Mambasa that morning and again found the street empty of trucks. The mechanic was sitting in the same spot across the road, looking more morose than ever. He had run out of money and was waiting without the balm of beer. The street remained empty, no trucks were coming from either direction, which meant that the road toward Uganda also must have been mired. When Tim went back to the mission to get us some lunch, I stayed at the little bar with the refrigerator and cold beer to watch the road just in case.

The condition of the road we had just traveled warranted revolution, not to mention all the other hardships of life in Mobutu's Zaire. Part of the reason no one has succeeded in ousting Mobutu has been his symbiosis with the United States, his willingness to carry out American wishes in return for American allegiance to his dictatorship.

One of the first big services Mobutu rendered to the United States was helping out in Angola where American strategists were trying to install a pro-Western government. Three African groups were fighting to oust the Portuguese from Angola, including the leftist Popular Movement for the Liberation of Angola, or MPLA, and the American-favored National Front for the Liberation of Angola, or FNLA

In the years before Angola won independence from Portugal in 1975, Mobutu allowed the FNLA and also CIA to operate from convenient headquarters and bases in Zaire. The CIA was providing covert aid to the FNLA, while the Soviets were aiding the MPLA. The Chinese, hostile to the Soviets and warming to the West, were aiding both the FNLA and a third group, the National Union for the Total Independence of Angola, or UNITA. This group was tainted in black Africa because it also was collaborating with the apartheid government of South Africa, but that did not deter China, and later the United States, from getting mixed up with it.

As the date set for Angolan independence approached and the MPLA appeared to be winning, Mobutu dispatched Zairian troops into Angola, and South Africa invaded from Angola's southern border. The United States funneled arms and tens of millions of dollars into the conflict and the CIA sent military advisers and hired mercenaries. But the American-backed Zairian offensive was rebuffed at the gates of the capital by MPLA fighters together with their own Zairian allies, former Katangan gendarmes who had fled into Angola a decade before. Mobutu's troops, the FNLA guerrillas, and the South Africans were beaten completely when Cuban troops joined in the fray on the side of the MPLA.

Mobutu had proved his fealty to the United States, despite the fact that his troops were defeated and the MPLA had gone for help to Cuba, whose troops would remain in Angola for years to come. The American project had succeeded only in pushing the Angolans closer to the Soviets. Mobutu also had certified his greed. The CIA had given him more than a million dollars to pass to the leaders of the FNLA and UNITA, who desperately needed it to pay debts. But, true to form, Mobutu pocketed the money for himself.

The Katangans resurfaced two years later when they invaded southern Zaire in an effort to retake their home province and to topple the Mobutu government. A few thousand Katangans, equipped with weapons from the MPLA, forged across the border in 1977. Mobutu's ill-disciplined army retreated in front of the invaders, who in a month were closing in on Kolwezi, the country's chief copper-mining city.

If any place in Zaire is worth fighting over, Kolwezi is it. The government's mining company, Gecamines, has its headquarters there. Originally owned by Belgians and other Europeans, Gecamines was nationalised in 1972 but has retained strong links with Belgium. The mining company produces about $120 million worth of minerals a month, about $1.5 billion a year, enough to support a considerable amount of corruption.

In all likelihood, the Katangans would have overrun the city and kept going if the Western powers had not intervened. France provided a fleet of military transport planes to airlift a Moroccan expeditionary force to Kolwezi. Clearly superior to the Katangans, the Moroccan soldiers in a matter of weeks retook the territory that the Zairian army had relinquished.

Punished though they were, the Katangans did not concede the struggle. A year later, they mounted another invasion and seized the center of Kolwezi itself, hoping to shut down copper production and cut off the Mobutu government's principal source of revenue. But the invading Katangans were unable to control the situation. Jobless young men along with the invaders went on rampages, terrorising and killing African civilians as well as Europeans who ran the mines. The takeover lasted only a week. The Katangans were driven out of Kolwezi by French legionnaires and Belgian paratroopers flown in on US planes. No American troops were used, but the Americans strafed the city from their planes.

Small groups of armed rebels have continued to operate on Zaire's eastern periphery, although they have never been able to threaten Zaire the way the Katangans did in the two Shaba invasions. These insurgents in eastern Zaire represent the remnants of Lumumba's followers, who were pushed deep into the mountains by government troops. They make occasional raids against army garrisons but haven't the force to make trouble that Mobutu's army, poorly disciplined as it is, cannot suppress.

While I was waiting by the empty main street, Tim got to the mission to find the equivalent of a small miracle, a message waiting in reply to the one we had sent from Kisangani. It had traveled by telephone, telex, radiophone, and finally to Mambasa by long-distance radios operated by the Catholics. The reply was sympathetic to our need for a few more weeks, although we likely would need more than that given the way things were going.

Buoyed by the message and thinking our luck was turning, Tim hurried back to town, expecting that a truck would have arrived. But nothing had happened, so Tim bought a beer, handed me some bread he had brought from the mission, and sat down to wait. Neither of us wanted to spend another night with Père Carlo.

Although we had left Kisangani with a bulky supply of Zairian money, we were running out of cash and needed to get more. There were no banks around, but all we needed was to find an entrance to the black market. With a couple of inquiries and within a couple of minutes, Tim found an Indian merchant across the street willing to trade zaires for dollars at a rate higher than the official one, dollars that the merchant could then use to purchase imported merchandise or to hoard as a profitable hedge against the inflation-prone Zairian currency. Changing money in Zaire takes a lot of work, given the number of deflated bills that must be counted, so Tim went with the Indian to his house a short distance from the street.

He was settled there, preoccupied with counting through stacks of bills, when he heard a rumbling coming from the direction of the highway. Having heard it also, I walked out into the middle of the highway as Tim came running in from the other direction with a plastic bag full of uncounted money, to see the tourist truck rolling into town. The tourists had stayed to rest by the Epulu and were just catching up to us.

We left Mambasa and Père Carlo with the unlikely tourists, who were adventuresome enough to attempt the traverse of Africa from top to bottom and timid enough to want to do it in a group. The tour leader was a Britisher adept in trans-African travel, who drove, repaired the truck, and organised the food. The tourists were able to travel through some of the most difficult regions of Africa without venturing outside their membrane of protection, for they carried with them everything they needed to survive. They had canned hamburgers and powdered milk, flashlights and batteries, sturdy tents and fold-up cots, patching materials for the truck's tires as well as spare parts. Unfortunately, the better outfitted they were and the more independent they were of the local peoples, the more removed they were from what they saw. They knew no African languages and almost nothing about African politics.

One of the New Zealanders, a red-headed bear of a man who was a butcher by trade but gentle by temperament, marveled at our travel methods. 'If I had known I could have made it without riding all day in some bloody big truck, I'd have tried it on my own,' he told us.

For us, the truck was an interlude of comfort, and we enjoyed it. So did the children along the road, who went into paroxysms of glee and horror at the sight of so many foreigners arrayed in the back of a truck. Some ran down the road after us until they were winded, or until the truck disappeared around a corner or over a rise.

The second New Zealander on the truck was an animal lover who kept trying to buy captured monkeys in order to set them free. The two New Zealanders were buddies, but a chronic argument had developed between two of the other travelers, a Dutch medical student and a South African who worked for a mining company. The Dutchman, who was trying to learn some Swahili and who had plans to return to the continent to work as a doctor, was constantly trying to figure out the local customs as the tour truck sped through region after region. He sampled African food, like manioc, and that got the South African irritated.

'You're not going to do any good mixing like that,' the South African advised. 'Blacks and whites just cause each other trouble, just look at what happened to the Congo. As soon as the Belgians gave up the country, you had the blacks going on rampages killing white people. If we let our blacks get out of control, they'd do the same thing. The races are different and they aren't meant to be the same. You can't change that by eating their food. You're not doing them any good by eating their food. All you're doing is leaving less for them.'

The Dutchman responded, 'It is not the differences of race that make the problems. It is the history of colonialists who have used the blacks to their advantage that has created an anger, and a hunger for revenge and for equality. They don't understand us, and there is no reason they should, and we also don't try to understand them.'

Neither one of them budged toward compromise. They paused at times but did not quit until the late afternoon when the driver halted to make camp in a wide gulch that led off the road. In a drill practiced to perfection over the weeks, the tourists unpacked the truck and its dozen compartments and set up an elaborate camp. They washed off the day's dirt from a faucet that fed from the truck's water supply. Dinner was made from rice, canned sausage, and rehydrated gravy. We slept that night under one of the tents and fell asleep to the screaming of forest hyraxes, a sound that we still had not identified but one to which we had become accustomed.

We woke to a display of dead forest animals that some enterprising local people had carried to the edge of camp, guessing that the foreigners might want to buy some fresh game if not some well-cured pelts. They were offering the best that they had – the flayed carcasses of dikdiks, away from which they were shooing flies, and the skins of flying squirrels and forest wildcats. No one bought anything, but several of the locals stayed around to watch the rather fantastic sight of a pack of foreigners eating an enormous breakfast.

Pots of coffee and tea were brewed on a gas stove. Bread, butter, jam, and jugs of powdered milk, plates, and tableware were arrayed on a long table, camping seats were drawn up, and a vat of sugared oatmeal bubbled on a fire the New Zealanders had built. We ate heartily, consuming as many calories each as an African might during an entire day.

After we all had finished with breakfast, half the oatmeal as well as a jug of milk was left uneaten. The tourists wanted to give away the leftovers and recruited me to explain in Swahili. A naked child was dispatched and returned breathless carrying an enameled washbasin to receive the oatmeal. With the concentrated dignity of an acolyte bearing a weighty holy candle, the child lifted the basin onto his head and walked away. The others followed in procession.

Lunch, which we had down the road, drew another audience of Africans, who watched as the table was set up and laden with tinned salmon, bread, and a big salad of tomatoes and onions purchased at a village and washed in a special disinfecting solution of purified water and Clorox bleach. From among the onlookers, several children sidled shyly toward the table. Several came as close as they dared and stretched out their hands for the emptied cans. After they got the cans, they ran off smelling the fishiness and reaching inside to scrape the last fibers of salmon from the bottoms and the sides. One boy had a large can that had held milk powder and pranced off with it, holding it to his chest and beating on it as if it were a drum. The cans were good for many things, for drinking cups, ladles, cooking pots if they were large, or for carrying water and storing food. They also could be rolled out flat and used for roofing, charcoal stoves, or lanterns.

Shortly after the drive resumed, the road began climbing in long rolls up out of the forest. At Kisangani, we had been at an altitude of about 1400 feet, and now we were climbing toward a 6000-foot plateau, a farming region that stretches along Zaire's eastern edge and forms a lip of the Congo Basin. Almost imperceptibly at first and then more obviously, the vegetation was thinning out and getting fringier. Here and there, a few bold farmers had cleared sizable, sun-drenched fields.

As we proceeded, fingers of grassland reached into the forest greenery, promising of savannas to come. The driver of the truck pulled off into one of these grassy openings and yelled for us to get out of our seats in the back. He was exclaiming about something out in front of the truck, a sight that took my breath away when I saw it.

Piercing through a pile of clouds in the high distance was a range of mountains crowned by snowslides. Against the profound blue of the peaks, the snow glinted like treasure. We were looking at the Ruwenzoris, the Mountains of the Moon. They are Africa's tallest range of mountains, their highest summit almost scraping 17,000 feet, and beyond them lies Uganda. Only lone peaks, like Kilimanjaro and Mount Kenya, are taller.

With the appearance of the Ruwenzoris, space had returned to the landscape. The forest was behind us. Hills tumbled down from the mountains onto the high plateau and they were covered with grasslands and the small fields of peasant farmers. A few clumps of trees stood like apprehended intruders on this suddenly generous land. The air was clear, so clear that the mountains looked much closer than they were, their sheer size adding to the deception.

The Ruwenzori Mountains are a piece of natural extravagance. They rise transcendently from the warm farmland to snowbound peaks in a work of nature that binds the extremes of alpine ice and tropical fields. Lying just thirty miles north of the equator, the Ruwenzori massif collects huge volumes of rain, which combine with high altitudes and equatorial sunlight to produce some of the strangest vegetation on earth. On the mountains' upper slopes, heather bushes reach dozens of feet in height, herbaceous lobelia become trees and groundsels flourish like gargantuan cabbages. Streamers of Spanish moss hang from the trees, adding strangeness to a strange landscape.

The Ruwenzoris run south into the volcanic Virunga Mountains, the habitat of the mountain gorillas that had served as a lure in enlisting Tim for the trip. But now that we were within a day or two's journey of the Virungas, the idea of detouring to see the world's only remaining mountain gorillas seemed frivolous. We were too intent on reaching Goma. That afternoon the road veered south, ending our push eastward that had begun in Kinshasa.

THIRTEEN

It was still daylight when we rolled into Beni, where the tourists were heading east into Uganda, whose border was now very close. Trucks from Uganda and from Kenya beyond were lined up on Beni's central street. The Indian Ocean coast rather than the Atlantic held sway over the town. Although we were still within the pull of the Congo's watershed, we felt something of the cheerful influence of the Swahili coast and the high open plains of eastern Africa.

Beni was the biggest town we had been in since we left the river. Its main street was tarred for a stretch and it had a big market square. Across from the market, a government building was falling down. Its windows were falling out, piece of glass by piece of glass, and manioc had been planted on the former lawn. Beni, for all the beauty of its site in the aura of one of the world's most spectacular mountain ranges, was another collapsing town. But it had a hotel with beds and a shower that worked. The hotel also supported the only restaurant in town that served real meals.

The other eating places had identically stark offerings: omelets and bread. The fare was the same even at the place down at the end of town that served as a truckdrivers' eatery, whorehouse, and cheap hotel. Two prostitutes were lounging out in front of the place waiting for repaired roads to bring some business, and we asked them if we could get something to eat there.

They nodded and one said, 'Yes. Eggs or bread.'

We were asking them about other restaurants in town when we heard a familiar voice from inside. It was Andrew from the boat, and Elly was there too, staying for a couple days to rest after their weeks in the mud. Andrew looked ill now, rather than just unhealthy, thinner and somehow paler under his sunburn. They had been eating bread and eggs, so we invited them up to the hotel and bought them dinners with soup and meat.

They, too, had had a hard time finding transportation into Beni and had spent the past two nights on the road, sleeping in a roadside hut with some villagers.

'It was nice enough of them to help us out,' Andrew said. 'Except for their chickens, a bloody nuisance they were.'

At night the villagers had kept their chickens inside the hut to protect them from predators. Andrew and Elly had rolled out their sleeping blankets on the floor and the chickens had woken them repeatedly, clucking and squawking and walking on them.

(Months later we learned that Andrew never made it to Dundee, South Africa. He died of malaria in Botswana, one country short of his goal.)

Staying at the hotel with us were some government and United Nations officials who had flown in from Kinshasa to give a seminar on business management.

The senior United Nations man, a Swiss economics official, had no illusions. He had been in Zaire for six years working on a project to teach Zairian businesses the techniques of accountability and efficiency. He readily admitted to us the absurdity of his task, for he had pondered it many times before, the ludicrousness of teaching Zairians to keep accurate books when the national economy was operating on a wholly corrupted structure of embezzlement and black marketeering, when it was swamped with cheating, trickery, nepotism, and theft.

'All I can do is teach them the techniques. It is up to them to decide whether they want to use them,' he said.

Given his familiarity with the swamps of the Zairian economy, the UN man was not sanguine about the latest set of economic reforms Mobutu had imposed at the behest of the International Monetary Fund.

'This is an economy that has been deformed by corruption and predation. If you try to apply classical methods of monetary reform to a perverse economy, you are making a mistake. All you are going to do is stifle the economy, stifle its uniquely corrupt creativity, damage commerce, and hurt the little man who makes little deals. The big deals are going to continue,' the UN man said.

'Just take a look at the customs system. You run into officers at the Uganda border posts here and they are driving Mercedes, and living very high. They don't officially get paid much, but they make a huge amount in bribes. It is a well-paid job after all. I wish that these people with the IMF in Washington [where the IMF is headquartered] would come out here and see how things really work. How can they understand the twists of this economy? How can they understand how the people suffer? They should come here and study the theories of bribery. They should come here and travel the roads. They should see how big the distance is between their theories and this reality.'

As we spoke to the UN man on the veranda of the hotel, two uniformed policemen, one a bemedaled officer, pulled up in a battered green Land Rover. They unloaded a crate of soft drinks, carried it into the hotel, and departed with a case of empties. They were peddling soft drinks, making ends meet in the Zairian way.

Foreign specialists tried before to reform Mobutu's Zaire. One of the more determined efforts was made by Erwin Blumenthal, a West German banker who was sent with a team of international experts to Kinshasa to watchdog the country's finances for the IMF. Mobutu himself was very much aware of the corruption that was dragging his country into ruin, having made a speech about 'le mal Zairois,' the Zairian sickness of greed. He criticised some members of his own inner circle, but he never took any meaningful steps to clean things up.

Almost immediately upon his arrival in August 1978,

Blumenthal attacked the pervasive corruption at official levels,
extending his reach to Mobutu's family and political entourage.
Having taken over as the principal director of Zaire's central
bank, Blumenthal cut off all credit and foreign exchange to
Mobutu's powerful and wealthy uncle Litho. In addition, fifty
Zairian companies, owned by Mobutu, his family, and close
associates, were banned from doing any business with the bank
until they paid long-overdue loans.

Blumenthal also put controls on the foreign exchange earned
from Zaire's copper and cobalt exports, the source of most of
the country's revenue. Some of the revenues were designated
for paying off the country's debt, with most of the rest for
buying food, medicines, spare parts, and raw materials.
Blumenthal wanted to see the money used to improve the
health of people and industry.

In the course of trying to straighten out Zaire's finances,
Blumenthal faced down an important army general who demanded a handout of foreign exchange, refusing the demand
even when several of the general's soldiers menaced him
with machine guns. But after eleven months of difficulties,
Blumenthal quit, leaving in a huff before completing his contract
with the IMF. As his final act, Blumenthal wrote a report
condemning Mobutu and his inner circle.

'There will certainly be new promises from Mobutu and
members of his government. The foreign debt, which does not
stop growing, will receive new rescheduling. But there is no,
I repeat, not one, chance on the horizon for Zaire's numerous
lenders to recover their funds . . . There was and is yet
a single major obstacle which annihilates all perspective of
improvement: the CORRUPTION of the ruling group,'
Blumenthal wrote, spelling out in capital letters what had so
frustrated and disgusted him.

He went on to note that there had been an apparent improvement in the country's 1980 economy, the first year it had not
declined since 1974, hypothesising sardonically that the small
upturn could be accounted for by the fact that the plundering
Mobutu had been absent from the country for much of the
year.

This did not mean that Mobutu was particularly austere in his habits when traveling abroad. When he traveled to the United States in 1982, he amused himself and his traveling group of eighty people, including twenty-one children, at the expense of the Zairian people. The trip cost $3 million and included a stopover at Florida's Disney World and a week of travel that ended in New York. The Mobutu party stayed at the Waldorf Astoria Hotel, occupying an entire floor.

When he visits the United States, Mobutu usually calls on Maurice Tempelsman, the American businessman who has benefited handsomely from his long-standing friendship with the Zairian president. Tempelsman is a billionaire, an international diamond and mineral magnate who was in the Congo during the early 1960s laying the groundwork for business deals involving diamonds and copper. To make sure that he does not lose Mobutu's all-important ear, Tempelsman has hired none other than Larry Devlin, the former CIA station chief who played such a crucial role in getting Mobutu into power and keeping him there. Once Devlin had helped install a dictatorship in Zaire that was acceptable to the US government, he moved up the ranks of the CIA to the top of the Africa division before leaving the agency. Because of his relationship with Mobutu, he is the perfect man to manage Tempelsman's interests in Zaire.

Mobutu's corruption has not frightened off Tempelsman, but other American companies have shied away. Overall American investment in Zaire is relatively small, amounting to about $250 million. Some major American corporations, including Gulf Oil, General Motors, Good Year, Continental Grain, Texaco, and Mobil, invested heavily in Zaire during the bright days of the 1970s when high copper prices camouflaged the disease eating into the country's economy. Many of these American undertakings have been crippled in recent years by the rotten economy. More significant to the Zairian economy is the $5 billion the country owes to Western governments, Western banks, and Western-dominated international organisations.

America's financiers are more entangled in Mobutu's regime than America's industrialists.

After one day in Beni, we took the only regular public transport to Butembo, a town twenty-four miles south on the way to Goma. Along with animals, children, men, and women with heavy bundles, we boarded the Butembo Safari Bus. It was a vehicle of extraordinary ricketiness. The bus did not roll but rather lunged forward, and each lunge was accompanied by a thousand metallic shrieks and mechanical groans. The body of the bus twisted and bent as if fastened together not with bolts and sodder but with hinges. Its sole windshield wiper dangled crazily in front of a cracked windshield. The bus seemed driven not so much by its machinery as by the sheer will of the driver reinforced by the peasants who needed to get their things moved down the road.

Although only a track, the road to Butembo was in better shape than the highway through the forest. Only twice during the three-hour trip did the bus get stuck in muddy spots, where the passengers all had to get out and walk while the driver and his several helpers threw grass and palm fronds under the wheels. The road was mostly dry and dusty, since the rains were not heavy here as they had been in the forest, and the bus raised a plume of dust behind it as it wound southward through a jumble of hills. Off to the east the land rose toward the Ruwenzoris and then edged toward the gulf of the Rift Valley; to the west, it fell off in waves to the great forest that stretched across the midriff of the continent back to the Atlantic coast. Catching the sunlight, the whitened trunks of the big trees turned silver and they looked like slender candlesticks against the greenery.

Nearer to the road, though, were whole areas where nothing grew, neither trees, nor grass, nor crops. The land once was forested, but tree cutters and charcoal makers had done their work, harvesting the wood to satisfy the unending demand for fuel. Power lines carrying electricity stopped at the edges of the larger towns, leaving the people of villages and farmsteads to create light and warmth as best they could. That the forest was irreplaceable, that its thin soil could not bear much erosion, that its loss could bring disastrous drought and flood to the Congo Basin, did not matter so greatly in the face of daily necessity. Fires had to be built and trees cut.

When the bus arrived at Butembo, it shuddered to a halt, sighing and clanking as if it truly had made its final journey. Butembo's dusty main street was lined with rough plaster-faced storefronts. Longhorned cattle grazed on patches of weedy grass growing on the banks of a meandering river that cut under the street. Bold hills rose around the town, tearing rents in the mists that clung to their ridgelines, and piebald ravens peculiar to the highlands of East Africa rode the currents of air that came twisting down the valley in which Butembo rests.

The town was flung down among the hills like some settlement in the American West of a century past, except for the polished Mercedes Benz sedans and the shiny Toyota pickup trucks cruising back and forth down main street. In either direction, hundreds of miles of bad roads cut Butembo off from any major city or port, but the town's bigtime gold smugglers simply had their fancy cars airlifted in. It did not matter that the cars were of little use in the raw and rugged territory beyond town. It was enough to drive in high status from one end of main street to the other end, two miles away.

Gold has made Butembo. Some of the country's richest gold deposits are found near the town and smuggling gold across the border into Uganda has become its pivotal business. Much of it was being painstakingly garnered by smalltime prospectors working the swampy rivers outside town. Any place where easy gold might be found attracted a small horde of prospectors, whose methods were reminiscent of the days of the California gold rush. With pants rolled up, the gold seekers panned in the swampy rivers outside town, sieving the water and sieving it again. Or they dug down into the soft earth of a potentially auriferous spot, hoping always to find sudden wealth. Mostly, they found nothing or just a few golden grains.

The smugglers would buy even small amounts of gold and they were the ones who made the big profits. Avoiding government restrictions on private mining, they bribed passage across the border. With the money from selling the gold, they would buy goods from Kenya, lotions and soaps and manufactured clothes, to stock Butembo's stores. Butembo was another place where the country's natural wealth was leaking away.

We had a hard time getting a ride onward. Tim walked the length of the main street, asking the drivers of every truck he could find if they were heading south. Having no luck, he returned to the front veranda of our little hotel and began a vigil of the street in hopes that a long-distance truck or bus would come rolling in. Figuring that the odds were against any good transport showing up soon, I set out on a walk up above town.

I went for miles, following a road that turned into a path winding through hills that had been deforested but replanted with eucalyptus trees. Favored for the speediness of their growth, the spiring eucalyptus perfumed the hill breezes with a mentholated sweetness. From the right vantage point I could see for miles across the hills, and looking westward, I could no longer see the forest. The sense of unencumbered space was tonic after so many deep weeks in the Ituri, where no view was unhindered and no space unthreatened by vegetation. Over my head, ravens flew, cawing, in acrobatic loops. It began to rain, but I kept going, getting wet but not cold. The slog back to Butembo did not seem long, and from the hills, misted with the rain, the town looked inviting, its tin roofs making a cascade of silver down the valley.

Tim had watched the raindrops come plunking down onto the road, settling the dust and then wetting it into a sheen of mud. He was thoroughly tired of the road, whether muddy or dusty. He stared glumly at me as I came up happily shaking the rain out of my hair. The only vehicles heading south toward Goma were small trucks running to nearby towns, but they were all so overloaded with sacks of goods and people that passengers stood on the rear bumpers and clung to the tail-gates.

After a couple of days of unfruitful road watching, we decided that the best spot from which to try to catch a ride was at the far end of town. No vehicle could move south toward Goma without passing this spot. We hauled our gear down the long main street and settled down with it beneath a tree. Other people with the same idea were waiting there, too, dozing and perhaps dreaming in the shade cast by the tree. Goats had eaten away the leaves from its lower branches and moved on to more exciting pasturage. Across the roadway a food vendor with a cart of carefully arranged fruits and tinned food did no business and seemed to doze on his feet.

Into the somnolence that hung more deeply than the shade over the roadside spot, a pair of soldiers came swaggering, one of them brandishing a semiautomatic rifle. They announced that they were going to Goma, that they were going there on an army mission and had to find their own way because no military trucks were available. The one with the rifle played with its loaded clip.

'We need somewhere to sit and something to drink,' the one with the rifle said, looking at the group but focusing on no one, the way a sergeant would give orders to his squad. The flat tone of the soldier's demand allowed for no argument or disobedience. Someone brought out a low wooden bench for them to sit on. A few young men came over and supplied the soldiers with a beer bottle filled with Zaire whiskey. The soldiers accepted the tribute as if it were their due and started drinking from the bottle, taking big swigs and passing it back and forth.

The one without the rifle noticed the vendor across the way and yelled at him to bring something to eat. The man did not budge, but kept sleepily looking at the ground as if he had not heard. Both soldiers got up and crossed the street. One of them reached into the cart and took some oranges and a can of condensed milk, while the other held the rifle. The vendor did not protest.

We sat edgily on the ground by the tree, following the movements of the soldiers and pretending not to watch lest our eyes attract their attention. They sat back down on their bench to eat and continue with their drinking. So we were sitting when a new Office des Routes dumptruck came roaring resplendently down the street carrying about thirty people in the back. A mound of gunnysacks rose in the midst of the passengers and two goats stood on the sacks. The soldiers leaped into the road, the one with the gun holding it low to his hip and pointing it toward the truck. It stopped and they clambered aboard. Nothing else of any size came by that day.

Our transport out of Butembo finally turned up the next morning in the form of an aging bus that set out at dawn's first light in hopes of making it the 120 miles to Goma before nightfall. The bus was packed and the seats extra-small so that a bench meant for two left one person half off the seat. It was impossible to get comfortable, even when the bus was still. When the bus started moving, we discovered that its suspension system was practically nonexistent. Each pothole that the bus hit sent a jolt up through the seats.

The countryside through which we were riding was pleasurable, though. The farmers' huts were thickly thatched and the dirt yards were swept clean and demarcated with neat hedgerows of the sort you might find in an English hamlet. Although the farms were small, the land was rich and well husbanded. Shortly after we passed over the equator for the second time in our journey from Kinshasa, we stopped at a town called Lubero, a quiet place set in a cradle of hills whose green was greener than emeralds.

A score of women crowded around the bus, commercial supplicants balancing baskets of fruit and food on their heads to sell through the windows of the bus. In the midst of the buying and selling, the two soldiers from Butembo suddenly showed up and clambered aboard, ignoring the consternation of the bus driver. The dumptruck that the soldiers had ridden from Butembo had turned off the main road and our bus was the next thing to come along. The conductor of the bus stood in the aisleway and told the soldiers that they should get off because he had no more room. But they laughed at him and sat down on the bench of some passengers who had gotten off to stretch their legs.

The soldiers would not budge from the seat and turned deaf ears to the arguments of the conductor and the driver, both of whom eventually disembarked. Since they could not refuse the soldiers, they were going to wait them out, an often useful tactic in Africa where time is pliable and can be turned as a weapon upon the impatient. The soldiers seemed to pay no attention to time's passage, first one hour and then another and another. The passengers wandered about the town square or slept, upright on the seats or sprawled near the bus in the shade of a porch wall. The driver and conductor had disappeared.

There was no choice but to wait. Tim and I sat on the wall for a while. An aloofness to setbacks is essential for traveling in many parts of Africa. If you forget that you cannot count on anything, that the bus isn't going to come or the truck isn't going to work, then you get in trouble either by uselessly trying to hurry things up or by working yourself into a terrible mood.

If your reflexes have been tuned in the West, patience is not an easy thing to learn. One of the earliest lessons in patience that Africa taught me took place during my first year in Ethiopia. I had traveled with a friend to an out-of-the-way town that was supposed to host a market so wonderful as to be worth a trip up the mountain on whose shoulder it was located.

The market turned out to be dismal, the town turned out to be an uninspired huddle of mud shacks lining a street that sloped sideways as if it would one day come loose and slide down the mountain, and rain was falling without cease, hard, cold Ethiopian mountain rain. We had taken a local bus up the mountain and been informed by the townspeople that it would be heading down the mountain the next day, which was not too soon for us. At dawn, we were up and poised at the front door of a miserable teahouse that served only stale bread and tea, ready to bound out to the bus.

The bus did not come that morning or that day, however, or the day after that or the one after that. Unable to stand any more waiting, we set off on foot on the long road down the mountain, cursing the bus as we went. The road descended in long switchbacks, which we shortcutted by scrambling straight down from switchback to switchback. It was when we were on one of the shortcuts that we heard the bus grinding along the stretch of road above us. We ran and leaped down toward the road but arrived to see the tail of the bus disappearing on the switchback below.

At Lubero, the only choice we had, other than being patient, was getting aggravated, which Tim did. He had been dismayed at the soldiers' reappearance and their delay of our bus turned his dismay to helpless anger. He felt as frustrated as he had when Amisi mired the Land Rover in the mudholes or when the Ugandan truck blew out its gearbox. He had been patient, very patient, for a long time, and he had reached his limit.

'What in the hell are we going to do now?' he asked rhetorically, knowing I had no good answer.

I said nothing.

'We're stuck again,' he said succinctly.

'It's not my fault,' I said, knowing he was blaming me for originating the whole idea of the Congo journey. 'You thought it was a good idea, too.'

He stopped talking.

'Anyway, we've almost made it. It shouldn't be hard to get a plane once we get to Goma,' I said, trying to make the future seem less interminable.

He said nothing.

'We could be back in Kinshasa by tomorrow.'

'There probably won't be a plane for a month,' he said.

'There's supposed to be one every few days. That's when they're scheduled,' I said.

He said nothing and I said nothing. We both knew how stupid my last statement had been. We knew that schedules had nothing to do with the reality through which we were traveling.

After a while, he told me that his back was hurting, that the bumping on the bus had inflamed old pains. Tim had hurt his back years before when he was thrown down during a scuffle in Cairo. The bumps that were jarring for me were agony for him.

The stalemate with the bus continued. The soldiers refused to get off and the driver did not intend to drive if they were aboard. Having nothing better to do, I walked over to the bus and bought from one of the women vendors a couple of roasted ears of corn. They were large, tough-kerneled ears of corn of the type that are eaten across Africa, one of which can make a meal. Not seeing much point in trying to talk to Tim, I got back on the bus and walked toward our seat, which was behind the one seized by the soldiers. As I moved past, one of the soldiers grabbed an ear of corn and glared, daring me to challenge his brigandage. He shucked it and began popping the fat kernels into his mouth.

'This corn is good,' he said.

I said nothing, continuing back to settle gloomily into the seat. Tim stayed on the wall. Nothing happened, except for an occasional mutter from one passenger or another, until the siege finally was broken by the arrival of a pickup truck. Realising that they were not getting anywhere with the bus, the soldiers got off and then climbed into the back of the truck, carrying their rifle and forcing the people already there to make room. The passengers got back on the bus and when the pickup pulled out of town, the driver and conductor reappeared.

A young man in the seat in front of us leaned back and whispered, 'They are bandits. They prey off the population. They take whatever they want, food, money, whatever. The soldiers act as if we are their conquered people.'

The bus wound on through the hill region, through another section of the land that had recently been deforested. Past the devastated hills, the bus entered a region supporting tea plantations. The estates had been cleared and planted during colonial days when the Belgians thought in grand terms of the profits that could be made in their Congo. Gardens of tropical flowers announced the plantations' main driveways and beckoned the eye away from shanties at the road's edge where the common workers lived. After the forest and Butembo and the peasant farmsteads of the surrounding countryside, these vast plantations were out of keeping, as if they had been created by some misplaced imagination. Off in the distance on the top of a gumdrop-shaped hill, I saw a white mansion that seemed even more unreal than the rest of the landscape. Rolling past the foot of the hill was a trail of lava leading off to the base of a volcano that rose against the horizon with finality.

Although we had been traveling parallel to the edge of the western arm of the Great Rift Valley since leaving Beni, we had not been close enough to see into it. Goma lay on the valley floor, though, and the road there negotiated the Rift escarpment, where the land sheers away from the Congo Plateau in a cascade of steep slopes, down and down almost a mile to the valley floor.

At the lip of the valley, just as the bus was nosing its way down the first of what would be an exhausting series of switchbacks, I strained to get a look only to have my vision swallowed by the vastness of what lay below and beyond. I could see neither the valley floor nor its far wall, which rose more than thirty miles away to the east. What I did see was space, that thick blue sort of space that appears to the eye when emptiness piles up over distances. Despite the descending road's vertiginous bends and tucks, the bus driver drove fast, speeding on the straight sections and braking hard on the curves.

The faster we went, the worse the bumping became. When the bus whammed through a particularly bad pothole, it felt as if someone were hitting us hard with a fist in a boxing glove. The worst jolts knocked our breath out. By the time the bus got to the valley floor, Tim was in serious pain because of his back, but he managed to see beyond it to the magnificence of the valley.

The valley looked like an unending plain. High golden-yellow grass swept to the far outlines of a chain of volcanoes rising like a shoreline from a dry sea. The volcanoes, eight of them known together as the Virunga Mountains, are restive, sometimes belching smoke and lava.

The air in the valley was more than transparent, it was

luminous, as if it were entrapping the tiniest particles of sunlight, iotas of light rays, and holding onto them for the barest fractions of seconds before letting them continue with their headlong rush to earth. Cumulus clouds wreathed the mountain peaks, as if some giant or some god had been trying to embroider immensity but gave up without finishing the edging of even one corner. In the near distance, the middle distance, and the far distance, herds of gazelles and other antelope were grazing. Those nearby lifted their heads to look at the bus on the narrow dirt highway, only briefly before dropping their heads and discounting the ungainly passage of the bus, an ephemeral interloper in this valley whose geological birth occurred in the Eocene era, tens of millions of years ago.

The Rift Valley is older than anybody can truly comprehend. Geologists have determined its age and analysed the stupendous tectonic forces that shaped it. But knowledge is one thing and comprehending the vast quantities of time that have collected in the valley is another. Who can understand a million years? The human mind has trouble with a score, forgetting the details of events as one year slides into the next. Who could bear to comprehend a million years, much less several upon several millions?

Down in that valley, which runs much of Africa's length and which I have visited several times at various points on that length, I always feel as I do at the edge of the ocean. I feel the presence of a force greater than anything I am capable of grasping with logic. Some germ within the depths of my subconscious shouts out in recognition of the ocean, the environment from which all earthly life has evolved, but those shouts are unintelligible to the more sophisticated strata of my consciousness where words and thoughts are formed. In Africa's great valley I feel that same sense of belonging even though I have come as a foreigner to the continent.

It was in the Rift Valley that the earliest ancestors of man roamed and flourished. Millions of years ago, when northern Europe and Canada were covered by ice caps, Africa's climate was balmy and conducive to life. Africa was growing drier gradually and its forested regions shrinking, leaving whole new regions of savanna. The scattering of trees that grew on these open grasslands was poor habitat for the monkeys and apes that had evolved in the heavy forest, but eventually new classes of primates moved into the savanna and the valley, which was jeweled with strings of deep lakes. The monkeys evolved into baboons and the apes into the ancestors of the Australopithecines, the simian men who, learning to chip tools from rocks and to speak, established the fundamentals of human civilisation. Modern man evolved from them.

The sky that day we arrived at the foot of the Rift escarpment arched above us in an azure dome enclosing everything, the golden grass, the browsing antelope, the far purple mountains. The sky was big, impossibly big, bigger than the encircling horizon would logically permit, rounder somehow than 360 degrees. The bus, as it moved out across the valley floor, was made miniature by the breadth of the earth around it and the sky above it.

This phenomenon, of the sky and the land overwhelming the usual three-dimensional reality in which the figure of a man has stature, is not peculiar to the Great Rift Valley. It occurs in other parts of Africa. In the semiarid bush country of Somalia, you can see rainstorms coming across the huge landscape and looking like pillars holding up the huger vault of the sky. Standing on the high plains of Kenya, you can see a hundred miles in any direction, south over the border to Tanzania where Mount Kilimanjaro rises its snowy cone or north the same distance to the jagged peaks of Mount Kenya. This is the land of the Masai, a people equal to the majesty of the eastern African savanna. Tall, proud, and wearing red robes, they have shunned the beguilements of modern-day Kenya to keep herding their cattle across the lofty steppe.

Tim and I were taking turns standing in the bus's aisleway where you could go into a half crouch, holding onto the side of the seat and, flexing your knees, and ease the shock of the bumps. The other passengers bumped along without complaining, conditioned as they were to a harder existence. The other passengers, that is, except for an exhausted Spanish mountaineer who had just come from scaling the highest peak in the Ruwenzoris solo. Brawny and bearded, he looked the part of a daredevil mountaineer, although he had fallen asleep as gently as a baby while crammed bolt upright between two other passengers.

From the crouching position in the bus's aisle, you could still watch the scenery and look for the animals that abounded. Wild boar fled from the bus into the scrub, their tails held straight up in alarm. Hippopotamuses slept in the rivers that lazed across the savanna as if they had all the time in the world. Elephants trudged along in groups, gray hummocks rising up in the grass, one of them occasionally swinging toward the bus and flapping its ears in warning.

Evening came as the bus jounced across the savanna, trying to beat the sinking sun. We had not reached Goma by the time darkness fell, which is when we realised why the driver had hurried so after the delay at Lubero. The bus's headlights did not work. The driver went stalwartly on through the quickly disappearing dusk and then the twilight, feeling his way the last few treacherous miles into Goma.

Goma is situated in a fine spot, sitting on the shores of Lake Kivu in the middle of the valley floor, with a pair of volcanoes named Nyiragongo and Nyamuragira rising like sentinels from its suburban plain. Nyiragongo erupted without warning in 1977, killing scores of people who could not escape the rivers of molten lava cascading down from the volcano's cone, and the volcano's caldera still cups a lake of molten lava.

In happier times, the town was a favorite of vacationers who wanted to see the valley wildlife and also the gorillas in the nearby Virungas. The place to stay in town was the Hôtel des Grands Lacs, to which we dragged our wearied bodies as soon as we could get off the bus. The hotel, with its grand entrance and sweeping verandas, promised more comfort than we had had in a long time. As we were checking in, though, we became embroiled in an argument with the receptionist, who tried to cheat us on the exchange rate for our dollars, and then became entrapped by the Spaniard. The mountaineer had expected to meet a friend at the hotel, who was supposed to be tending to his luggage and loyally awaiting his return but who had disappeared somewhere without leaving a message.

'Hijo de puta,' he swore. 'Son of a whore.'

Almost out of money, the Spaniard had been counting on his friend to help him out. We ended up offering him space for the night on the floor of our room.

'My god! Now I am saved,' he said, being a man of emphatic expression.

Since the Spaniard was the dirtiest of the three of us, we agreed that he rightfully should enjoy the first hot bath. Upon entering the room, he immediately paced off a rectangle on the floor as if he were about to set up camp, threw down his rucksack, and headed for what we all thought would be a bathroom of as regal a style as the rest of the hotel.

'Son of a whore,' he shouted a moment later.

The bathroom was indeed regal, but its marble sink and marble bathtub were both filled to the brim with cold water. A bucket on the floor was meant for dipping out water for flushing the toilet, for there was no running water at that hour anywhere in the hotel. There was no running water anywhere in town, for that matter. We found out that although Lake Kivu makes a perfect reservoir, the town of Goma could no longer afford to run its municipal water pumps for more than three hours each morning. So when the water was flowing the hotel staff filled up all the bathtubs and sinks.

Grumbling and smelling highly of soured sweat, the Spaniard gave up on the idea of a bath, unrolled his sleeping bag on the floor of the room, crawled in, and was snoring within minutes. I took a bath anyway in the standing water, which left me shivering and covered with a scum of soap that had not washed clean in the chill water. But Tim and I were soon collapsed in our beds, Tim grateful to rest his back, and both of us sleeping as if we had been robbed of rest for days.

In the middle of the night, the Spaniard sat up in his sleeping bag, yelling hysterically in Spanish. He was fighting his way through a nightmare.

Tim sat up in his bed and yelled, 'Yaaaa!' In his half-awake state, he thought some intruder was trying to murder the Spaniard.

By the second yell, I was wide awake, too, in the room whose entire atmosphere now smelled of sour sweat. The Spaniard apologised profusely for waking us, but his contrition was little comfort for the time we then spent tossing and turning in search of further sleep. Soon after dawn, we were awake and hurrying off in a taxi in search of an airplane.

Three planes sat out on the airstrip of Goma's little airport, but only one of them was loading. The other two were glinting motionlessly in the bright morning sun. No one inside the terminal seemed to know the itineraries or schedules for any of the airplanes. About three dozen dispirited people were sitting on plastic chairs, which were pegged together in rows in the universal style of modern airports. They were would-be passengers on an Air Zaire flight that was two days' late arriving in Goma. Some passengers were more resigned than others to the indeterminate delay typical of the government airline that goes by the nickname 'Air Peut-Être.'

One of the more fretful members of the group held hostage to the vagaries of Zairian air travel was a large man who was pacing back and forth in the limited space of the waiting room. We interrupted the man's fretting to ask him if he knew when the next flight would depart for Kinshasa.

'I am booked on the next flight to Kinshasa,' he said, his tone brimming with frustration. 'I have my ticket, and I have not the slightest idea when it will leave. The clerks at Air Zaire say the same thing every day. For three days, they said the plane is coming. The first day, they said there was a problem with a spare part and a repair. The second day, they said there was a problem with fuel. The third day, they talked about the spare part again. The only truth is that the plane is not here.'

The man was a Zairian who ran a small-time trading business in African arts and crafts. He was returning from Kenya where he had bought cleverly woven straw baskets, big cream-colored ostrich eggs, and Masai jewelry strung with thousands of tiny beads. He was particularly vexed because he was losing money each extra night he had to stay over in Goma. To make matters worse, his partner was expecting him, he said, as was his wife, who must be thinking he had gone off on a binge in Nairobi with the Kenyan whores who lay in wait for tourists and other foreigners.

We did not bother to buy tickets at the Air Zaire counter, where a message scrawled on a blackboard announced that the flight to the capital would arrive and depart this same morning, but at an hour that had passed already.

Taking the initiative, Tim folded some money into the palm of his hand and quickly bribed a customs official guarding the gate out to the airstrip. He was hoping somehow to finagle passage aboard the plane that seemed to be preparing for departure. It was an old passenger jet, a Boeing 707, on whose fuselage WOLF had been spelled out in large letters. We were in luck. In charge of the sweating crew loading a cargo of potatoes was a sweating Belgian who readily agreed to take us if we paid roughly what it would have cost for the fickle service of Air Zaire. The Belgian said that the plane, which was run by a private cargo company, would take off as soon as the last of fifteen tons of potatoes were on board.

Potatoes, such humble fare in the West, are valuable items in the market at Kinshasa, where vegetables are in chronic short supply due to the miseries of overland transportation. That it was worth hauling tons of potatoes by jet the breadth of the Congo Basin is one of those economic truths peculiar to Zaire.

We were about to climb a set of unsteady metal stairs to the plane's front door when our frustrated acquaintance came running across the tarmac, his arms full of baskets, followed by a boy carrying a box of ostrich eggs and another of assorted crafts. He too bargained a place on the Wolf plane and settled into the space behind the cockpit where a dozen old seats were stapled into the floor. Beyond these seats, the interior of the plane had been stripped down to its structural strutwork and filled with gunnysacks of potatoes. Our acquaintance paid no heed to the potatoes and continued with his plaints about Air Zaire.

It was just about then that the pilot and copilot of the Wolf plane arrived, looking anomalously natty in navy pants and clean white shirts. As soon as their conversation became audible, though, that sense of properness was punctured.

'Okay, okay, old boy, let's cut the talk and get this fucking crate cranked up,' the pilot, a Britisher, was saying in a clipped accent to his copilot, a Belgian.

The Belgian had the florid, unhealthy look of someone who has lived too many years in the tropics swinging from extremes of indulgence to extremes of hardship. The pair went back to their argument as they arranged themselves in the cockpit.

'We bloody well aren't going to pay them more than three hundred dollars, US, and we bloody well aren't going to pay them in dollars. If they want the money, they can bloody well take it in zaires or not take it at all,' the pilot said, referring to some sort of fee or bribe they were supposed to pay to airport officials.

'Damnation,' the copilot said. 'Damnation.' Whether he was responding to the pilot or just commenting on the situation in general, we couldn't tell.

'I told you last time that I thought it was a mistake to pay them off in dollars. Now they expect to get dollars. Before you know it, they're going to be trying to set up some sort of foreign currency regulations for their goddamn matabeesh,' the pilot continued.

That argument tailed off into a discussion of a piece of good fortune that had come their way that morning. An Air Zaire officer had traded them an extra ration of jet fuel in return for flying his nephew with the handful of paying passengers to Kinshasa. We speculated about whether this would leave the Air Zaire plane without fuel, immobilised once it finally arrived in Goma. Down on the tarmac, meanwhile, one of the men in the loading crew had gotten into an altercation about his pay, shouting that it was not enough. The pilot heard the dispute mounting, got up, and yelled from the airplane's door.

'Hey there. Hey. If you don't like your wages, don't take

them. Just remember, you're fucking well lucky to get paid anything at all. You're lucky to get a job.'

With that he slammed the door shut, locked it, and went forward to the cockpit.

'Let's get this fucking crate cranked up,' he said again. 'Let's get this operation on the road.'

The plane's engines whined up to a full throttle and drowned out the cockpit conversation. The last words we were able to hear were about whether they had overloaded the plane by taking too many potatoes. The plane took off reluctantly, like an overweight duck heaving to get aeronautical traction.

'Oh no! Oh no!' yelled the arts-and-crafts man as the fellow in charge of the cargo heaved a gunnysack of potatoes onto the top of his box of preserved ostrich eggs.

The old jet bumped once and then lumbered into the air, climbing laboriously, arcing over Goma's outlying slums. Under the mid-morning sun, the tin roofs of the hovels looked like patches of silver that had spilled out from the gleaming amplitude of Lake Kivu. Free of clouds, the volcanoes stood resolutely by, their steep slopes a solemn indigo, monuments to the earth's quiescent power.

Shortly, the savanna dropped from view behind us and the cargo jet crossed the eastern periphery of the great forest, moving over the band where fields and trees interlocked in a reticulation of variegated greens. Then there was only the undulating green of the ancient forest whose beginnings reached back far into the remoteness of time. The idea of time itself did not exist back then. Time was as alien to the silences and the animal howls of the forest as the men who arrived bearing the concepts of past and future. In sudden contrast to the arboreal green below, the Upper Congo snaked northward, cutting an aqueous brown course through the forest, the stretch of river that the early explorers thought must feed into the Nile. Yellow sandbanks splotched the river, broad and shadeless and undoubtedly dotted with dozing crocodiles. From the air, it was impossible to see the mud-and-wattle huts and little villages clinging to the banks, the settlements built on that tenuously habitable edge between river and forest.

The view from up in the cockpit gave the impression that the forest had no limit and had made no concession to the advent of man. After the plane crossed the Upper Congo, not a road was visible, not a town, not a settlement, nothing broke the green except more mud-brown looping tributaries of the great river.

'What if a plane develops some kind of mechanical trouble and has to make an emergency landing? What do you do?' I asked the pilot, once the plane had leveled into steady flight and the squabbling had receded.

'If you are blessed with the luck of God, you are flying a small airplane and you push for the nearest road or one of those little landing strips they still have next to the missions. You have to know where the landing spots are,' the pilot said. 'You memorise where they are.'

He leaned back in his seat, taking his hands off the semicircular wheel and nonchalantly letting the plane fly itself.

'On the other hand, if you're jockeying around in some big aeroplane, you're pretty well doomed, I'd say. About all you can do is crash-land on top of the forest and hope the canopy will hold you up and let you skid along until you stop. Which it won't, particularly if you're in one loaded to its gills with spuds.'

The copilot laughed and said, 'You pray to the dear mother of God that you don't get lost, or you're finished. All these damned trees look the same when you're lost.'

If a steward had come around selling drinks on the plane, we would have had a couple for courage's sake. The airplane did not falter, though, and within another hour we began seeing chartreuse swaths in the deeper green of the forest. These were the swamps that dominate much of the terrain in the regions of the river above Malebo Pool.

We were almost back to Kinshasa. The distance had taken us nearly two months to travel on the way out, traversing the swamps and the forest aboard the chugging *Mudimbi*, inching our way along the road through the Ituri, struggling to find transportation in the fertile hills of the eastern highlands. We had covered the same distance by air in less than three hours.

FOURTEEN

It was pure luxury taking hot baths once we got back to the hotel in Kinshasa. We lounged in the bathtub, scrubbing off layers of red dirt and tension, sweat and frustration. Life was suddenly easy again, and we were regaining that sense of existential security that comes from believing that the future holds no abrupt surprises. All we had left to do was conduct a few interviews before flying back to Belgium, then the United States and a world where things worked as they were supposed to. We had made it through the heart of Africa and had found the going difficult but certainly not so formidable as we had feared. We had found Africa's geographic center, that legendary heart of darkness where history has marched so sullenly, leavened by people who possessed good measures of laughter and courage.

For breakfast that first morning back, we treated ourselves at a swanky little restaurant near Kinshasa's main boulevard patronised by the city's elite – Europeans, Americans, and those Zairians grown wealthy under Mobutu's rule. Some barefoot boys were hanging around the entrance to the restaurant, attracted by the patrons who would occasionally toss them a little money or pay them to run an errand. Ignoring the reality that the boys represented, we took seats on the restaurant's outdoor terrace and, in the protecting shade of a profusion of tropical plants, ordered croissants and big glass mugs of coffee and cream.

We hadn't finished the last croissant flakes when the boys took off in a pack up the street. We could not see over the edge of the walled terrace beyond which more people were shouting and running, so we gulped the creamy remainder of our coffee and rushed out into the street to find out what was happening.

Soldiers were brandishing rifles and chasing men down the main Boulevard de Trente Juin and across the central traffic circle at ex-Albert Place. The soldiers pursued them past the brick pedestal that once supported King Albert's statue, past the ivory market, and past the cages that held the red-tailed parrots and cowering monkeys from the rain forest. The chase had begun in front of the large building housing the offices of ONATRA, the government transportation authority, where the soldiers had broken up a bunch of striking transport workers who normally would have been running the riverboats and barges. They were protesting the soaring cost of food and other basic necessities caused by the devaluation. They were telling Mobutu that this move was intolerable. But strikes are illegal in Mobutu's Zaire, as is any kind of political opposition or protest whether voiced singly or en masse, so the soldiers had been called out.

The transport workers had dared a protest, had dared to force a crack in the veneer of Mobutu's control, and had dared to face the consequences. They knew, as did the soldiers, that beneath that veneer lay a repository of discontent that could blow up into widespread anger. We knew this, too, and were astounded by what we saw happening on the boulevard. Our expectation of an easy few days was paling quickly.

When the strikers scattered beyond their reach, the soldiers regrouped in front of the ONATRA building under a tree that had littered the ground with yellow blossoms. Across the avenue stood the publicity billboard of the US Information Service, displaying a set of glossy color photographs of Mobutu hobnobbing with President Reagan and other influential American officials taken during one of Mobutu's visits to Washington.

The next morning, the bank workers also went on strike. One of the struck banks was on a normally quiet side street down near the port, which we passed as we made our way toward the center of town. Standing around the entrance to the bank were more soldiers and men carrying walkie-talkies and looking shifty-eyed behind dark sunglasses, who we guessed were members of the security police. The bank employees, more circumspect than the transport workers, were nowhere in sight, but the street was tense. People were crossing the street to avoid walking past the guarded entrance of the bank and modulating their voices to whispers.

Adding further to the tension in the capital was a report that the soldiers had killed one of the transport workers. The report was circulating on the *'radio trottoir,'* the so-called sidewalk radio, spreading by word of mouth in the restaurants and offices and on the streets and sidewalks of the city. The couple of newspapers that did actually circulate in Kinshasa printed nothing to displease the government and people had learned to depend upon the unofficial grapevine for much of their news.

The transport workers tried to keep publicising their discontent. Soldiers were stationed all around the ONATRA building the second morning when the workers arrived to protest, dozens of them standing in the open backs of two big cargo trucks, all of them yelling and shaking their fists. The trucks cruised by the building, turned around, and cruised back the other way, the soldiers watching and clenching their rifles. But the trucks kept going, the strikers evidently too afraid of Mobutu's army to risk venting their anger at his governance.

I silently cheered the strikers, hoping that they would succeed in their protest, because they were giving voice to the unhappiness we had seen at every turn of our journey across the country. It was possible that this was the beginning of something that would spread across the breadth of the land, that people everywhere would join to declare an end to their various plights under the Mobutu regime. The mood all over the city was on edge as we went about our final interviews with diplomats, economists, and others who provided us with their explanations of the Zairian reality.

One of our interviews was with an American diplomat, who explicated the reasons for the continuing American alliance with Mobutu. We met with him in a restaurant near the center of Kinshasa, which had improvised a German decor and menu.

Seated in a Bavarian-style booth, we ate sausages and
sauerkraut and listened to the diplomat talk.

'The reasons are obvious enough, whether or not you agree
with them,' he said. 'First is that Zaire provides a strategic
footing. It is a big country right in the middle of Africa. Zaire
borders nine countries, among them Angola, which has caused
great nervousness in Washington because it harbors Cuban
troops. Second is that Mobutu is a guaranteed anti-Communist
who will help out from time to time.'

Zaire serves as a crucial base for spying on Angola next door
and funneling support to dissidents. Angola in recent years has
been the subject of immense concern to the CIA and the
Reagan administration's Africa experts, because from 15,000
to 25,000 Cuban soldiers have been stationed there. They
believe the Cubans are a terrible Soviet-inspired threat, even
though the Angolan government initially invited the Cubans to
their country to counter the aggressions of South Africa and
South African-backed rebels.

Besides helping out in Angola, Mobutu has dispatched Zairian
troops to Chad to defend against incursions by Libya's Muam-
mar Qaddafi. As long as Mobutu is in charge, American policymakers can count on the heart of Africa's being out of bounds
for the Soviets.

The diplomat continued, 'Third, Zaire has got minerals, lots
of cobalt and copper, which are considered strategic items.'

Zaire's cobalt, between fifty and sixty percent of the world's
supply, is crucial in producing the high-performance alloys
needed for the manufacture of jet engines. Zaire also is the
world's leading producer of industrial diamonds and has offshore
oil and an array of other minerals such as zinc, silver, manganese, cassiterite, gold, coal, wolframite, and germanium.

All of these minerals have been put to use in the industrial
world. Manganese is essential in manufacturing most steel
and also is used in making aluminum and dry-cell batteries;
cassiterite is a chief source of tin; from wolframite comes
tungsten, vital to electrical systems; and germanium is used in
transistors, lasers, and missile guidance systems.

'Fourth, is that some think that Mobutu's the best person

around for the job, and those who don't aren't sure they want to take a risk on an unknown.'

The diplomat did not mention that the reason so few Zairians come to mind as potential leaders is that Mobutu has quite thoroughly repressed any of his citizens who have demonstrated political skill and independence. He reminded us rather that Mobutu, repressive as he might be, had kept the country intact. Another ruler, a less ruthless one perhaps, might have failed to hold Zaire together. He did not pause to worry about the unpredictability of the future in a country whose political system is a crude dictatorship, a country with ethnic and regional fault lines that threaten to split into chasms, a country with a whole generation that has grown up knowing both corruption and privation.

As I took notes about what the diplomat was saying, I thought about what we had seen aboard the dilapidated *Mudimbi* and along the torturous road through the Ituri. I thought about the Mercedes Benzes that the smugglers flaunted on Butembo's main street and the payoffs at Goma's airport. I thought about what a shambles Mobutu and the Americans had made of Zaire.

Of all our interviews, we saved the riskiest for last, so that if trouble ensued it would not ruin our trip. Wanting to talk to one of those rare Zairians who has taken the risk of publicly criticising the Mobutu regime, we went looking for someone from the Group of Thirteen, the name given to thirteen members of the national parliament who broke with Mobutu back in 1980 by writing an open letter to the nation, and the world, deploring the conditions in Zaire and calling for democracy. For this, they were stripped of their civil and political rights and banished, exiled in Zaire's interior. The ex-parliamentarians have stood out among opponents of the Mobutu regime because they have not fled the country but have stayed to take the consequences.

A year later, they entered into negotiations with the government about establishing a second political party, the Union for

Democracy and Social Progress, or UDPS, to challenge the absolute power of Mobutu's own party. But this was too much for Mobutu to tolerate and he had them arrested, found guilty of conspiracy to destroy the Zairian constitution, because it outlaws any political party except Mobutu's, and sentenced to fifteen years in prison.

Mobutu dealt with the parliament as a whole, too. He set up a party central committee, whose hundred-odd members he nominated himself, giving it power to overrule the parliament. Mobutu made himself president of the committee and turned parliament into a rubber stamp for whatever he wanted. He ensured the allegiance of the committee by paying them enormous salaries, twenty times as much as a high-ranking civil servant or medical doctor makes.

Discontent was quieted for a while, even though the economy remained in trouble and life difficult for ordinary Zairians. Mobutu was aware of the country's growing economic troubles and in late 1977 announced a major three-year development plan, called, of course, the Mobutu Plan. The plan was supposed to give high priority to agriculture and transportation, to increase food production, and to improve roads so that farmers, large and small, could get their crops to market, but it faded away like so many of Mobutu's official endeavors.

By 1980, Erwin Blumenthal had given up trying to clean up the national bank and the economy was in even worse shape, so bad in fact that Mobutu had been forced to the humiliation of asking back the Belgians and others whose businesses he had nationalised. Mobutu also invited Europeans back to take charge of the taxation and transportation departments and the customs operation. Even so, the country's difficulties did not lessen. The downward momentum was too strong.

As the thirteen parliamentarians put it in their 1980 letter:

Today, on the other hand, it can be said that corruption, misappropriation of funds, embezzlement, and greed have reached their peak. It could even be said that they have been institutionalised. Never has the country been robbed of so much and the people exploited so much.

The parliamentarians also wrote in their letter addressing Mobutu:

> We know that you are allergic to honesty and truth . . . After these fifteen years of unshared rule, we find ourselves in the presence of two absolutely distinct factions. On one side, a few privileged people, scandalously rich. On the other, the mass of the people wallowing in misery and counting only on international relief to survive as best they can. And when relief reaches Zaire, the rich manage to embezzle the goods for their own profit.

They were bound to anger Mobutu with the remarks they made about people being reduced to eating dogs:

> Might your intelligence services be embarrassed to tell you about the new phenomenon which can be observed in the capital for example: Sanitary services have almost completely disappeared, yet no trace can be found of dogs and cats run over on the streets on the very next day following their death. What becomes of them? Well, your population makes good use of them!

Fortunately for the purposes of our interviewing, the imprisoned members of the Group of Thirteen, who included some of Mobutu's best known critics, had been released several months before we made our trip. Their release was part of an amnesty for political prisoners that Mobutu had agreed to under pressure from human rights groups and his American diplomatic patrons. After they were amnestied, some members of the group returned to their homes in Kinshasa, where they were being allowed to live quietly for the most part, though under the constant scrutiny of the security police.

No other American journalists had interviewed any of the group as far as we knew, but without much trouble we were able to locate one of the leaders, a man named Tshisekedi wa Mulumba. He lived on the main Boulevard de Trente Juin, a few miles out from the center of town in a neighborhood where the United Nations has its offices and wealthy people live in houses hidden away behind high walls.

Anyone who has survived for very long in Zaire has developed a sense, similar to paranoia except that its basis is real, that warns against doing anything to provoke the government's wrath. Even as visitors, we had developed enough of an appreciation of this sense to be nervous about going to see Tshisekedi, although we believed that no one would bother us. Meddling with American journalists would only bring Mobutu bad publicity, of which he already had a surfeit.

But because of our nervousness on the afternoon we went looking for Tshisekedi, we tried to dissemble a bit by having the driver of our taxi stop a few hundred yards beyond our destination. We walked back to the gate of the house we believed was Tshisekedi's. The maneuver would not have confused the most simple-minded detective, but it made us feel better. With luck, no one might have noticed our hasty arrival at the gate, which was opened by a polite boy who trotted off into the house with the message that we were American journalists desiring an interview. A masonry wall shielded us from the street and we breathed more easily as we waited by the house, which was as modern and spacious as anything you can see in an affluent southern California suburb.

The boy came back, led us upstairs to a second-floor balcony that looked out over the wall to the street, and asked us to stay there. Down on Trente Juin, people were walking along the edges of the boulevard trying to stay in the shade of the street-side palms. Other people clustered at bus stops, ready to scramble onto overcrowded buses. Some others just stood about under the trees as if they had nothing to do, looking like the unemployed young men who kill time on the corners of America's cities of a hot summer afternoon.

I was enjoying the activity on Trente Juin until I realised that those young men loitering under the palms might not be as nonchalant as they looked. The two of them nearest us kept glancing up at the balcony through dark heavy-framed sunglasses that dominated their faces. Something about them wasn't right. I pointed them out to Tim.

'Do you think they're security police?' he asked.

'I don't think so. They wouldn't be out in the open like that. Anyway, it doesn't matter. They wouldn't be dumb enough to do anything to us,' I said, convincing myself if not Tim.

After several more minutes, the boy showed us into a study where Tshisekedi was waiting for us. He was a big man who carried his weight sternly, as if he were still one of the most powerful figures in the government of Zaire. He was a lawyer by training and had been once the minister of the interior and once the minister of justice. But that was before his falling out with the regime. Tshisekedi greeted us calmly, as if we had showed up for a routine appointment to get legal advice and, after asking us a few questions, told us to sit down so that we could hear his story.

We took seats on either side of him in a room that clearly belonged to a man familiar with the trappings of power and intellect. Law books lined one wall of the office and a rug of zebra skin graced the floor. Despite the comfortable setting, none of us relaxed. Rather, we huddled together like a trio of conspirators.

The first thing Tshisekedi did was hand us a color photograph of himself taken right after a beating he had taken from Mobutu's men. It looked as if someone had thrown a bucket of blood at him. A white handkerchief tied around his head was drenched red, his face was bruised and swollen, and his white shirt was soaked with blood. A woman held his arm, her head thrown back in anguish.

'They used Israeli army belts to hit us with. That's how we knew it was members of Mobutu's presidential guard. They were dressed like civilians, but they had those belts,' he said, explaining the photograph.

(The elite soldiers who guard President Mobutu are products of Israeli training and outfitting, a favor Israel has done for Mobutu, tactician that he is, in return for Zaire's diplomatic recognition of its statehood. Although most of black Africa has broken off polite relations with Israel, Mobutu has tried to use

Israel's quest for diplomatic recognition to his advantage. After he encountered resistance in Congress on the issue of continuing aid to Zaire, Mobutu re-established ties with Israel in hopes of bringing the pressure of the potent Jewish lobby to bear on Capitol Hill in his favor. But even this lobbying did not sway most of the congressmen concerned about conditions in Zaire.)

'They used the buckles to hit us,' Tshisekedi went on with his story. 'They used the sides of their bayonets. They threw me to the ground and beat me. Then they grabbed me and five or six of the others and dragged us to their jeeps. They took us to the prison, the one that Mobutu has near his palace. They beat us again, with clubs.'

The beating incident actually was the end of an episode that had begun with a uniquely Zairian protest prompted by the arrival of American congressmen on a tour of several African countries in the summer of 1983. What they wanted to find out in Zaire was whether economic and military aid should be curtailed to express displeasure with Mobutu's government. For Mobutu's critics, the visit by the delegation from the House Subcommittee on Africa offered an unusual opportunity to make their views known. Members of the Group of Thirteen, including Tshisekedi, went to the airport to greet the congressmen. They showed up wearing proper ties and suit jackets, in bold affront to the decree that loyal citizens dress in Mobutu suits rather than resort to the cultural fashions of the West. But what the protestors did next was considered inexcusable. Still flaunting their ties, ten of them met at the Intercontinental Hotel with the congressmen and their aides.

As fearful of its citizens as they are of it, the Mobutu government refused to sanction the group's meeting with the American politicians. Mobutu did have reason to worry. Many of the congressmen were liberal Democrats inclined to believe that the United States should be distancing itself from the Mobutu government. The Group of Thirteen certainly was going to try to buttress the argument for an aid cutback. Mobutu knew this and so did the Americans staffing the Kinshasa embassy, who had been working hard, although with little success, to reform Mobutu's ways and maintain him as an ally. The American diplomats in Kinshasa were anxious that the congressional visit go smoothly.

After Tshisekedi and the others finished the meeting, they were greeted in the front parking lot by a hundred sympathisers who cheered and waved banners proclaiming the event a victory for the outlawed second party. The congressmen left the hotel for other appointments, except for Representative Mickey Leland, who happened to stay behind. Leland, a black Democrat from Texas with a record of promoting civil rights, later wrote down in his report what he saw of the beating of Tshisekedi and others:

Several men were wielding large cinder blocks to destroy a car in the parking lot. Standing near me was an American hired by the US Embassy to handle transportation for the delegation's visit. He said that I should ignore what was happening, dismissing it as 'typical African behavior.' Suddenly people were running in the parking lot and about 20 men emerged from jeep-like vehicles and began to kick and beat several people. I saw one man being whipped by three men. Another was grabbed by two or three men, thrown to the ground, and beaten with what appeared to be chains. I did not understand what was going on or who was being beaten until I noticed one of the victims being yanked by his necktie and slammed to the ground. It was one of the ex-parliamentarians we had just met . . . I headed down a ramp from the hotel entrance to help him but the Embassy employee grasped me and warned that I might be beaten or killed. I asked him where the police were and he pointed out a policeman who was watching the beatings without interceding. I then checked with Embassy personnel in the control center set up in the hotel to coordinate the delegation's visit and found that several of them had witnessed the destruction of automobiles and the beatings. I hurried to the Embassy where the American Ambassador attempted to dismiss the beatings by characterising them as behavior which 'happens all the time.' He told me this was a different society from ours and I did not understand it.

The delegation protested the treatment of the Zairian pro-testors, but the American ambassador to Kinshasa, a career diplomat named Peter Constable, tried to smooth things over but failed. A report filed by the subcommittee upon its return home made no apologies for its undiplomatic conduct in snub-bing the Zairian president:

'Sadly, our own Ambassador unsuccessfully sought to per-suade our delegation not to protest too vigorously the beatings and arrests and to reconsider its decision to spurn a luncheon aboard the Presidential yacht less than 24 hours after the violence.'

The congressmen had learned firsthand about Mobutu's treatment of dissent and the official US attitude toward it. Mobutu had learned that all Americans could not be trusted, that some of them could cause a lot of trouble in addition to being rude.

The Group of Thirteen can hardly be called revolutionary. Tshisekedi has not dedicated himself to the overthrow of the government or the end of free enterprise in Zaire. He told us that various members of the Group of Thirteen held anti-Soviet and pro-West views similar to his own, being eager to adopt the democratic values upon which the economic and political systems of the West were founded. In fact, democracy was precisely what they wanted.

As he talked with us, Tshisekedi toned his deep voice down into a half-whisper. Only five months before he had been locked away in prison, where he had been for fourteen months. But prison had not changed his mind about the benefits a second party would bring to Zaire. He thought that if Mobutu's absolute power could be shared with another political party, giving people a means to voice their grievances, life in Zaire would have to change.

'A second party would put the brakes on the corruption of the clique around Mobutu,' he said.

From his years in the inner circle of power, Tshisekedi had come to believe that Mobutu would never, and could never, change of his own volition.

'Mobutu truly has a malady. He is a kleptomaniac. Zaire is

ruled by an uncontrolled thief. It is a kleptocracy,' he said.

Tshisekedi told us that many Zairians would be glad enough to be rid of the burden of Mobutu, but that most are practiced at hiding their feelings. Tshisekedi placed limits on how much he would tell us. When we asked him how many followers the Group of Thirteen and its UDPS could claim, he backed away from answering.

'We have ways of organising and spreading political ideas,' he said, and that was all.

It was impossible for us to gauge the strength of popular sympathy for Tshisekedi and his fellows, since fear of government retaliation has quieted so many tongues. The Group of Thirteen is the only vocal opposition within the country to Mobutu, but it also was a group dominated by a single tribe, the Baluba of Kasai Oriental Province in south-central Zaire. A tribe of achievers formerly favored and promoted by the Belgians, the Baluba are resented by members of other tribes.

Tshisekedi talked with us into the late afternoon. To help us better understand the principles of his proposed party, Tshisekedi gave us a copy of a lengthy document describing the UDPS and its aim of transforming Zaire into a democratic state. I tucked it away in my camera bag with our lenses and notebooks.

As we got up to leave, I asked Tshisekedi about whether the security police were surveilling his house.

'Oh, I am sure they are watching me, but I can't tell you exactly who they are because they move around. Sometimes they are parked in cars. Sometimes they are standing or walking along the street. But they are always there. They stop my friends and question them when they leave,' he said.

But he went on to assure us that Mobutu's agents would not bother us. They were certainly more clever than that.

'No, they won't want you to be able to write a personal story about repression in Zaire. I don't think they'll dare to do anything to you,' Tshisekedi said. He walked out onto the porch with us.

'But if they do, it would be good for me.' He smiled.

On the way out, we got a look at a car Mobutu's men had smashed during the Intercontinental incident, Tshisekedi's Jaguar sedan, still unrepaired with crumpled roof and broken glass. Sitting in the driveway next to it was his other car, a shiny Mercedes Benz. The underlying irony about Tshisekedi – and the other leaders of the group – was his wealth, which he had gained through the same system that he now denounced.

We hailed a passing Fiat cab and headed back for the center of town. Engrossed in assessing our interview, neither Tim nor I paid particular attention when a man in dark glasses flagged down the cab and joined us as a passenger since it is customary in Zaire for cabs to take several fares at once. His face was gaunt, sunken into concavities beneath his cheek-bones, and he was carrying a hardpack box of Marlboro cigarettes, a costly item by Zairian standards.

The man directed the driver to a side street off the main boulevard where I expected he would get out before we continued on into the center of town. He told the cab driver to pull up and stop in front of a pair of tall metal gates, the entranceway to some formidably walled compound. The gates swung inward instantly, opening into a courtyard alive with men.

'Drive in,' the man with us in the cab ordered.

The driver didn't budge.

'Drive in now,' the man ordered more harshly.

The driver still didn't budge.

Realising too late that we were in trouble, probably extremely serious trouble, Tim and I scrambled to get out of the cab.

'You can't do that,' the man shouted furiously at us. 'You must stay in the cab. You must cooperate.'

We both jumped out and ran back into the street, with the men from the compound swarming after us. They were the dreaded security police and they were all coming for us. The one who had hijacked our cab held a card up at Tim's face that identified him as an agent of the Centre National pour Recherche et Investigations, the National Center for Research and Investigations, the name of the civilian security police. He kept shouting, saying that we had no choice, that we had to come with him.

Pushing at the police agents and hitting them away with my hands, I backed down the street away from the gate. They insisted that they wanted me to come with them so that they could ask a few questions. They wanted to know why I was being so uncooperative. I imagined the worst, that we would disappear forever in the bowels of Mobutu's apparatus of repression. Not for a second did I hesitate to invoke my nationality, something I am normally quite circumspect about in African countries like Zaire that have suffered the unhappy effects of US foreign policy.

'*Je suis Americaine,*' I shouted at the agents sidling down the street after me. 'I am an American! *Je suis Americaine!*'

With every ounce of vehemence I could muster, I insisted that if they wanted to question me, they could do it at the American embassy. As they moved in to try to grab my arms, I slapped at them as if I were utterly indignant that they dared to accost a citizen of the United States.

'*Je suis Americaine,*' I continued to shout, as if that somehow would put me beyond their reach and automatically protect me. The arrogance of the tactic did not occur to me then – imagine an African being arrested by the DC police and shouting, 'I am a Nigerian!' to ward off his tormentors. But it helped to keep the agents at bay.

Beneath my vehemence, I felt sickeningly helpless. That comfortable rug of guarantees that is a birthright of middle-class Americans had been jerked out from under our feet. All assumptions were off. The security police were not going to read us our rights or call a lawyer for us. The fear returned, the fear that we had carried with us to the Congo and then laughed at during the highest moments of the river trip. We had stumbled into the Congo's mythic darkness. Mobutu's security police were capable of anything – from detaining prisoners without charge and treating them with mild cruelty to torturing them, starving them, and even executing them.

My apprehension built into anger, crossing that boundary between fear and outrage. I started swearing at the police agents who persisted in trying to maneuver me back toward the gate. Tim had adopted cooler tactics, trying to stay calm and reason with the police agents who surrounded him. He figured that resisting would make the situation even worse by aggravating the agents whose raw power flowed from Mobutu himself. He thought he might be able to explain the purpose of our interview with Tshisekedi, assuming that was what they were so upset about, and convince them to release us. He let a couple of them grab his arms. Although I was a distance down the street by then, he shouted to me and said he would go along, leaving me free to go summon help.

I started swearing afresh, not at the agent who had a lock on Tim's arm and was pulling him away, but at Tim. The idea of his sacrificing himself made me furious. So did a corollary thought, strange though it seemed amid this high drama, that he was trying to save me because I was the woman and he the man. Chauvinism had been the last thing on Tim's mind, but my outburst killed his plan.

Just as I was not beyond invoking American citizenship, I was not beyond appealing to the postcolonial Belgian presence in Zaire. Down at the end of the street I spotted several Belgians chatting with each other. I yelled at them at the top of my voice. Husky men in khaki safari suits, they came sauntering over and started questioning the security police, who tolerated their interference and backed off a step, perhaps in lingering deference to historical tyranny. But the police were not about to give up. Tim had worked his way up the street toward me and twenty of them clustered around the two of us, making an opening in their ragged circle to accommodate the Belgians.

While all this was going on, a motorcylist came down the side street, slowing to a putter in order to take a look at the commotion. He looked European so I yelled at him in French and Tim, who was nearer the center of the street, hastily pleaded with him to take a message to the American embassy that two journalists from Baltimore were in trouble. Getting a message out was crucial, because the police could do with us what they liked so long as no one with diplomatic authority knew our whereabouts. The motorcyclist, who was a young Frenchman, disappeared down the street.

The standoff in the street continued. A couple of the CNRI agents were telling the Belgians that as agents of the government they had the prerogative to take us for interrogation.

'This isn't the Belgian Congo, this is Zaire,' one of them reiterated. 'You have no right to interfere in our business.'

Finally, the Frenchman reappeared, returning as a passenger in a reassuringly big and shiny Chevrolet jeep in the company of the American embassy's security chief, its vice consul, and a Zairian soldier assigned to patrol the embassy. The soldier stepped between us and the CNRI agents and led us to the safety of the jeep. We thought we were saved.

We weren't. Within minutes we were securely in the grasp of the security police. After a hurried conference in the street, the Americans decided it best if we went with the agents. Our hopes of safety were dashed. We were alone and we were captive.

A squad of agents escorted us through the high compound gates and clanged them shut triumphantly. They led us through the courtyard to a building, through a large foyer eerily empty of furniture and people and into a smaller room where a fat man in a Mobutu suit sat waiting for us. His suit was unbuttoned in the front, allowing room for his belly to protrude under a white T-shirt. He pointed to some chairs opposite the desk.

'Please be comfortable. You must sit down and relax. You have plenty of time and I have plenty of time,' the man said. His eyes remained stone cold, boring into us from behind obese eyelids that drooped of their own weight. His name was Adambu, we would learn later, and he was a high official at CNRI, reporting to a man named Seti Yale, one of Mobutu's most trusted and well rewarded loyalists. Yale was one of those privileged members of the inner circle who could embezzle money directly from the national bank. The building was CNRI's secretariat, one of the principal places where Zairians who fall into political disfavor are detained and tortured.

Our bags – my purse and camera bag and the shoulder bag in which Tim carried his notebooks and money – were laid out on the desk and Adambu started picking through them. We wished we had been more careful, knowing that our antagonists had their hands on the notes from some of the most negative conversations we had had about Mobutu.

Adambu made me take the cameras apart, take the lenses off, the lens caps, the filters, so that he could peer through each piece. He spilled the contents of my purse out on the desk. Then he dumped pills out of pill bottles, assiduously opening up random antibiotic capsules to ascertain that nothing was secreted inside. He was enjoying his power.

He found a box of matches and dumped those out, too. He took my sunglasses out of their case and peered into it. He flipped through our notebooks, including one that contained most of Tim's writing from the trip, and sent them off to be translated into French. He pulled money and then several notes from my wallet, unfolded and laboriously scrutinised each one. One consisted of notations about the riverboats' supposed schedules, another notations about the forest as we had seen it from the potato plane. Each scrap of paper, each camera lens, each pen, each pill bottle was passed along the desk to an assisting agent who listed and labeled each item. The evidence grew into a small pile.

Flies were buzzing around the room and around Adambu, who periodically leaned back from his toil and slapped at the ones audacious enough to circle near his head and shoulders, more often than not missing them but whacking himself. It was like a scene from some poorly realised slapstick comedy except that there was no laughter, only the stares of the half-dozen agents who lingered at the edges of the room. They were all thin, almost cadaverously so, and nervous – entirely different people from the many Zairians whom we had met in the interior, people who loved to laugh and who hated the government that had brought them so much suffering. Not a single one of the CNRI agents, including the fat Adambu, looked normal.

'So why were you talking with Tshisekedi wa Mulumba?' Adambu asked, speaking in French with exaggerated slowness and politeness.

Tim answered, saying we were journalists and had wanted

to interview a member of the opposition to balance out our reportage. I was imagining what Adambu must be like when he was not being polite. I pictured him lunging across that desk and hitting some unfortunate prisoner with his hammy fist.

'So you are not denying what you have done,' Adambu said with a conclusive smile.

Adambu smiled again when he pulled from a side pocket of my camera bag the document Tshisekedi had given us that described the UDPS and the pluralistic philosophy of the Group of Thirteen. He passed the document to his assistant, who also smiled unpleasantly when he understood what it was, numbered it, and handed it around for the edification of the other agents. They all knew that the UDPS document was a piece of treason.

Turning his attention back to us, Adambu said, 'We want to know what your purpose is. We have some questions to which you must give us answers. That is the end to what I have to say to you.'

Adambu left the room. Then several of the agents led Tim away. Two of them stayed behind with me and I demanded, with as much confidence as I could fabricate, that they explain where they were taking Tim.

'Just to another place for some questions,' one said.

They were separating us and I was horrified. There is comfort, immense comfort, in having good company in bad situations. But they had separated us.

Adambu's agents had taken our watches and I no longer had a good idea of what time it was. I didn't know how long Adambu had been going through our things in the windowless room, except that it had seemed like a long time. I guessed that evening had fallen.

Eventually, another man came into the room and sat down in Adambu's seat. He started talking to me in halting and nearly unintelligible English. After several futile tries at making himself understood, he switched into French and explained that he was the interpreter come to translate for the pair of CNRI agents who wanted to interrogate me. He spoke English *en principe*,' and I acted as if I hardly spoke French, matching my pretended against his real incompetence. My interrogation proceeded with extreme difficulty, as I seemed to misunderstand most of the questions and then answered them in French that recalled grammatical mistakes worthy of a grade school student.

'*J'ai ne parle Français non bien.* I have not speak French not good,' I told the interrogators.

'*Qu'est-ce que vous allez écrire de Zaire?*' the interpreter asked in French.

'I am not crying,' I answered.

The questioning went on at a lame pace for perhaps two hours, during which little was established except that I was an American reporter. They finally gave up their effort altogether and leaned back in their chairs, talking to each other in Lingala and assuming I would not understand. But I caught enough to realise they were telling the would-be interpreter about the earlier street scene, about my vehement refusals to cooperate.

'*Azali mwasi matata.* She's a tough woman,' one of them said.

Tough was the last thing I was feeling. I sat there worrying about what they were going to do to me next and about what they were doing to Tim, whom I had kept demanding to see.

Tim was having a more difficult time of it with a batch of CNRI agents who were treating him like a serious criminal. He told me later about how his interrogators had armed themselves with politically incriminating quotations from his notebook. In response, Tim stated and restated that his purpose was merely that of a journalist, to find out information about Zairian politics. He told them that talking with Tshisekedi was not the same as siding with him. They refused to accept this claim to journalistic neutrality.

'You work for a newspaper in the United States. Is this newspaper Democrat or Republican?' the middle one of his three questioners asked. They had placed him in a chair and sat opposite him along a table like three judges.

'Neither,' Tim answered.

'Did it recommend Reagan to be president?'

'No.'

'Aha,' the middle questioner cried with the enthusiasm of discovery. 'So your paper is against the government.'

Tim's protests and explanations were interrupted by the second questioner, an agent who wore his sunglasses even in the dim light of the CNRI secretariat and who had been leafing through Tim's confiscated notebook. The first line in that notebook, written out plainly, was the old warning of the hotel watchman: *'Les gendarmes sont les grand voleurs.'* The notebook was shown down the length of the table and back again. Tim was dismayed. Since he couldn't plausibly deny that this was his handwriting, he began envisioning the worst of consequences.

'Your attitude is against the government of Zaire,' he was sternly told by the agent with the sunglasses.

Tim leaned across the table and pointed out the many passages, the many essays he had written in his notebook about the beauty of the river, the grace of the canoeists with their lanceolate paddles, the strength of the *commerçants*, the natural wealth of Zaire.

'*Ça, c'est la nature,*' the third interrogator responded. 'That is merely nature.'

Then they leafed over to another page where the one with the sunglasses found and read out loud the most damaging line possible: 'Mobutu is the biggest thief of all.'

The agents, first one and then another, demanded to know who had said this terrible thing. Tim said he did not remember back that far, too many weeks had gone by. The words were those of the friend who had shown us around the slums when we were first in Kinshasa. We had taken care not to record his and others' names in our notes; otherwise several Zairians would have been in grave trouble. The questioning became more hostile.

'Where did you hear of this man Tshisekedi?' the middle interrogator asked.

'The Group of Thirteen is well known in the United States, ever since the incident at the Intercontinental.'

The one with the sunglasses pushed back his chair and stood up. 'From whom did you learn of this affair?' he asked.

'From the congressmen's accounts in the newspapers,' Tim replied.

'From which congressmen?'

'Well, one of them, Parren Mitchell, is from my city.'

'So, Parren Mitchell sent you here to talk to Tshisekedi,' the agent declared.

He sat down again and began writing furiously on the top sheet of a stack of blank paper. Tim could not disabuse his questioners of the notion that there was some plot afoot between us and the congressmen of the House Subcommittee on Africa or the officials staffing the American embassy in Kinshasa. They asked dozens of questions about the embassy officials and the subcommittee members, and the agent with the sunglasses kept scribbling away on his stack of paper.

The interrogation became no less nonsensical as it went on. Tim was despairing. His initial hope, which was that truthfulness would satisfy his interrogators and convince them to let us go, was extinguished.

As the hours dragged by, I had little to do save worry about Tim, and myself, and watch the flies. I had given up asking the agents where Tim was and when we would be let go. The flies helped to pass the time. Three of them were dominating the space at the center of the room, buzzing about in erratic loops and circles, and landing sporadically on the desk. As a diversion, I set about trying to keep track of the three flies, not confusing them with others that dodged in interloping circuits across the center of the room.

Mobutu has established not one, but two security police branches, one of them civilian and the other military. Because of the habit of these police of taking suspected political dissidents into custody, holding them without charge while often mistreating and torturing them, Amnesty International has put Zaire high on its list of human-rights violators. Over the past decade, Amnesty has documented thousands of cases of abuse and torture in Zaire.

A recent bulletin on Zaire published by the human-rights organisation described the treatment meted out by Mobutu's police:

> Both political and ordinary prisoners in Zaire are frequently beaten and subjected to other forms of ill-treatment as a routine part of their punishment. The most frequently reported forms of ill-treatment are the most crude: beatings and starvation. These are reportedly used at most prisons and detention centres in Kinshasa. Political detainees are routinely beaten, particularly on the face, ears and chest. Many are also held in tight handcuffs known as *krakras*. Torture techniques vary between the different detention centres. They include whipping (with electric flex), beatings (with various blunt instruments), electric shock treatment, burns, hanging upside down and being beaten, and submersion of the head in water for long periods. Women are also reported to have been raped and one male prisoner has reported that in order to make him supply information, his [security police] guards persuaded his wife to come to the prison where he was held and she was raped by three guards in her husband's presence.

Some of the best information about atrocities in Mobutu's Zaire has come from members of his regime who have fled the country. From exile, Bernardin Mungul-Diaka, who had been a ranking party official, put together a list of massacres and executions that he claimed had occurred since Mobutu took power. The compilation began with Lumumba's killing and went on to detail a dozen bloody incidents.

The list included the 1966 hanging of four former cabinet members for plotting against Mobutu. The four were executed in front of 50,000 spectators, making it abundantly clear what could happen to those who opposed Mobutu. A decade later, Mobutu still was executing those who would challenge his dictates. In 1978, he had eight military officers and five civilians shot by a firing squad for purportedly trying to overthrow him. That same year, fourteen ringleaders of a revolt in a province near Kinshasa were executed at another public spectacle, hanged one at a time on separate gallows.

Mungul-Diaka's list also included the massacre the following year of several thousand rebel soldiers in Shaba who were burned, buried alive, or thrown to their deaths from helicopters; the 1969 killing of several hundred university students; the 1970 killing of about 500 villagers in retaliation for the killing of a soldier who had been caught stealing a chicken; and the 1979 massacre in Eastern Kasai of at least a few hundred villagers who had dug secretly for diamonds considered to be the property of Mobutu or his cronies.

Nguza Karl-I-Bond confirmed in his testimony to the House subcommittee that the reports published by Amnesty International were true 'despite the denials I was forced to issue officially as Foreign Minister and Prime Minister.' He also said that he himself had been arrested and tortured by Mobutu's agents in 1977 on a charge of treason or political dissidence.

For all I knew, anything could be happening to Tim. I could only hope that the CNRI agents were aware that harming either one of us could mean bad publicity and diplomatic trouble. I was thankful that we were not Zairian detainees.

The agents kept questioning Tim for hours, during which he detailed for them our entire itinerary across Zaire. Finally, they led him downstairs and back into the room where I was waiting. When I saw that he was all right, I refrained from rushing to him. I did not want them to know how frightened I had been.

The agents bundled us into a car and drove us back to our hotel, leaving us with orders to return the next morning for further interrogation. They kept the belongings they had confiscated from us, most particularly our passports, without which we could not legally cross any border.

Our night was not over. We were whisked off by an American embassy chauffeur to the residence of the deputy chief of mission, where several ranking American diplomats were huddled around the dining room table. Ambassador Constable was away from the capital visiting Kisangani. When we sat down at the polished wood table, first they offered us plates of sandwiches and glasses of red wine, good French wine that went down like an antidote to the miserable hours we had spent since the CNRI agent hijacked our cab. We had gone from Zaire's underbelly to an immaculately kept American house.

Fearing that our arrest might snowball into further diplomatic trouble, the Americans had gathered at the deputy's house to find a way to get us released as quickly and quietly as possible. The problem was that the two of us had stumbled into a morass of trouble that had been stagnating ever since the Group of Thirteen began speaking out against Mobutu's dictatorship and had been made much worse by the incident at the Intercontinental, which had aroused all sorts of suspicions about some American-type cabal to overthrow the regime. As soon as the agents surveilling Tshisekedi's house had seen us, they must have visualised a vast plot in the making and rejoiced at having discovered it.

The diplomats told us how they planned to deal with the predicament. The bad part of it was that we were supposed to continue to report to the security police. The good part of it was that embassy officials would pull what diplomatic levers they thought they could to get us out of CNRI's clutches.

The next morning, filled with reluctance, we got ready to turn ourselves back over to Adambu and his agents. To make matters worse, I found myself struggling with a ridiculous sartorial issue: What do you wear to an interrogation if all your clothes are filthy from weeks of traveling in the Congo watershed? I would have found the quandary amusing if I had not felt more than equally grim about the coming session. I decided on my cleanest cotton dress, sponged off most of the dried mud, and safety-pinned its torn seam closed.

We reported as we had been ordered to CNRI headquarters, a place that made the secretariat building of the night before seem pleasant. From the gate, we were shepherded by armed guards into a room outside Adambu's principal office. Some miserable prisoners were already there when we arrived, and the three available battered chairs were occupied. The rest of the prisoners stood, waiting, leaning against the walls, enduring the passage of time until they were ushered into the big man's office to learn their fate. Sunlight filtered in through curtains of a begrimed leopard-skin print, dimly illuminating two parallel rows of smudges along the walls where prisoners had leaned their heads and shoulders, during thousands upon thousands of hours.

Accompanying us that morning was Sally Beth Bumbrey, the embassy consul, who was charged with the frequently difficult task of getting Americans out of trouble in Zaire. She was a young black woman from Texas who performed her duties with a determined style, dressing fashionably and keeping her cool, undaunted by the scenes around her. When the guards at the CNRI gate had demanded a bribe of cigarettes, she ignored them. When they told her she needed special authorisation to enter, she told them they were mistaken. We would have been happier if her efficiency were getting us out of CNRI headquarters rather than into it, but her presence took some of the edge off our considerable trepidation. The consul looked out of place in the dingy room next to Adambu's office, too bright and American a personality, too optimistic amid the pessimism.

Besides the chairs, the furniture in the room consisted of two desks, a derelict one propped in a corner and one piled with folders behind which sat a dour young man in a spotless white Mobutu suit. The man was Adambu's secretary, keeper of the office doorway, and the folders were the files of detainees. Since there was nowhere else to sit, the three of us clambered onto the other desk to await our summoning for the further interrogation.

The dour man looked up from his files and told us coldly that we had to get down from the desk. Tim pointed out that there was nowhere else to sit.

'It is not allowed. You must not sit there,' he said and looked back down at his files.

Tim bridled and retorted, 'You are very impolite.'

Even though we had to stand, I felt momentarily cheered by Tim's small show of bravery.

We had been tense when we arrived, steeled for immediate questioning and determined not to provide any useful information to our questioners. Late into the night before, Tim and I had discussed how we could best protect ourselves and the many Zairians who had helped us and talked to us. We expected to be separated again, so that the CNRI agents would be able to check whether our stories matched. Since it was impossible to lie under those circumstances, we decided to pretend that we had seen very little and forgotten much. Yet for the moment, no one was paying much attention to us.

Agents came and went, grim-faced men who kept their eyes hidden behind sunglasses, dealing with various unsavory businesses in the streets or the prison cells behind the building. The hours dragged past and the waiting room grew hotter. A barely functioning air conditioner churned away above a door that led onto an overgrown courtyard, from which other doors led off to offices or more cells. The air conditioner was leaking and someone had set a tin bucket underneath it to catch the drips, which acted like an erratic metronome counting an unnatural time. An old map of the country hung on one of the walls, so dated that it still called the place the Belgian Congo. The leopard-print curtains hung lifeless in the breezeless room, like symbols of the ruined grandeur of the country.

We heard no screams as we sat there, but the misery of the prisoners, suspects, and supplicants with whom we were waiting was loud enough. Perhaps a dozen other unfortunates, Zairians and a couple of foreigners who looked down on their luck, waited with us. But there was no sense of comradeship in the room. We did not want to share each other's pain and did not dare to ask each other's crimes.

Tim had advanced a theory earlier in the morning that Adambu and his henchmen would be letting us go immediately, that the pleasure of arresting us would have been ruined overnight by the hassle of having diplomats from the American embassy hovering over our case. His theory lapsed with the morning. The only improvement in our lot consisted of gaining monopoly of a chair in the waiting room, which we had been able to take over from a prisoner who was summoned into Adambu's office. None of the other prisoners had moved to take the chair, perhaps hoping that if they did not move they might not attract unwanted attention to themselves. The three of us took turns sitting on the chair.

Although prisoners and agents came and went, it was impossible to get a good sense of what was going on. Because of the caution the CNRI agents employed when they opened doors, I could not get any kind of look inside Adambu's office or inside a second adjoining room. With high stealth, an agent would open a door only wide enough to stick his head into the office and then, in one sinuous maneuver, would slide sideways through the narrowed entrance and close the door with a quick thunk.

Consul Bumbrey had brought with her a capacious basket whose contents included American magazines. The three of us, two standing and one sitting on the chair, flipped through copies of *Time* and *People* and *Esquire* as if we were merely waiting in the anteroom of a dentist's office, as if everything were normal, as if we would have our appointments and then be gone about the business of everyday life, as if we had a choice about what we were going to do.

The longer Adambu kept us waiting, the more Tim and I worried about the contents of the confiscated notebooks. We worried whether CNRI was passing its information along to Mobutu, who certainly would not be pleased to find himself described as a kleptomaniac in our notes.

We waited for hours, and kept waiting after Consul Bumbrey got up and left, saying she had to check on another American who, for the moment at least, was in worse straits. He had been thrown into Makala, Kinshasa's main prison, for passing bad cheques around the capital.

Dark reports periodically emanated from the prison, including stories documented by Amnesty International about prisoners starving to death or suffering in overcrowded cells. The prison was designed to hold 900 prisoners, but in recent years its average population has gone as high as 3000. Several years ago, after forty Makala prisoners reportedly starved to death, the Zairian Minister of Justice was convicted of embezzling money from the prison's food budget. The place was so poorly run that prisoners sometimes were lost there, languishing after they had served their terms or been found innocent. We later heard a reliable report about one wretch who was found innocent of his alleged crime but did not know it because, as was often the case, he had not attended his own trial. Makala did not have enough vehicles to transport all its prisoners to their legal hearings and its system of keeping records was abysmal. Not knowing of his innocence, the prisoner waited two extra years until some Catholic nuns were able to sort out his record and have him freed.

In her cheerful Texas accent, Consul Bumbrey told us about another American who had tried to commit suicide while imprisoned in Makala, not realising the effect her words were having. My fear, which had been numbed by the waiting, revived. Tim's jaw was clenched. For all the two of us knew, we would be in the same place by afternoon.

We continued our uneasy wait. The minutes piled up into half hours and the half hours slid into hours. Adambu's secretary shuttled in and out of the office, delivering files and escorting prisoners. One man was crying into his hands as he was led out. After many hours, Adambu ordered us in.

The office was large but its space was filled with a desk piled high with more folders, hundreds of them of different colors, interspersed with desktop bric-a-brac, including a heavy cut-glass Pierre Cardin cigarette lighter. Giving us a big smile, Adambu leaned back in his chair as if to show off his overfed midriff, which threatened to pop open the jacket he had buttoned over it. He began berating us, lounging in his chair and telling us we had stupidly come to the wrong office, that our interrogators had been waiting at the secretariat office for us all morning, that our stupidity would mean a delay in resolving our case, that since it was lunchtime we should go eat and return at four.

'Well, we have tickets for a flight to Brussels tonight,' Tim said.

'And so?' he said.

'We expect to be on it,' Tim replied, hoping that Adambu would be glad to see us go.

'Come back at four,' he repeated. 'I don't want to hear about your itinerary.'

We returned at four. By the time Adambu summoned us, it was eight at night and the flight to Brussels had departed. He told us we would not be leaving Zaire right away since his agents had much work to do yet on our case. Since the coming day was a holiday, we were ordered to return to CNRI in two days. He then opened his eyes as wide as he could before narrowing them to slits.

'Go out and eat a big dinner. Drink lots of beer. Go to a nightclub to dance,' he said.

'We want to get on the next flight to Brussels,' Tim said.

'I don't think you understand very well. We have very good nightclubs and very good music in Zaire. You have no choice. Enjoy yourselves.' He curled his lips into a grin that offered no comfort.

We spent the night at our hotel worrying. We worried about whether we were going to end up in Makala, about when we would finally be released, about whether the CNRI agents were going to insist we identify the Zairians with whom we had talked. Having been doggedly optimistic much of the day, Tim by then was feeling defeated.

'They could keep us for weeks, months. They can keep us as long as they want to,' Tim said.

'Maybe they will,' I said.

'What I should have told Adambu was the opposite,' Tim said half jokingly. 'I should have told him that we wanted to stay in Zaire for a longer time, that we had to do a lot more reporting and research. Then he would have made us leave tonight.'

'We could have told him that we wanted to finish interviewing all the other members of the Group of Thirteen,' I added.

'We could have told him that we were grateful for the

chance to get a tour of the inner workings of security-police headquarters,' Tim said.

As Adambu had mandated, we turned ourselves back in at CNRI headquarters after the holiday. We saw no interrogators that day. We returned to the dismal building the next two days and, as before, we waited, waited, and waited. The waiting became a purgatory. Each day, we were told that the agents were not yet ready to question us again. Each day, we became less optimistic. Sometimes Consul Bumbrey waited with us, and sometimes we waited alone in Adambu's anteroom or another largish room among whose furnishings was a chair that had no legs left. The days dragged by and the nights back in the hotel room were not much happier. We learned that CNRI had sent translations of some of the nastiest remarks from our notebooks up the chain of command to Mobutu. Meanwhile, Ambassador Constable had returned to the capital and met with Mobutu, finding him suspicious of our intent and personally upset by the quotation from our notes that vilified him as the country's greatest thief.

That evening we began considering the time-honored route of escape for Zairian political prisoners – fleeing across the river at night in a canoe, dodging Zairian patrol boats, and making it to the Republic of the Congo. From the balcony of our room, Tim and I could see the river and the string of lights marking the Brazzaville riverfront a couple of miles away. Like a pair of conspirators we whispered to each other, wondering how often people actually did sneak across.

That night neither of us could sleep. I was frustrated and my confidence was eroding at its essence. I lay in bed thinking about how we would celebrate when we finally got on a plane to Brussels. Then I started thinking about how foolish it was to think about this celebration when we had to report again to Adambu first thing in the morning. I wondered whether a canoe crossing really would be possible. If we made it to Brazzaville, Adambu still would have our passports. We would need to get new ones. Would the Americans staffing the Brazzaville embassy refuse to help us? Would Ambassador Constable want us sent back to Kinshasa?

Our room had two single beds, but I needed some refuge from my thoughts so I got up and crawled into Tim's bed. But Tim also had been lying awake and did not have any comfort left to give. Trying desperately to sleep, he got up and resettled himself in the bed I had been in. After lying alone in the dark for a while, I tried again, moving back to my original bed. Tim responded by getting up and going back to his bed, grumbling about how it was my fault. I didn't know if he was complaining about the whole trip or just the fact that he wasn't getting any sleep. I did not try again.

FIFTEEN

We felt more and more isolated as the days passed. In the evenings, when we were let go by the security police, we found most people unwilling to associate with us lest they be accused of conniving in whatever grand conspiracy we were supposed to be abetting.

The wife of one of the American diplomats whom we had met earlier expressed her sympathy by sending us a package of homemade cookies. A more relevant, and perhaps far more useful, present was passed along from Angier Peavy, the genial, Tab-drinking cultural affairs officer. She sent us a fetish, a charm sewn into a square of embossed leather, whose purpose was to ward off troubles. It was impossible to tell what was inside the stiff leather, whether the charm was made of bits of bone or dried plants or pieces of a snake's skin. It could have been anything. Willing to look toward any possible source of help, I tied it around my neck.

By the end of the week, we had made no discernible progress toward getting released. Ambassador Constable and his deputy had been working behind the scenes, talking with Mobutu and his foreign minister, a man named Kamanda wa Kamanda, but nothing they did seemed to be working. Adambu was not budging. He had said only that we would be released when CNRI finished investigating and interrogating us.

The ambassador, however, had been hatching a plan aimed at proving to Mobutu that we were serious journalists. Over the days, he was able to convince Mobutu of the wisdom of allowing us to interview a high-level government official as an antidote to what we had heard from the politically noxious Tshisekedi. We sprang at the opportunity, a rare one, since

Mobutu and his henchmen hardly ever give interviews. The original candidate for the interview was Kamanda wa Kamanda.

We never did get an interview with Kamanda, though. Mobutu decided against it, apparently because he thought it inappropriate to have his foreign minister speaking officially with a couple of CNRI prisoners. Mobutu's eventual choice as the man to represent the government was Vunduawe te Pemako, an official recently dismissed from the government in disgrace. Vunduawe was deputy prime minister until he became the most prominent casualty in one of Mobutu's campaigns to supposedly reform the government. Accused of corruption and stripped of his cabinet status, Vunduawe was climbing back into the circle of power.

Although the campaign to reform the government proceeded with much fanfare against several dozen unhappy officials, it signified little in this country where millions survive by bribe taking, smuggling, and black marketeering. It was being used by Mobutu and his official American defenders to prove that Zaire could be relied upon to clean up its act and repay its loans. All this left us in an ironic situation; we were going to get our official briefing from a man who personified the corruptness of Mobutu's regime.

The morning of the interview was a Sunday, five days after our arrest by the security police. A government car was to pick us up at the US embassy in the morning. The car was late and Tim and I debated what it would look like if it finally did arrive.

'They're probably going to send an old Volkswagen,' Tim said. 'Maybe an old Fiat, something equal to our status.'

'No, they won't. They're going to try to impress us. It'll be a Mercedes,' I said.

A few minutes later, a blue-gray Mercedes Benz rolled up and assuming that the driver was a government chauffeur, we both climbed into the rear seat.

'Excuse me. I would prefer that one of you sit in the front,' the driver said, speaking not in French but in English so precise and beautifully accented that it was clear he was no ordinary chauffeur.

Chagrined by our gaffe, Tim hurriedly got out and into the front seat next to the driver, who was wearing a curious costume – a baseball cap, a Hawaiian-style sports shirt, and formal striped pants such as a British parliamentarian might don. He was smoking a long, expensive cigar. Politely, we introduced ourselves and he responded by telling us his name was Kamanda. That was the foreign minister's name, but we were certain that the Kamanda wa Kamanda himself would not be chauffeuring us around Kinshasa. Instead of inquiring whether he was the foreign minister, Tim tried to finesse the problem by asking whether he was a member of the government. He answered ambiguously, saying he was a member of the hierarchy of Mobutu's political party. We were too immersed in decorum to press him for further information.

He dropped us off at a gateway in the Binza hills that led into a compound with a newly built split-level house. When we had climbed the front stairs that led into a marble-floored foyer, a servant showed us to a living room where several people were waiting. Not being sure how we were going to be treated, whether we were there because we were journalists or criminals, we stepped forward hesitantly. Immediately, though, Vunduawe stood up and waved us to a sofa. His wife also stood and handed around a plate of food suitable for a party, things like baked cheese balls and pretzels. That it was not yet midday did not stop her from also offering us an array of aperitifs, from which I selected coffee liqueur. We were not going to be treated like criminals.

Vunduawe was dressed in a Mobutu suit of black-and-gold brocade that would have looked better on a Louis XIV chair. He was a smallish man with a melon of a potbelly. Sharp lines of concentration or worry marked his forehead. We sat down around a coffee table and were introduced to the two other men, the chief of one of Kinshasa's uncourageous newspapers and a professor of economics from the Kinshasa university. Zairian music played softly in the background and no one was frank. We certainly were not going to bring up CNRI or Tshisekedi, and Vunduawe was not going to elaborate on why he had been expelled from office. The cocktail-hour atmosphere magnified the pretense.

We tried to chat. Vunduawe's wife told us she had toured the United States and enjoyed it, although she was much more familiar with Europe. She spent a lot of time in Paris where she had studied and now was interested in improving the legal rights of women in Zaire, not addressing the more significant point that neither men nor women have much guarantee of civil liberties here. We talked about how much we had enjoyed touring Zaire.

We all were nervous. The hors d'oeuvres were passed again and I had another glass of the cloyingly sweet liqueur. Neither Tim nor I was going to risk asking a serious question.

Unprompted by us, Vunduawe turned the conversation to politics. Undoubtedly having received instructions from Mobutu about what we needed to be told, he launched into a lecture about the rationale behind Zaire's one-party state. Vunduawe was an articulate man, a jurist who taught law at the University of Kinshasa when he was not performing some political job.

'You need to understand the logic of the government here. It is different from some other governments, but that doesn't mean it is to be condemned. Certainly, there is in this world no universal way of government,' Vunduawe said.

'The political regime is the result of the history of our people. Over in the United States, it is different, the history is different. In the United States, you have separation of powers, because you have the historical memory of the absolute power of the British king, an event that you want to protect against ever happening again. Even your religion influenced the political history – you had various religions and a pluralistic society. It is necessary to understand that we have another political and sociological history. We know the other systems, yours, the French, the Belgian. But we have another system because we have our own unique history. Historically, we are a people who were humiliated.'

I found myself agreeing with what Vunduawe was saying.

Tim also was nodding his head. Vunduawe described the humiliation Zairians suffered before independence.

'The black people of this country were treated like intelligent animals. House servants weren't permitted to be in Belgian residential quarters after six in the evening. A black could not have a post as an official or go into certain stores. At the university, only a handful of blacks were accepted as students. Without educations, Zairians were necessarily given secondary posts. One of the only ways to get an education then was to become a preacher. There was no law school at independence. Our law was Belgian law, a law that was prepared by the Belgian parliament.

'The system of 1960 [the parliamentary system arranged by the departing colonial Belgians] was not practical. It was a thing from the West and the people didn't understand it. With that system, they were incapable of directing their nation.'

He said that Mobutism was almost inevitable, that the 1965 coup d'état was the best way to end the conflicts and confusion that had engulfed the country after independence. The coup was not the idea of Mobutu alone, he said, but rather a plan concocted by a bunch of young politicians who were known as the Binza group after this same prosperous neighborhood where most of them lived. Vunduawe theorised that Mobutu had not seized control of the government because he was power-hungry but because the Binza group, backed by members of the army's high command, realised that the country needed a strongman to end the chaos. After all, he said, Mobutu originally had promised to take power for a limited period of time while restoring a democratic system.

His logic began to lose me here. Mobutu has proven himself to be one of the most power-hungry men in the world. Vunduawe talked on into the afternoon, ignoring the lunch hour. We all kept eating cheeseballs and pretzels, washed down with liqueurs.

The only tumult in the afternoon was the work of nature. A storm came lashing down around the house, a tempest that beat on the roof and threw sheets of water against the windows. Its fury, though, was short-lived and Vunduawe kept talking.

He broached the subject of Tshisekedi, but never let on that he was aware of our troubles because of this same man. The charade went on. Vunduawe knew Tshisekedi well, for the two had been colleagues in the Mobutu government before they parted political ways. Vunduawe also had represented Mobutu in talks the government held with members of the Group of Thirteen just before they were imprisoned.

Vunduawe advised us to take a look back into the past and see what Tshisekedi was doing when he was minister of the interior. He had been with Mobutu when the general was consolidating his dictatorial hold on the country and creating his one-party state.

'As for Tshisekedi's case, when one is in power, all goes well. When he had power as minister of the interior, he wanted to prevent others from getting to power with a second party. Tshisekedi acts like he is white, like he is pure, but when he had power, he used it, he arrested men arbitrarily. It is today when he has no power that he claims to be a champion of the rights of the people. The thing you need to know about Tshisekedi is that he is jealous. Tshisekedi has formed an opposition because he is jealous and wants to get back into the circle of power, not because he is so loyal to his high ideals.'

Vunduawe's argument would have been convincing if Tshisekedi had fled the country to avoid the punishments that Mobutu metes out. But Tshisekedi has not had an easy time of it.

'It would be a mistake,' Vunduawe said, 'to consider Zairian politics without considering the fact that the country has so many ethnic groups, each with its own internal identity. You also must consider the fact that communications are difficult across the country. If we had more than one party, the parties would split on tribal lines. In one region, you can find several tribes. Even among the Balubas, there are divisions. The answer is to have a strong government. Zaire must have a strong government or it will be taken over by outside powers. Look what happened after independence. Mobutu has saved the country by his strength. He is the cement of Zaire. The people know that.

'If there were a devaluation in the United States like the one we have just had, everything would stop, people would march, there would be trouble. But here, because the chief is so loved, that doesn't happen. He is not loved for his *beaux yeux*, no, but because he has constructed a peace for the country.'

Tim and I could have argued that the peace Vunduawe described, being based on fear, had no truth to it, that it was a violent peace, but we didn't. We wanted to be agreeable. Vunduawe seemed to have sensed our unspoken skepticism.

He sat up straight in his chair and gave us a sharp look.

'In any case, Mobutu has no intention of sharing his power. Why give the opposition a gift? There is an old tribal saying that power is like the skin of a leopard. Two people can't sit on a single spot.'

The others in the room had said little, allowing Vunduawe to defend Mobutu interrupted only by occasional careful questions from us. But as the hours passed, some of our wariness wore off. Everyone was relaxing, or at least getting sodden from the glasses of sweet alcohol.

A tangent of Vunduawe's defense of Mobutu was that the United States should give him more aid, rather than less, as Mobutu's critics in Congress have been advocating as a way of gaining distance from his debauched government.

'You can't play too long with fire before you have a forest fire that you can't stop. The people of Zaire are reaching the limits of their endurance. They need help before it is too late. The United States needs to give that help. The United States and Zaire are political friends and they should be economic ones as well. We have to depend on the goodwill of the United States, because we have no strength relative to you. Certainly the United States wants our copper and minerals, but they are sold on your market. We can't determine the price for our minerals. Zaire is like a faithful woman who waits for her husband to come home again to her,' Vunduawe said.

Then, as if reading our thoughts, one of the newspaper men broke into the conversation and started talking about corruption, to the embarrassed surprise of both ourselves and our host.

'You have probably heard much talk about corruption in

Mobutu's government, but this is not something so unusual. In every country in the world, people cheat in order to make money,' the newspaper man said.

Vunduawe nervously agreed, and led the conversation away from Mobutu.

'It wasn't the Zairians who planted corruption in Zaire. It was introduced by the Belgians, the French, and then the Americans. They all tried to manipulate this country for their profit. That is corruption of the deepest sort. You must remember that we have had a long relationship, ever since 1884 [the United States was the first country to diplomatically recognise Leopold's Congo Free States], and it would be a hard day if it ended,' he said.

The Zairians continued to avoid mentioning CNRI, and we refused to bring up the matter of the corruption, so we parted like friends. Vunduawe and his wife insisted on driving us back to town.

'When are you leaving Zaire?' the wife asked.

'Oh, in a few days,' Tim answered graciously, instead of saying, 'Just as soon as your torturers give us back our passports.'

We thought our painstakingly careful interview with Vunduawe would help us get out of Zaire, that we too were on the road toward rehabilitation. We thought also that American clout with Mobutu's government might help. During our trip on the river, several Zairians had told us in all seriousness that Mobutu consulted the American ambassador every morning so that he would act in accord with American interests. We knew Mobutu didn't function with such complete obsequiousness to the American wish, but we hoped, at least temporarily, that he did.

The next morning, however, Adambu's men were as charmless as ever. They shuffled us off to a secondary waiting room, the one with the legless chair. The room was hot by mid-morning and torpid by midday. A CNRI guard, carrying a semiautomatic rifle over his shoulder, patrolled back and forth, repetitively passing and passing again the two windows of the corner room. Beyond him and above the walls of the compound the flowering crowns of trees were visible. The scene could have been an image from a dream of psychic frustration.

We had no clear idea anymore, or even any good hypotheses, about what was going on. We could not guess what Adambu's plans were or what his orders were from those above. Over the week we had heard conflicting rumors, that we would be freed the next day or that we were far from being freed.

Not until the late afternoon did Adambu summon us to his office. As soon as we were seated in front of his desk and had asked the usual question about getting our passports back, he launched into a monologue.

'You still have some things to learn. You don't know very much about me but I am going to tell you a little. I come from a tribe that lives in the forest. It is a tribe of hunters and of meat eaters, not of farmers. It is a tribe of strong men. But what I want to tell you, what is relevant to your case, is a saying that comes from my tribe: "Meat spoils. But problems never spoil." That is the saying and that is my answer to you.'

He was telling us our case would drag on.

After Adambu let us go for the day, Tim went over to the US embassy to tell Ambassador Constable about our session with Vunduawe and to see if he could learn any new details about our plight. He came back with a strange bit of news. As soon as our ambassador heard Tim's description of our Sunday chauffeur, he confirmed that the ridiculously dressed man was indeed the foreign minister, Kamanda wa Kamanda, incognito, the man responsible for the country's relations with foreigners, the man who held our passports to freedom. Kamanda had wanted an unofficial look at us.

The next day, Adambu's agents took us to a room we had not seen before. Consul Bumbrey had come to CNRI with us that morning but the agents insisted that she not accompany us, that we go alone to this new room three doors down in the row that opened off the littered courtyard. A lone palm tree grew in the yard and a purple-tailed lizard skittered up its trunk. As soon as the door locked behind us, we knew we were in a place designed for unpleasant interrogations and worse. All four walls of the room and its ceiling were padded and soundproofed so that prisoners' screams would not carry into the courtyard. A desk and a chair furnished the room. In the middle of the wall behind the desk, a one-way mirror stared down at us, unartfully camouflaged with a picture frame glued to the wall around it. In a small act of defiance, we sat on the desk. I watched the door, praying that no torturer would open it.

'Well, it's better accommodations than Makala would be,' I tried to joke. Tim did not laugh.

'There's only one reason to put us in a soundproofed room,' Tim said. Our conversation ended.

We figured out that this was CNRI's notorious Cell Three, a place where many Zairian detainees have been tortured.

There was nothing to distract me from my thoughts as we waited for Adambu's orders, whatever they were, to be carried out. This cell was indeed the heart of darkness, the corruption of Africa's essence, the place where human reason failed. We had traveled into the center of Zaire, looking for a legendary darkness, but found rivers and forests that were home to millions of people who had not forgotten how to laugh or dance even as they fought every day to survive. Zaire's darkness was not geographic. It was not a fruit of the entangling forest, but a creation of man. The dark legacy of the Portuguese slavers who betrayed the Mani Kongo has carried through the years of the tyrant Leopold, to Mobutu and his system grounded in torture, repression, and corruption. Those who put Mobutu in place and have kept him there have been foreigners, first among them the American policymakers, who can pretend, as the Belgians and the other Europeans did, that they have been bringing light to the darkness. They can pretend, but perhaps not forever, that shoring up one of Africa's premier dictators is going to make the world more democratic.

We never learned if Adambu had been toying with the idea of beating us up a little or whether he merely had been trying to scare us. Without explanation, we were let out of the cell and shuttled back to the waiting room. We stayed there until evening, when we were again escorted off by CNRI agents.

This time we were taken upstairs and separated, each of us led to cubicles by our original interrogators. They had translations of our notebooks written out on sheets of paper. My questioners concentrated on trying to get names from me. 'Mobutu is the biggest thief of all,' one of the interrogators read. 'Who is the man who said this to you?'

I told them I did not remember his name. When they demanded a description, I lied. If the man was fat, I said he was thin. Tim, meanwhile, was being asked the same litany of questions that had been put to him a week before. When they finally let us go that night, the misunderstandings had not lessened.

Back in the hotel that night, we talked again, and more seriously, about crossing to Brazzaville. If the CNRI agents were going to question us until we told them something useful, we would be detained for some time.

The following morning, electrifying news was buzzing around the American embassy and the *radio trottoir*. The word was that Mobutu had shuffled his cabinet again and that Kamanda, who had seemed so confident when he chauffeured us to Binza, had been ousted as foreign minister. Cabinet shuffles were not unusual news in Mobutu's system of political control, but this one was accompanied by a rumor that we might be freed. Something was supposed to have happened, but we did not know what.

Sally Beth Bumbrey came by our room to tell us she had been summoned to see Adambu, but without us. We waited for hours for her return, not budging from our room, other than to venture out on the balcony and look over the tops of the port warehouses to the river. When the consul did come back, she did not have much to report. Adambu had kept her waiting in the anteroom, only to eventually inform her that we were still under detention and that he would send word when he wanted us.

Tim and I went out for lunch to the little restaurant across the street, where we had sat out on the sidewalk on an evening when we were first in Kinshasa and watched people light fires on mounds of garbage. We were in low humor, tired of waiting, tired of being helpless, tired of Zaire's rotten politics, when Consul Bumbrey showed up again, but this time with some solid news. There indeed had been a cabinet shuffle, and at a hastily arranged ceremony to install new cabinet members, Mobutu and Seti Yale and Ambassador Constable had coincided. From what we could gather, the ambassador had made another plea to Mobutu on our behalf. Mobutu, perhaps in good spirits about getting rid of his old cabinet, decided to comply and informed the security police chief that we must be released.

Adambu sent word for us to meet him late in the afternoon back at the secretariat where we first had been detained. On the way over, we reminded each other not to be hopeful, that Adambu would not want to release us. When we arrived, the building was all but deserted. In the foyer, though, we encountered an old man whose job was to tend the door. His face brightened into a dance of wrinkles.

'Ah, I saw you when they tried to take you. You gave them a really hard time. You told them off. Oh, it was wonderful,' he said with glee, repeating the words I had screamed in the street.

After years of watching political prisoners being shuffled in and out, he was cheered that anyone would stand up to his employers and too old to worry about the consequences of saying so.

When Adambu arrived, he took us to the same barren room and started returning our confiscated things, one by one, shoving them from a pile on his side of the desk over toward us. When he came to the notebooks, he said he would keep them. We badly wanted them back and Tim argued.

'The American ambassador said we would get all our things back,' he said.

'But the American ambassador does not run Zaire,' Adambu replied.

Tim mustered his best French and haughtiest demeanor.

'But Seti Yale told the American ambassador that we could have everything back, and Seti Yale is your boss.'

Adambu's face hardened.

'Those are not my orders,' he replied.

We did not get back the notebooks or the roll of film Adambu had taken from the camera. That was a loss, but we had forty more rolls of film and many more notebooks back at the hotel.

One from among the police agents hovering near Adambu's bulk took mugshots of us, front and profile. It seemed we were criminals. Adambu told us never to come back to Zaire again.

'I am declaring you persona non grata,' he said.

Free of Adambu, we hastily reserved seats on a flight out of Zaire that night and rushed back to the hotel to get our gear. Given the amount of paranoia we had stored up in the previous week, we suspected that police agents at the airport customs barrier would dissect our luggage and take anything they found interesting. At the last minute we were able to arrange to have the notebooks and film smuggled out by another route.

Soon enough we were whisked off to the airport in a Chevrolet van driven by a chauffeur for the American embassy, where a collective sigh of relief had accompanied the news of our imminent departure. A second van filled with embassy guards led the way. Bouncing on the springy seat as the van sped through the slums of *La Cité* toward Njili airport, I turned around to look back and saw that two jeeps, filled with men who could only be security police, were tailing us.

Their jeeps pulled in right behind us at the airport entrance, where we shouldered our bags and marched in, wanting desperately to blend in with the other passengers and escape attention. Somehow, we did get through customs without a microscopic search and boarded the plane to Brussels.

After the jet took off, we basked in the thankful knowledge that we were safe, heading back to a world where we would be able to write and say what we pleased, unlike the Zairians we were leaving behind.

EPILOGUE

Two years after our journey up the river, we had the pleasure of seeing Gabriel once more. By that time, Tim had taken a new job as a foreign correspondent in the Middle East, while I planned to stay on in Baltimore to finish this book. But Tim had not yet left the United States when Gabriel arrived from Kisangani. He had come to do some academic research and he brought predictable news about the state of affairs in Zaire's interior.

According to Gabriel, Kisangani was faring as badly as ever. Soldiers still were ranging the nighttime streets and robbing citizens. The road into the Ituri was as dauntingly pot-holed as ever. Teachers were not getting paid. Disillusionment with the government was equalled by fear of the security police.

Gabriel had lost none of his humor and curiosity, though. He had an endless supply of questions, wanting to know why in the rich cities of the United States so many people live in slums, for instance, or why there aren't more black Americans in Congress, why everyone drives instead of walking, how African issues are decided in Congress, what Americans think about Africa, why more Americans don't know more about Zaire given the wealth of information they have, who is going to be elected the next President, or what foods Americans like most to eat.

We answered his questions, including the last one. With some persuading, Gabriel went with us down to Baltimore's seafood market to sample for himself the city's premiere delicacy, the Chesapeake Bay oyster, served raw on the half shell. For him, oysters were equivalent to some of the strangest things we had eaten in Zaire, such as sautéed tree grubs or monkey legs.

When he saw his first oyster opened on the seafood bar, the grayish flesh of the creature lying in a slimy pool in the hollow of the shell, Gabriel rolled his eyes in protest. It was only after smothering the oyster in horseradish sauce that he managed to swallow it. He refused a second, backing away from the bar and arguing that the first oyster had tasted as unpleasant as it looked.

Other Zairians whom we had met on our journey had not fared as well as Gabriel.

Shortly after we interviewed Tshisekedi wa Malumba in November 1983, he was banished from the capital along with others of the Group of Thirteen, as Mobutu made use of the old Belgian method of relegating political opponents to remote spots in the bush. More than a year passed before Tshisekedi was allowed to return to Kinshasa, where he soon ran afoul of Mobutu's regime again.

By January 1986, he had been sentenced to another term in prison, this time charged and convicted of 'insulting the head of state' by talking about his political opinions to a French news reporter. Arrested and convicted with Tshisekedi was another member of the group, Kanana Thsiongo. Kanana was staying at Tshisekedi's home when a squad of soldiers barged in. According to Amnesty International reports, Kanana in his anger at what was going on shouted that Mobutu was a cannibal and had stashed in refrigerators the flesh of members of the Baluba tribe, to which both Tshisekedi and Kanana belong. This was Tshisekedi's fifth arrest since he started disagreeing with Mobutu's policies.

Following the arrests of Tshisekedi and Kanana, government police carried out a series of nighttime raids against suspected supporters of the would-be second political party, beating them and ransacking and burning their homes. More than one hundred people were detained.

A group of rebels provoked a more brutal response when they briefly took control of a town in eastern Zaire. After retaking the town, Mobutu's army retaliated by torturing and killing dozens of people. Some were whipped with barbed wire and some were executed without any form of trial.

Meanwhile, Vunduawe te Pemako was climbing back up the rungs of the regime's hierarchy from his days of dishonor, which was when we had our official, uncomfortable interview with him. Vunduawe recently made it back to the top, his crime of corruption forgiven or forgotten. Mobutu named him minister of territorial administration this year as part of the same cabinet shuffle in which he established the brand-new position of minister 'for the rights and liberties of citizens.' What this new minister is supposed to do in Mobutu's Zaire is anybody's guess.

But there is no better example of how Mobutu has been playing the surreal strings of his power than the story of the return of Nguza Karl-I-Bond, who seemed to have ended his roller coaster political career by fleeing the country. But after publicising Mobutu's greed and brutality in devastating detail while abroad, Nguza abruptly went back to Zaire. It is not known exactly what blandishments Mobutu used, but Nguza was in Kinshasa for the twenty-fifth anniversary of independence from Belgium. Shortly thereafter he was named ambassador from Zaire to the United States.

Since our journey up the Congo, two other US-backed dictators have been overthrown, Ferdinand Marcos in the Philippines and Jean-Claude (Baby Doc) Duvalier in Haiti. Before the peoples of the Philippines and Haiti revolted, both Marcos and Duvalier appeared to be as entrenched as Mobutu and as assured of American support. It would seem obvious that underneath the violent sort of peace Mobutu has clamped on Zaire, the people there also are seething with desire for a better government.

It is now about three years since we were in Zaire, and Mobutu has just been in Washington again. He came on a state visit to see President Reagan, who was still willing to ignore the Zairian ruler's rottenness.

During his visit, Mobutu also was feted by his old friend, Maurice Tempelsman, the diamond magnate whose interests in Zaire are supervised by Larry Devlin, the ex-CIA man who worked so energetically to assassinate Patrice Lumumba. Tempelsman hosted a tasteful banquet for Mobutu at the Willard Hotel, a posh establishment even by Washington's glittery standards. Mobutu arrived at the hotel accompanied by his traveling retinue of politicians and relatives and an escort of nervous Secret Service men. In the reception line, where he greeted the dozens of American businessmen and diplomats who had been invited to the affair, he wore his emblematic leopard skin hat.

He took off the hat for the luncheon itself, which was held in one of the Willard's formal chambers graced by chandeliers and marble columns. All the tables were decorated with bowls of tall, freshly cut flowers. Seated at the head table with Mobutu were Tempelsman and John Silcox, president of Chevron's overseas petroleum corporation. The first course was chilled salmon eaten with white wine, followed by filet mignon with red wine and completed by a dessert of berries in thick cream.

Afterward, Mobutu, Tempelsman, and Wilcox gave speeches, the Zairian emphasising how much he wanted to reform his country's economy and the Americans touting Zaire as a place to make investments. The audience applauded. No one mentioned that Zaire is falling apart, that its people are desperately poor, or that Mobutu ranks among the world's most vicious dictators.

Ronald Reagan treated Mobutu with equal comradeliness, promising to keep sending military and economic aid that has been running at about $70 million a year, for a total since World War II that is approaching the billion-dollar mark. Reagan also praised Mobutu as 'a voice of good sense and good will,' a stunningly hypocritical description if I ever heard one. More accurately, Mobutu has continued to serve as a prostitute to American interests in Angola and elsewhere on the African continent.

SUGGESTED READING

This list includes books that have been vital to my putting together a history of the Congo region and describing the politics of modern day Zaire. It also includes books whose ideas have been important to me and books that I have enjoyed.

BOOKS ABOUT THE HISTORY OF THE CONGO:

Anstey, Roger. *King Leopold's Legacy: The Congo under Belgian Rule*. Oxford: Oxford University Press, 1966.

Davidson, Basil. *The African Slave Trade: Precolonial History 1450–1850*. Boston: Atlantic Little, Brown, Boston, 1961.

——. *Let Freedom Come: Africa in Modern History*. Boston: Atlantic Little, Brown, 1978.

——. *The Lost Cities of Africa*. Boston: Atlantic-Little, Brown, 1959.

Forbath, Peter. *The River Congo: The Discovery, Exploration and Exploitation of the World's Most Dramatic River*. New York: Harper & Row, 1977.

Morel, E.D. *King Leopold's Rule in Africa*. New York: Funk & Wagnalls, 1905.

Rotberg, Robert I. *Africa and Its Explorers: Motives, Methods and Impact*. Cambridge: Harvard University Press, 1970.

Slade, Ruth. *King Leopold's Congo: Aspects of the Development of Race Relations in the Congo Independent State*. London: Oxford University Press, 1962.

Stanley, Henry Morton. *The Congo and the Founding of Its Free State* (2 vols.). London: Sampson Lowe, 1885.

——. *In Darkest Africa* (2 vols.). London: Sampson Lowe, 1890.

——. *Through the Dark Continent* (2 vols.). London: Sampson Lowe, 1872.

Twain, Mark. *King Leopold's Soliloquy*. Boston: P. R. Warren, 1905.

Zdzislaw, Najder. *Joseph Conrad: A Chronicle*. New Brunswick, New Jersey: Rutgers University Press, 1983.

BOOKS ABOUT THE POLITICS OF ZAIRE:

Fanon, Frantz. *The Wretched of the Earth*, trans. Constance Farrington. New York: Grove Press, 1965.

Gran, Guy, ed. *Zaire: The Political Economy of Underdevelopment*. New York: Praeger, 1979.

Heinz, G. and H. Donnay. *Lumumba: The Last Fifty Days*. New York: Grove Press, 1969.

Hoare, Mike. *Congo Mercenary*. London: Robert Hale, 1967.

Kalb, Madeleine G. *The Congo Cables: The Cold War in Africa – From Eisenhower to Kennedy*. New York: Macmillan, 1982.

Kwitny, Jonathan. *Endless Enemies: The Making of an Unfriendly World*. New York: Congdon & Weed, 1984.

Mahoney, Richard D. *JFK: Ordeal in Africa*. Oxford: Oxford University Press, 1983.

McKown, Robin. *Lumumba: A Biography*. New York: Doubleday, 1969.

Nkrumah, Kwame. *Neo-colonialism. The Last Stage of Imperialism*. London: Thomas Nelson & Sons, 1965.

Nzongola-Ntalaja. *The Crisis in Zaire: Myths and Realities*. Trenton, New Jersey: Africa World Press, 1986.

Ray, Ellen, et al., eds., *Dirty Work 2: The CIA in Africa*. Secaucus, New Jersey: Lyle Stuart, 1979.

Rodney, Walter. *How Europe Underdeveloped Africa*. London: Bogle-L'Ouverture Publications, 1972.

Rotberg, Robert I., ed. *Rebellion in Black Africa*. Oxford: Oxford University Press, 1971.

Stockwell, John. *In Search of Enemies: A CIA Story*. New York: WW. Norton, 1978.

Weiss, Herbert F. *Political Protest in the Congo*. Princeton: Princeton University Press, 1967.

Weissman, Stephen R. *American Foreign Policy in the Congo 1960–1964*. Ithaca: Cornell University Press, 1974.

Young, Crawford and Thomas Turner. *The Rise and Decline of the Zairian State*. Madison: University of Wisconsin Press, 1985.

BOOKS ABOUT FORESTS AND ORIGINS:

Duffy, Kevin. *Children of the Forest*. New York: Dodd, Mead, 1984.

Forsyth, Adrian and Ken Miyata. *Tropical Nature: Life and Death in the Rain Forests of Central and South America*. New York: Charles Scribner's Sons, 1984.

Fossey, Dian. *Gorillas in the Mist*. Boston: Houghton Mifflin, 1983.

Leakey, Richard E., and Roger Lewin. *Origins: What New Discoveries Reveal About the Emergence of our Species and Its Possible Future*. New York: E. P. Dutton, 1977.

Myers, Norman. *The Primary Source: Tropical Forests and our Future*. New York: W. W. Norton, 1984.

Turnbull, Colin M. *The Forest People*. New York: Simon and Schuster, 1961.

BOOKS OF FICTION:

Conrad, Joseph. *Heart of Darkness*, in *Youth and Two Other Stories*. Garden City: Doubleday, 1923.

Greene, Graham. *A Burnt-out Case*. New York: Viking, 1961.

Naipaul, V. S. *A Bend in the River*. New York: Alfred A. Knopf, 1979.

Of importance in understanding the role the United States played in determining Zaire's fate is the report of the Senate committee chaired by Frank Church that investigated the CIA's efforts to subvert governments around the world:

Alleged Assassination Plots Involving Foreign Leaders: An Interim Report of the Select Committee to Study Governmental Operations with Respect to Intelligence Activities, United States Senate. Washington: US Government Printing Office, 1975.

For information about human-rights violations in Zaire, the reports of Amnesty International are continually excellent.

OTHER DOCUMENTS REFERRED TO IN THE BOOK INCLUDE:

Blumenthal, Erwin. *Zaire: Report on Her International Financial Credibility.* Manuscript, April 1982.

Thirteen Members of Parliament. *Open letter to the Citizen Mobutu Sese Seko, President of Zaire.* Manuscript, December 1980.

Leland, Mickey. Extract, *The Impact of US Foreign Policy on Seven African Countries.* Washington: The Committee on Foreign Affairs, US House of Representatives, US Government Printing Office, 1984.

JAMES HAMILTON-PATERSON

PLAYING WITH WATER
Alone on a Philippine Island

Every year, for a full third of the year, James Hamilton-Paterson lives alone, fishing for survival on the otherwise uninhabited Philippine island of Tiwarik.

In PLAYING WITH WATER he explains why. With a poet's insight and skill he examines our experience of the relationship between external and internal realities, while brilliantly bringing to life a remote, and, to the Western eye, strange part of the world.

'A wonderful inner journey in the outer light and colour of a remote coast, uncommonly well-written'
Peter Matthiessen, author of THE SNOW LEOPARD

'Rich, original, adventurous and very well-written'
Muriel Spark

'Unforgettable . . . The Philippine landscape and these remote islanders are crystalline and at the same time mysterious, the writing itself superb'
Ronald Blythe, author of AKENFIELD

'A classic travel book . . . entirely original: at once astringently and gorgeously written . . . everyone in despair at contemporary literature should read it'
Andrew Harvey, author of A JOURNEY IN LADAKH

'One of the most moving and beautifully written books of interior exploration that I have come across for a long time'
Selina Hastings

GEOFFREY MOORHOUSE

IMPERIAL CITY
The Rise and Rise of New York

'His portrait, assured, detailed, measured, perceptive, is imbued with the city's own energy and sense of exhilaration . . . He has seized the city'
Trevor Fishlock in the Daily Telegraph

'I can find no higher praise for IMPERIAL CITY than to say that it's a worthy successor to his CALCUTTA . . . Mr Moorhouse is superb'
Mervyn Jones in the Sunday Telegraph

'"New York can be disgusting, frightening, maddening, crude . . . it also is uplifting, exciting, enchanting, warm." To have written a book that reflects all those qualities is a substantial achievement'
Punch

'The excessive energies of New York vibrate on every page. His book is responsible, engaging and humane'
The Times Literary Supplement

'Required reading for all who would learn more about New York'
Newsday

'A rich and immensely readable account . . . deserves a place in anybody's transatlantic luggage'
New Society

KATIE HICKMAN

DREAMS OF THE PEACEFUL DRAGON
A Journey into Bhutan

'The world has few secrets left, but Bhutan is one of them.
This is why I went there'

Isolated from the outside world for three centuries, this
forbidden kingdom in the Himalayas provides the setting for a
bewitching adventure amongst widely varying people and
terrain.

'Magical and mysterious'

Daily Mail

'In the best traditions of the intrepid British traveller'
The Literary Review

'She evokes the spectacular scenery and atmosphere of this
extraordinary realm'

Daily Mail

'Absorbing . . . she describes the beauty and absolute foreign-
ness of Bhutan vividly. She makes the smells and the sounds
and the whole atmosphere come to life'

Susan Hill

Current and forthcoming titles from Sceptre

BERNARD LEVIN

**HANNIBAL'S FOOTSTEPS
TO THE END OF THE RHINE**

PETER SOMERVILLE-LARGE

**TO THE NAVEL OF THE WORLD
Yaks and Unheroic travels in
Nepal and Tibet**

CHRISTINA DODWELL

**A TRAVELLER ON HORSEBACK
In Eastern Turkey and Iran**

BOOKS OF DISTINCTION